Dedication

To my beautiful little son, Sean Michael: You are the light of my life. I will love you forever and for always.

Contents

Contents

Contents

Contents

Contents

Preface

Data structures: The term strikes fear into the hearts of many computer science students; any course that focuses on data structures is sure to be a hard one. Data structures are the backbone of serious computer programs, yet they are never seen by the user. They are probably the least exciting and conceptually difficult part of any application or systems program. By the same token, they are absolutely necessary if you are going to do more than write trivial, small programs.

A data structure is a programming construct that provides a way to handle multiple data elements (either simple data types, structures, or objects), organizing them in a predicatable way so they can be retrieved, sorted, and/or searched. A multitasking operating system, for example, uses a data structure known as a queue to hold processes waiting for access to the CPU. An application program that manages data—whether those data are customers or the current scores and status of a group of game players— must organize the multiple objects so that they can be found quickly when needed.

Data structures have been around for a long time. The basic algorithms that determine how they function are well known and well documented. However, until the past few years, most of the work on data structures has been in structured programming languages, such as Pascal or C. Today, data structures have been adapted to the object-oriented paradigm.

Many classic data structures are part of C++ libraries (in particular, the C++ Standard Template Library (STL)). You can use them without understanding how they work. However, if you are going to choose the correct data structures for your program, you should understand how the data structures work and what capabilities they provide. In some cases, you may even determine that you can't use the library-supplied data structures because they don't provide the specific functionality you need. Your only recourse will be to write your own.

This book covers classic data structures from an object-oriented perspective with specific C++ implementations. The first part of the book covers basic data structures, including arrays, vectors, linked lists, stacks, and queues. The classes developed for these data structures will be reused throughout parts three and four to create more sophisticated structures.

Part two of the book examines tree structures in depth, focusing on binary search trees, AVL trees, and B-Trees. The section finishes with a chapter on heaps and priority queues, which presents a very different way of looking at binary trees. Trees are algorithmically complex, but they are among the most widely used data structures to provide fast access to stored data. Traversals of the trees use data structures presented in Part one.

Part three of the book looks at additional techniques for ordering, accessing, and searching data. You will find a chapter with a wide variety of sort routines and a very fast search method known as a binary search. You will also read about hash tables and dictionaries. All of the sort and search methods in Part three are built using the basic data structures presented previously in the book.

Part four contains two sample programs that use a selection of the data structures discussed earlier in the book to organize and access data. The first program is RAM-based; the second works with disk-based data and therefore requires different types of organization.

If you examine college data structures texts, you'll almost always find a chapter on graphs. Graphs really aren't data structures; they're a mathematical concept that can be implemented using data structures. Mathematical graph theory is far more complex than what can be covered in a single chapter, and all that can be done in a data structures text is to skim the surface. Rather than provide you with incomplete and unsatisfying examples of graphs, I have made a conscious decision to leave them out of this book. You will instead find more depth on topics such as trees, which form the basis of so many data access methods.

Note: To find some in-depth information about graphs and graph theory, try one or more of the following titles:

- Giuseppe Di Battista et al, *Graph Drawing: Algorithms for the Visualization of Graphs*. Prentice Hall, 1998.
- G. Chartrand, *Graphs & Digraphs*. CRC Press, 1996.
- Robin J. Wilson, *Introduction to Graph Theory*. Addison-Wesley, 1997.

As far as I can tell, the sample code in this book is platform agnostic. Although it was written using CodeWarrior for Macintosh, I have tried to avoid using any langauge elements that are platform- or compiler-specific. The code is intended to work with Windows, Macintosh, and UNIX platforms.

What You Need to Know

To get the most out of this book, you should be proficient in programming using C++. You should be comfortable with writing object-oriented programs and be familiar with object-oriented concepts such as classes, encapsulation, and inheritance. You should also have a solid understanding of pointers.

There are a few advanced C++ concepts (for example, pointers to functions and handles) that are used in some of the data structure code. In those cases, you will find an explanation of those language concepts, just in case you haven't encountered them before.

Getting the Sample Code

You can download the code for the sample programs and the templates for the data structures classes from my Web site:

http://www.blackgryphonltd.com

Click on the Books button and then the name of the book. On this book's private page you'll find a ZIP archive with the source code. (Macintosh and UNIX users usually can unzip, but Windows users can't unstuff or untar.)

Acknowledgements

As always, it takes a host of people behind the scenes to bring a book like this to press. I'd like to take this opportunity to thank them in person:

- Diane Cerra, the editor who took over in the middle of the project and guided it so smoothly to completion. You are a delight to work with, Diane.

- Belinda Breyer and Mona Buehler, also on the editorial team. Thank you, ladies. Your support and quick responses to my questions was wonderful.

- The production team: Victor Curran (Publishing Services Manager) and Angela Dooley (Production Editor). It is always a pleasure to produce a book for Morgan Kaufmann. They have the greatest production people in the world!

- Adrienne Rebello, a copy editor with a sense a humor. Her good eye and light touch were so very welcome.

In addition, there were three technical reviewers who performed exhaustive reviews, for which I am very grateful:

- Karen Watterson: San Diego-based independent database consultant
- Mark Watson: Industry consultant
- Derek Jamison: Software Design Engineer/Test

(I never thought it would be great to have people find bugs in my code, but I am so glad these folks did!!!!)

Thanks all!

JLH

Part I: Basic Data Structures

Object-oriented programs have a specific strategy for implementing data structures. In this part of the book you first will be introduced to that strategy in the context of arrays. Why arrays? Because they are the first data structure (yes, Martha, they are data structures ...) to which most programmers are introduced. You already understand the way in which C++ arrays work. Arrays, therefore, are a great vehicle for demonstrating a new way of organizing your code.

The remainder of this part looks at the data structures that form the foundation of most studies of data structures: vectors, linked lists, stacks, and queues. As you read beyond this first part, you will see these data structures used repeatedly as the basis of more complex data structures. Therefore, it is vital that you understand the functioning of these basic data structures before moving on to the rest of the book.

CHAPTER 1

Introducing Object-Oriented Data Structures: Arrays

Object-oriented programmers have a unique way of handling data structures. Although the implementation details of the manipulation of the data structures are typically the same as those of classic data structures, the higher-level organization of data structure classes reflect object-oriented principles.

In this chapter you will find an introduction to the object-oriented way of viewing data structures. To make the transition easier for both experienced programmers and those who are new to data structures, the first examples will involve arrays, with which you should already be familiar.

When you learned about arrays, you probably weren't told that they were a data structure. However, they do meet the criteria for a data structure: Arrays allow you to store, organize, and manipulate multiple data elements of the same data type in a known and predictable way. Arrays therefore provide an excellent starting place.

> **Note:** One of the best things about an array (and a vector, which is discussed in Chapter 2) is that it provides direct access to the elements in the array. This means that when the data are ordered (sorted) you can use a fast search technique to locate specific values. There are a number of sort and search techniques that can be used on arrays and vectors, some of which are discussed in Chapter 9.

1.1   Container Classes and Iterators

One of the fundamental principles of object-oriented programming is encapsulation, through which the implementation details of how an object does its work are hidden from other objects. Object-oriented data structures extend this concept to the functioning of an entire data structure. The details of how the data structure organizes and manipulates data are hidden from all objects outside the structure.

Classes known as *container classes* manage data structures. Typically, a container class does the following:

- Contains the elements or references to the elements managed by the data structure.
- Accepts elements (or references to elements) and inserts them into the data structure.
- Provides one or more ways to locate elements within the data structure.
- Returns data values from an element in the data structure. This may require a "find" operation to locate the desired element.
- Deletes elements (or references to elements) from the data structure.

A container class may also support modifying data values stored in the data elements. What is required for modification depends on the data structure, how it is organized, and the nature of the elements being stored. You will see examples of this throughout this book.

A container class does not perform I/O, with one exception. If the objects managed by a container class are *persistent*—the objects continue to exist after the program that created them stops running—then the container class may coordinate file I/O, although the actual read and write code is part of the persistent objects themselves. Examples of how container classes interact with persistent objects can be found in the sample applications in Chapters 12 and 13.

Notice that a container class does not support retrieving the elements in the data structure in order (*traversing* the data structure). Data traversals are handled by a special type of class known as an *iterator*. An iterator object provides the object using the iterator with one element of a data structure at a time, in some predetermined order.

The iterator object keeps track of its position in the data structure, independent of the data structure itself. This means that more than one iterator object can exist at any given time for a single data structure, each retrieving elements in a different order from different places in the data structure.

Iterators greatly simplify the traversal of some of the more complex data structures, such as binary trees. Once the iterator classes are written, you never have to worry about the logic of traversing the data structure again. You simply create an iterator object that returns values in the desired order and ask it to give you one element after another from the data structure.

1.2 *Handling Arrays of a Simple Data Type*

In Figure 1-1 you will find the user interface of a simple program that demonstrates the use of a container class for an array that holds a simple data type (in this case, integers). Like the rest of the demonstration programs in this book, it doesn't perform meaningful work, but does provide access to all member functions of the container class as well as use any iterator classes that accompany the container.

```
You can:
    1. Add an item
    2. Delete an item
    3. Retrieve an item by its position in the structure
    4. Find ordinal position of element
    5. List all items
    6. Get size of structure
    9. Exit

Choice: |
```

Figure 1-1 The user interface of the array demonstration program

The declaration of the container class—the *array manager*—can be found in Listing 1-1. The array manager class stores the total elements in the array, the maximum elements the array can store, and a pointer to the array itself. The member functions support adding an element, retrieving a single element, deleting an element, and finding an element.

```
#ifndef MGR
#define MGR 1

class ArrayMgr
{
    private:
        int total_elements, max_elements;
        int * theArray;

    public:
        ArrayMgr (int);  // pass in value for max_elements
        ~ArrayMgr ();
        bool addElement (int); // pass in a single element
        // pass in ordinal position of element; return element value
        bool getElement (int, int &);
        // pass in ordinal position of element
        bool deleteElement (int);
        // pass in element value; return ordinal value
        bool findElement (int, int &);
        int getSize (); // return total elements in the array
};

#endif
```

Listing 1-1 The declaration of an array manager class for an array of a simple data type

The implementation of this class appears in Listing 1-2. The constructor accepts the size of the array as an input parameter and allocates storage for an array of integers. Although storage for the array is being allocated dynamically, this is *not* a dynamic array. In other words, once space for the array has been allocated, the size of the array cannot be changed.

```
#include "ArrayMgr.h"

ArrayMgr::ArrayMgr (int iMax)
{
    max_elements = iMax;
    total_elements = 0;
    theArray = new int [max_elements];
}
ArrayMgr::~ArrayMgr()
    { delete [] theArray; }

bool ArrayMgr::addElement (int newValue)
{
    bool result;
    if (total_elements < max_elements)
    {
        theArray[total_elements] = newValue;
        total_elements++;
        result = true;
    }
    else
        result = false;
    return result;
}

bool ArrayMgr::getElement (int position, int & value)
{
    int result = true;
    if (position >= total_elements)
        result = false;
    else
        value = theArray [position];
    return result;
}

bool ArrayMgr::deleteElement (int position)
{
    bool result = true;
    if (position >= total_elements || total_elements == 0)
        result = false;
    else
```

Listing 1-2   *The array manager class for an array of a simple data type*

```
    {
        for (int i = position; i < total_elements - 1; i++)
            theArray[i] = theArray[i+1];
        total_elements--;
    }
    return result;
}

bool ArrayMgr::findElement (int searchValue, int & position)
{
    int result = true;
    int i = 0;
    while (i < total_elements)
    {
        if (theArray[i] == searchValue)
            position = i;
        i++;
    }
    if (i >= total_elements)
        result = false;
    return result;
}

int ArrayMgr::getSize ()
    { return total_elements; }
```

Listing 1-2 (Continued) *The array manager class for an array of a simple data type*

Note: Dynamic arrays are more commonly known as vectors. Vectors are discussed in Chapter 2.

1.2.1 Adding an Element

To add an element to the array, the array manager expects the object calling the <u>addElement function to supply the value that is to be inserted into the array.</u> The array manager then handles the element insertion in the following way:

1. Determine whether there is room in the array for a new element. If not, return `false`, indicating that the insertion failed.
2. Insert the new value into the array.
3. Increment the value of the total elements in the array.
4. Return `true`, indicating that the insertion was successful.

It is, of course, up to the calling function to interpret the boolean return value.

1.2.2 Retrieving an Element

To retrieve a single element, the array manager needs to know the ordinal position in the array from which it is to retrieve the value. It can then return the value in a reference parameter.

The array manager handles the `getElement` function in the following way:

1. Determine whether the requested position is within the range of array positions currently used. If not, return `false` to indicate that the retrieval failed.
2. Assign the value at the requested array position to the reference parameter (`value` in this case). = theArray[position]
3. Return `true` indicating that the retrieval succeeded.

1.2.3 Deleting an Element

Deleting an element from an array is slightly more complex than inserting one because you must move the values below the deleted value up to cover the "hole" left by the deletion. The `deleteElement` function therefore does the following:

1. Determine whether the position of the element to be deleted is within the range of valid array indexes. If not, return `false`, indicating that the deletion failed.
2. Begin at one position below the deleted element and move all elements from there to the end of the array up one position.
3. Decrement the number of elements in the array.
4. Return `true` to indicate that the deletion succeeded.

> **Note:** In most cases, a data structure should not delete from memory the element that is being removed from the data structure. Why? Because the data structure has no way of knowing if the element is being used by other data structures or if the program still needs to use that element. It should therefore be left up to an application program to decide how to handle an element removed from a data structure.

1.2.4 Finding an Element

Both the `getElement` and `deleteElement` functions require that the calling function know the array index of the element to be retrieved or deleted. The array manager must therefore have one or more `find` functions that search the contents of the array based on data values.

For this particular example, the code uses a sequential search to locate a specific integer value:

1. Assume that the search will succeed.
2. Begin at the first value in the array and check it against the search value.
3. Repeat step 2 until either the search value is found or the last valid value in the array has been compared to the search value.

4. When the search value is found, place its array index into the reference parameter (`position`). Return `true`.

5. If the search value is not found, return `false`.

> **Note:** There are certainly many more efficient ways to search an array, especially if the array is sorted. However, the sequential search is short and easy to understand. It is therefore just fine for this demonstration, where efficiency isn't an issue. You will read about other, more efficient search methods throughout this book.

1.2.5 Finding the Size of the Array

The `getSize` function returns the number of valid elements in the array. A calling function can use this value to control a loop that processes all the elements in the array, one at a time.

1.2.6 Using the Array Manager

You will find the declaration of the application class for the demonstration program that uses the array manager class we have been discussing in Listing 1-3. The implementation of that class appears in Listing 1-4.

```
#ifndef APP
#define APP 1

#include "arraymgr.h"

#define MAX_ELEMENTS 10
#define ADD 1
#define DELETE 2
#define RETRIEVE 3
#define FIND 4
#define LIST 5
#define SIZE 6
#define EXIT 9
```

Listing 1-3   The declaration of the application class for the demonstration of using an array manager

```
class AppClass
{
    private:
        ArrayMgr * testArray;
        int menu ();
        void add();
        void remove ();
        void retrieve ();
        void find ();
        void list ();
        void size ();
    public:
        AppClass ();
        void run();
};

#endif
```

Listing 1-3 (Continued) The declaration of the application class for the demonstration of using an

```
#include "appclass.h"
#include "arrayitr.h"
#include <iostream.h>

AppClass::AppClass ()
{
    testArray = new ArrayMgr (MAX_ELEMENTS);
}
void AppClass::run ()
{
    int choice = menu();
    while (choice != EXIT)
    {
        switch (choice)
        {
            case ADD:
                add ();
                break;
            case DELETE:
                remove ();
                break;
            case RETRIEVE:
```

Listing 1-4   The implementation of the demonstration application class

```
                retrieve ();
                break;
            case FIND:
                find ();
                break;
            case LIST:
                list ();
                break;
            case SIZE:
                size ();
                break;
        }
        choice = menu();
    }
}

int AppClass::menu ()
{
    int choice;
    cout << "\nYou can: ";
    cout << "\n  1. Add an item";
    cout << "\n  2. Delete an item";
    cout <<
        "\n  3. Retrieve an item by its position in the structure";
    cout << "\n  4. Find ordinal position of element";
    cout << "\n  5. List all items";
    cout << "\n  6. Get size of structure";
    cout << "\n  9. Exit";
    cout << "\n\nChoice: ";
    cin >> choice;
    return choice;
}

void AppClass::add ()
{
    int value;
    cout << "\nEnter a new value: ";
    cin >> value;
    bool result = testArray->addElement (value);
    if (result)
        cout << "\nElement added successfully." << endl;
```

Listing 1-4 (Continued) The implementation of the demonstration application class

```
    else
    {
        cout << "\nCouldn't add an element because ";
        cout << "the array is full." << endl;
    }
}


void AppClass::remove ()
{
    int pos;
    cout << "\nEnter the position to delete: ";
    cin >> pos;
    bool result = testArray->deleteElement (pos);
    if (result)
        cout << "\nThe deletion was successful." << endl;
    else
    {
        cout << "\nThe position was out of range. ";
        cout << "No deletion was performed." << endl;
    }
}

void AppClass::retrieve ()
{
    int pos, value;
    cout << "\nEnter an array position: ";
    cin >> pos;
    bool result = testArray->getElement (pos, value);
    if (result)
        cout << "\nThe value at " << pos << " is " << value
            << "." << endl;
    else
        cout << "\nThe array position you entered is out of range."
            << endl;
}

void AppClass::find ()
{
    int value, pos;
    cout << "\nEnter a value to find: ";
```

Listing 1-4 (Continued) The implementation of the demonstration application class

```
    cin >> value;
    bool result = testArray->findElement (value, pos);
    if (!result)
        cout << "\n" << value << " is not in the array." << endl;
    else
        cout << "\n" << value << " is in position "
            << pos << "." << endl;
}


void AppClass::list ()
{
    int value;
    ArrayItr *theItr=new ArrayItr(testArray,testArray->getSize());
    bool result = theItr->getNext(value);
    int i = 0;
    while (result)
    {
        cout << i+1 << ": " << value << endl;
        result = theItr->getNext(value);
        i++;
    }
}


void AppClass::size ()
{
    cout << "There are " << testArray->getSize()
        << " elements in the array." << endl;
}
```

Listing 1-4 (Continued) The implementation of the demonstration application class

1.2.6.1 Creating the Array Manager Object

The application class's constructor creates an object of the array manager class, passing in the number of elements to be allocated for the array. This is typical of classes that use container classes: The class using the container must declare an object of the container class for each data structure of that type it needs to use. If the container is to be used throughout the program, the most convenient place to create it is in a constructor.

Notice in Listing 1-3 that the array manager object is declared as a variable that is global to the class. Although the array manager object could certainly be created in the application class's run function, doing so would require passing the array manager object among the run function and the other application class functions. Therefore, if a data structure is going to be used throughout a program, it is more convenient to declare as one of the application class's variables.

1.2.6.2 Adding, Retrieving, Finding, and Deleting Elements

The application class functions that add an element, retrieve a single element, find an element, and delete an element are relatively straightforward. They all follow this pattern:

1. Collect the required data from the user. For example, to add a value to the array, the application class asks the user for the data value.
2. Call the appropriate array manager function.
3. Check the return value of the function to determine whether the operation succeeded.
4. Display a message to the user indicating the result of the operation.

The most important thing to notice when looking at the application class is that the application has no knowledge of the type of data structure into which Thing objects are being placed. The nature of the data structure (whether it is an array or something else) and the way in which it handles the data are completely hidden from the application. The application therefore could change the data structure simply by changing the container class from which it creates an object.

1.2.6.3 The main Function

In an object-oriented C++ program, <u>the main function is the only function that isn't part of a class.</u> Its job is to create an object of the application class and to call the run function. The function in Listing 1-5 is used for all the programs in this book and therefore will not be repeated.

```
#include "appclass.h"

int main ()
{
    AppClass * theApp = new AppClass ();
    theApp->run();
}
```

Listing 1-5 The main function used for all programs in this book

1.2.7 Using an Iterator Class to List Elements

The application class's list function uses an iterator object to step through the elements in the array one at a time. Although there is more than one way to write an iterator, for this simple first example the iterator is initialized to point to the first element in the array (0) when an object is created from the iterator class (Listing 1-6). Each call to the getNext function returns the next successive value in the array.

```
#ifndef ITR
#define ITR 1

#include "ArrayMgr.h"

class ArrayItr
{
    private:
        ArrayMgr * theArray;
        int numb_elements;
        int current_index;
```

Listing 1-6 The declaration of a simple array iterator class

```
public:
    // pass in the array manager and total elements
    ArrayItr (ArrayMgr *, int);
    bool getNext (int &);
};

#endif
```

Listing 1-6 The declaration of a simple array iterator class

As you can see in Listing 1-6, the iterator keeps track of where it is in the array (current_index). Therefore, there may be many iterator objects, each working on a different place in the array.

Notice also that the iterator will work with any object of the array manager class. The iterator's constructor (see Listing 1-7) not only sets the current index to 0, but initializes the array to be listed and the total number of elements in the array.

```
#include "ArrayItr.h"

ArrayItr::ArrayItr (ArrayMgr * inArray, int iElements)
{
    theArray = inArray;
    numb_elements = iElements;
    current_index = 0;
}

bool ArrayItr::getNext (int & value)
{
    bool result = false;
    if (current_index <numb_elements)
    {
        theArray->getElement (current_index, value);
        result = true;
        current_index++;
    }
    return result;
}
```

Listing 1-7 The implementation of a simple array iterator class

Most of the array iterator's work is done in the `getNext` function. It places the value of the "next" element in the array in a reference parameter, increments the pointer to the current index, and returns true indicating that a value is ready to be processes. However, if the current index is beyond the number of valid elements in the array, the function returns false.

The application class's `list` function therefore first creates an iterator object:

```
ArrayItr * theItr = new ArrayItr
   (testArray, testArray->getSize());
```

It then enters a loop that stops when `getNext` returns false. The body of the loop processes a successfully retrieved element. In this particular example, it simply displays the value of the element in a console window.

1.3   Handling Arrays of Objects

Although writing a data structure to handle a value of a simple data type is usually clean and straightforward, it's not particularly realistic. Most of the time data structures are used to manage groups of objects instead of individual values.

1.3.1 A Class to Be Managed

Throughout this book, we will be using a generic class—`Thing`—to represent any class from which objects can be created and then handled by a data structure. The declaration of the `Thing` class can be found in Listing 1-8; the implementation of the class appears in Listing 1-9. (The `Array-able` class is discussed in the next section, "Mix-In Classes.")

A `Thing` object has two data values: a name and an ID number. It has a default constructor that does nothing, a constructor that initializes the variables, and two accessor functions.

```
#ifndef THING
#define THING

#include "arrayable.h"
                         derived/inherited from
class Thing : Arrayable
{
    private:
        int thing_id;
        char thing_name [20];

    public:
        Thing ();
        Thing (int, char []);
        int getID ();
        char * getName ();
        int getKey();
};

#endif
```

Listing 1-8   Declaration of the Thing class

1.3.2 Mix-In Classes

The remaining function in the Thing class—getKey—is related to the Arrayable class from which Thing inherits. Arrayable (defined in Listing 1-10 and implemented in Listing 1-11) is what is known as a *mix-in class*. It doesn't represent the typical inheritance relationship of general-to-specific (the "is a" relationship). Instead, it adds functionality to a class.

When objects are part of a data structure, there must be at least one data value used to search and/or sort the objects. This represents an object's *key*. The container class must therefore have access to the key value, regardless of which data value it happens to be. The mix-in class, with its C++ virtual function, forces the Thing class to implement the getKey function. Any class whose objects are to be handled by the array manager class must inherit from Arrayable.

```cpp
#include "Thing.h"          // Listing 1-8
#include <string.h>

Thing::Thing ()
{

}

Thing::Thing (int iID, char iName[])
{
    thing_id = iID;
    strcpy(thing_name, iName);
}

int Thing::getID ()
    { return thing_id; }

char * Thing::getName ()
    { return thing_name; }

int Thing::getKey ()
    { return thing_id; }
```

Listing 1-9 *Implementation of the Thing class*

```cpp
#ifndef ARRAYABLE
#define ARRAYABLE

class Arrayable
{
    public:
        Arrayable ();
        virtual int getKey() = 0;
};

#endif
```

Listing 1-10 *The declaration of the Arrayable class*

```
#include "arrayable.h"

Arrayable::Arrayable ()
    {  }
```

Listing 1-11 The implementation of the Arrayable class

1.3.3 An Array Manager for Objects

The array manager class for objects (declared in Listing 1-12 and implemented in Listing 1-13) is very similar to the array manager for a simple
data type. However, the array now holds pointers to objects rather than
data values, and functions such as addElement and getElement, which
previously worked with data values, now use pointers to objects.

```
#ifndef MGR
#define MGR 1

#include "Thing.h"
#define MAX_ELEMENTS 10

class ArrayMgr
{
    private:
        int total_elements;
        Thing * theArray [MAX_ELEMENTS];

    public:
        ArrayMgr ();   // pass in value for max_elements
        bool addElement (Thing *); // pass in a single element
        // pass in ordinal position of element
        bool getElement (int, Thing * &);
        // pass in ordinal position of element
        bool deleteElement (int);
        // pass in key value; return ordinal value
        bool findElement (int, int &);
```

Listing 1-12 Declaration of the ArrayMgr class for objects

```
        int getSize (); // return total elements in the array
};

#endif
```

Listing 1-12 Declaration of the ArrayMgr class for objects

```
#include "ArrayMgr.h"

ArrayMgr::ArrayMgr ()
{
    total_elements = 0;
}

bool ArrayMgr::addElement (Thing * newObject)
{
    bool result;
    if (total_elements < MAX_ELEMENTS)
    {
        theArray[total_elements] = newObject;
        total_elements++;
        result = true;
    }
    else
        result = false;
    return result;
}

bool ArrayMgr::getElement (int position, Thing *  & element)
{
    int result = true;
    if (position > total_elements || total_elements == 0)
        result = false;
    else
        element = theArray [position];
    return result;
}
```

Listing 1-13   Implementation of the ArrayMgr class for objects

```
bool ArrayMgr::deleteElement (int position)
{
    bool result = true;
    if (position > total_elements || total_elements == 0)
        result = false;
    else
    {
        for (int i = position; i < total_elements - 1; i++)
            theArray[i] = theArray[i+1];
        total_elements--;
    }
    return result;
}

bool ArrayMgr::findElement (int searchValue, int & position)
{
    int result = true;
    int i = 0;
    position = -1;
    while (i < total_elements)
    {
        if (theArray[i]->getKey() == searchValue)
            position = i;
        i++;
    }
    if (position == -1)
        result = false;
    return result;
}

int ArrayMgr::getSize ()
    { return total_elements; }
```

Listing 1-13 (Continued)   Implementation of the ArrayMgr class for objects

Note: Although it is possible to create an array manager in C++ that stores the actual objects rather than pointers to the objects, it is usually not wise to do so. First, if you want the objects to be part of more than one data structure, you must duplicate them. Second, when you are moving objects from one location to another in the data structure, you must move entire objects, rather than just pointers. The result can be slower performance and memory fragmentation.

The other major difference between this version of the class and the original version is the use of the getKey function. When the findElement function attempts to find a single object in the array, it must use each Thing object's getKey function to retrieve the key's value so that it can be compared to the search value.

1.3.4 Using the Array Manager for Objects

The application class to test the array manager that works with objects rather than simple data types (Listing 1-14 and Listing 1-15) is only a bit different from the original version of the application class. The major change is in the user interface: The program must collect data for the object that will be stored and then create the object, which can then be passed to the array manager.

```
#ifndef APP
#define APP

#include "ArrayMgr.h"

#define ADD 1
#define DELETE 2
#define RETRIEVE 3
#define FIND 4
#define LIST 5
#define SIZE 6
#define EXIT 9
```

Listing 1-14 Declaration of an application class that uses an array manager for objects

```
class AppClass
{
    private:
        ArrayMgr * testArray;
        int menu ();
        void add ();
        void remove ();
        void retrieve ();
        void find ();
        void list ();
        void size ();
    public:
        AppClass ();
        void run ();
};

#endif
```

Listing 1-14 Declaration of an application class that uses an array manager for objects

```
#include "appclass.h"
#include "arrayitr.h"
#include "thing.h"
#include <iostream.h>

AppClass::AppClass ()
{
    testArray = new ArrayMgr ();
}

void AppClass::run ()
{
    int choice = menu();
    while (choice != EXIT)
    {
        switch (choice)
        {
            case ADD:
                add ();
```

Listing 1-15   Implementation of an application class that uses an array manager for objects

```
                break;
            case DELETE:
                remove();
                break;
            case RETRIEVE:
                retrieve ();
                break;
            case FIND:
                find ();
                break;
            case LIST:
                list ();
                break;
            case SIZE:
                size ();
                break;
        }
        choice = menu();
    }
}

int AppClass::menu ()
{
    int choice;
    cout << "\nYou can: ";
    cout << "\n  1. Add an item";
    cout << "\n  2. Delete an item";
    cout <<
        "\n  3. Retrieve an item by its position in the structure";
    cout << "\n  4. Find ordinal position of element";
    cout << "\n  5. List all items";
    cout << "\n  6. Get size of structure";
    cout << "\n  9. Exit";
    cout << "\n\nChoice: ";
    cin >> choice;
    return choice;
}

void AppClass::add ()
{
```

Listing 1-15 (Continued) Implementation of an application class that uses an array manager for

```
    int ID;
    char name [20];
    cout << "\nEnter a Thing ID: ";
    cin >> ID;
    cout << "\nEnter a Thing name: ";
    cin >> name;
    Thing * newObject = new Thing (ID, name);
    bool result = testArray->addElement (newObject);
    if (result)
        cout << "\nElement added successfully." << endl;
    else
    {
        cout << "\nCouldn't add an element because ";
        cout << "the array is full." << endl;
    }
}

void AppClass::remove ()
{
    int pos;
    cout << "\nEnter the position to delete: ";
    cin >> pos;
    bool result = testArray->deleteElement (pos);
    if (result)
        cout << "\nThe deletion was successful." << endl;
    else
    {
        cout << "\nThe position was out of range.";
        cout << "No deletion was performed." << endl;
    }
}

void AppClass::retrieve ()
{
    int pos;
    cout << "\nEnter an array position: ";
    cin >> pos;
    Thing * theThing;
    bool result =
        testArray->getElement (pos, theThing);
```

Listing 1-15 (Continued) Implementation of an application class that uses an array manager for

```
    if (result)
    {
        cout << "\nThe Thing at " << pos << " has an ID of "
            << theThing->getID();
        cout << "\nand a name of " << theThing->getName() << "."
            << endl;
    }
        else
    cout << "\nThe array position you entered is out of range."
        << endl;
}

void AppClass::find ()
{
    int ID, pos;
    cout << "\nEnter an ID to find: ";
    cin >> ID;
    bool result = testArray->findElement (ID, pos);
    if (!result)
        cout << "\nThere is no Thing with an Id of " << ID
            << " in the array." << endl;
    else
        cout << "\nThe Thing with an ID of " << ID
            << " is in position " << pos << "." << endl;
}

void AppClass::list ()
{
    ArrayItr * theItr = new ArrayItr
        (testArray, testArray->getSize());
    Thing * theThing;
    bool result = theItr->getNext(theThing);
    int i = 0;
    while (result)
    {
        cout << i+1 << ": ID = " << theThing->getID()
            << " Name = " << theThing->getName() << "." << endl;
        result = theItr->getNext(theThing);
        i++;
    }
```

Listing 1-15 (Continued) Implementation of an application class that uses an array manager for

```
}

void AppClass::size ()
{
    cout << "There are " << testArray->getSize()
        << " elements in the array." << endl;
}
```

Listing 1-15 (Continued) Implementation of an application class that uses an array manager for

1.3.5 Listing Values from an Array Manager of Objects

The array iterator (Listing 1-16 and Listing 1-17) has also been modified slightly. In particular, the getNext function returns a pointer to an object instead of a data value. As a result, the application class's list function must use Thing class functions to retrieve data for display.

```
#ifndef ITR
#define ITR

#include "ArrayMgr.h"

class ArrayItr
{
    private:
        ArrayMgr * theArray;
        int numb_elements;
        int current_index;

    public:
        // pass in the array manager and total elements
        ArrayItr (ArrayMgr *, int);
        bool getNext (Thing * &);
};

#endif
```

Listing 1-16 Declaration of an iterator class for an array of objects

```
#include "ArrayItr.h"

ArrayItr::ArrayItr (ArrayMgr * inArray, int iElements)
{
    theArray = inArray;
    numb_elements = iElements;
    current_index = 0;
}

bool ArrayItr::getNext (Thing * & nextObject)
{
    bool result = false;
    if (current_index <numb_elements)
    {
        theArray->getElement (current_index, nextObject);
        result = true;
        current_index++;
    }
    return result;
```

Listing 1-17 Implementation of an iterator class for an array of objects

1.4 *Making the Classes Generic*

There is one major problem with the way in which the container classes you have seen have been written: They are specific to one data type or class. If you write data structures in this way, you will find yourself rewriting the container classes and iterators for each class and data type you need to manage. This is certainly wasted effort, especially given that there is a way to write the code generically, so that a single class declaration and implementation can be used for any data type.

There is an alternative. For C++, you can create templates, a method of writing a class so that it can be assigned data types and/or classes when the program is compiled. A C++ template is a declaration of a class that includes placeholders for data types that are specified when an object is created from the class. The compiler actually generates the class implementation during the compilation process, using the supplied data types.

> **Important note:** Although you may want to write your own data structures using C++ templates, this book will continue to use the simple data types and/or the Thing class for examples when first presenting new data structures. In this author's opinion, C++ templates can be hard to read and their use would make it harder for you to understand how the container and iterator classes operate. However, many of the data structures later in the book make use of those presented earlier. Some templates therefore appear in the body of the book as they are used to support other data structures. Those templates that are not covered in the body of the book can be found in Appendix A.

1.4.1 Declaring a Template

Because a template is a declaration (and not specifically an implementation), an entire template class appears in a header file. In Listing 1-18, for example, you can find the template version of the array manager class. The declaration of the class appears first, followed by the "implementations" of all its member functions.

```
#ifndef MGR
#define MGR 1

#define MAX_ELEMENTS 10

template <class A, class B>
class ArrayMgr
{
    private:
        int total_elements;
        A * theArray [MAX_ELEMENTS];

    public:
        ArrayMgr<A, B> ();
        bool addElement (A *); // pass in a single element
        // pass in ordinal position of element
        bool getElement (int, A * &);
```

Listing 1-18   A C++ template class for the array manager

```
        // pass in ordinal position of element
        bool deleteElement (int);
        // pass in key value; return ordinal value
        bool findElement (B, int &);
        int getSize (); // return total elements in the array
};

template <class A, class B>
ArrayMgr<A, B>::ArrayMgr()
{
    total_elements = 0;
}

template <class A, class B>
bool ArrayMgr<A,B>::addElement (A * newObject)
{
    bool result;
    if (total_elements < MAX_ELEMENTS)
    {
        theArray[total_elements] = newObject;
        total_elements++;
        result = true;
    }
    else
        result = false;
    return result;
}


template <class A, class B>
bool ArrayMgr<A,B>::getElement (int position, A *  & element)
{
    int result = true;
    if (position > total_elements || total_elements == 0)
        result = false;
    else
        element = theArray [position];
    return result;
}
```

Listing 1-18 (Continued) A C++ template class for the array manager

```
template <class A, class B>
bool ArrayMgr<A,B>::deleteElement (int position)
{
    bool result = true;
    if (position > total_elements || total_elements == 0)
        result = false;
    else
    {
        for (int i = position; i < total_elements - 1; i++)
            theArray[i] = theArray[i+1];
        total_elements--;
    }
    return result;
}


template <class A, class B>
bool ArrayMgr<A,B>::findElement (B searchValue, int & position)
{
    int result = true;
    int i = 0;
    position = -1;
    while (i < total_elements)
    {
        if (theArray[i]->getKey() == searchValue)
            position = i;
        i++;
    }
    if (position == -1)
        result = false;
    return result;
}

template <class A, class B>
int ArrayMgr<A,B>::getSize ()
    { return total_elements; }

#endif
```

Listing 1-18 (Continued) A C++ template class for the array manager

The declaration begins with the keyword `template`, followed by identifiers for each of the data types that can be specified when an object is created. The list of identifiers appears within < and >, each preceded by the keyword `class`. Multiple identifiers are separated by commas. Within the declaration itself, you use the identifiers wherever data types/classes ordinarily would appear.

For example, in Listing 1-18 the identifier A represents the class being managed and B represents the data type of the class's key. Therefore, you declare the array being managed with

```
A * theArray [MAX_ELEMENTS];
```

The official name of a template class becomes

```
class_name<identifier1, identifier2, ...>
```

This means that wherever you would use the class name, you must include the identifiers for the variable data types/classes. For example, the default constructor for the array manager class has the default prototype

```
ArrayMgr<A, B> ();
```

The implementation of the member functions follows the same pattern:

- Each member function name is preceded by the keyword template and the specifications of the variable data types/classes.

  ```
  template <class A, class B>
  ```

- Each time the class name appears to qualify a function name, it is followed by identifiers for the variable data types/classes.

  ```
  bool ArrayMgr<A,B>::deleteElement (int position)
  ```

- Data types/classes are replaced by their identifiers within function headers.

  ```
  template <class A, class B>
  ```
  ```
  bool ArrayMgr<A,B>::findElement (B searchValue, int &
      position)
  ```

> **Note:** When you create generic data structures in C++, you will run into a problem when the search or sort key for an object is a string unless you use a string class where the relationship operators (for example, == and >) have been overloaded to function as they do with other data types.

1.4.2 Using a Template

To use a template, include the header file in which the template is declared in any file in which an object is to be created from the template class. Use specific classes and/or data types for the identifiers when creating an object. For example, in our sample program, you would specify the Thing class for the object being managed (A) and int as the data type of the key (B):

```
testArray = new ArrayMgr<Thing, int> ();
```

The C++ Standard Template Library (STL) is built from templates such as the one you have just seen. You can also build your own template library by writing and storing reusable template classes.

1.5 Summary

In this chapter you have been introduced to the use of container classes to manage data structures in an object-oriented program. A container class hides the details of the data structure from the object using the data structure.

You have also read about iterator classes, which traverse data structures to provide an object using the data structure with one element from the data structure at a time, in some prescribed order. Because an iterator keeps track of its own position in the data structure, it is possible to have multiple iterators at the same time, working on the same data structure.

Finally, you were introduced to a technique for writing generic container and iterator classes. In C++, the mechanism is to use templates. Templates are declarations of classes and their member functions that use placeholders instead of data types. The data types are supplied when you create an object from the template class. The compiler then generates the actual class and the source code for the member functions for you.

CHAPTER 2

Vectors

One of the problems with arrays as data structures is that they are fixed in size. Either you waste space by making an array so large that you don't use all the elements or you run the risk of the array becoming too small. Instead, it would be nice to have a data structure that is the equivalent of a dynamic array, which could be expanded or shrunk as needed. Such a data structure is known as a *vector*.

In this chapter you will discover how you can extend an array manager to create a container class to handle vectors. As in Chapter 1, this chapter begins with an example that uses a simple data type and follows with a more general container class that manages objects.

Note: This will be the last time you will see an example using a simple data type. The remaining chapters in this book focus on handling objects only.

The sample program is controlled by the text menu in Figure 2-1. Notice that it has all of the same functionality as the array demonstration program, but also includes an option for resizing the vector.

```
You can:
    1. Add an item
    2. Delete an item
    3. Retrieve an item by its position in the structure
    4. Find ordinal position of element
    5. List all items
    6. Get size of structure
    7. Get number of elements in structure
    8. Resize the structure
    9. Exit

Choice:
```

Figure 2-1   *The controlling menu for the vector demonstration program*

2.1 *Handling a Vector of a Simple Data Type*

The declaration of a vector manager class can be found in Listing 2-1; its implementation is in Listing 2-2. The VectorMgr class includes all the functions that were part of the array manager, plus functions to return the number of elements in the vector, whether the vector is empty, and to resize the vector.

```
#ifndef VECTOR_MGR
#define VECTOR_MGR 1

class VectorMgr
{
    private:
        int total_elements, current_size;
        int * theVector;
    public:
        VectorMgr (int); // pass in initial size
        ~VectorMgr ();
        bool addElement (int); // pass in a single element
```

Listing 2-1   *Declaration of the vector manager class for a simple data type*

```
      // pass in ordinal position of element
      bool getElement (int, int &);
      // pass in ordinal position of element to delete
      bool deleteElement (int);
      // pass in element value; return ordinal value
      bool findElement (int, int &);
      int getNumbElements (); // return total elements in vector
      int getSize (); // return current size
      bool isEmpty (); // true if vector is empty
      void resize (int); // pass in new size
};

#endif
```

Listing 2-1 (Continued)   Declaration of the vector manager class for a simple data type

```
#include "vectormgr.h"
#include <iostream.h"

VectorMgr::VectorMgr (int size)
{
    theVector = new int [size];
    if (!theVector)
    {
        cout << "\nCannot create vector.";
        return;
    }
    // holds next array index as well as total elements
    total_elements = 0;
    current_size = size;
}

VectorMgr::~VectorMgr ()
    { delete [] theVector; }

bool VectorMgr::addElement (int value)
{
    if (total_elements == current_size)
        return false; // vector is full
    theVector [total_elements++] = value;
```

Listing 2-2   Implementation of the vector manager class for a simple data type

```
    return true;
}

bool VectorMgr::getElement (int element, int & value)
{
    if (element >= total_elements)
        return false;
    value = theVector [element];
    return true;
}

bool VectorMgr::deleteElement (int element)
{
    bool result = true;
    if (element >= total_elements)
        result = false;
    else
    {
        for (int i = element; i < total_elements - 1; i++)
            theVector[i] = theVector[i+1];
        total_elements--;
    }
    return result;
}

bool VectorMgr::findElement (int value, int & element)
{
    int result = true;
    int i = 0;
    while (i < total_elements)
    {
        if (theVector[i] == value)
            element = i;
        i++;
    }
    if (i >= total_elements)
        result = false;
    return result;
}
```

Listing 2-2 (Continued) Implementation of the vector manager class for a simple data type

```
int VectorMgr::getNumbElements ()
    { return total_elements; }

int VectorMgr::getSize ()
    { return current_size; }

bool VectorMgr::isEmpty ()
{
    if (total_elements == 0)
        return true;
    return false;
}

void VectorMgr::resize (int newSize)
{
    char yes_no;
    if (newSize < total_elements)
    {
        cout <<
    "\nThe new size is too small to contain all existing elements."
            << endl;
        cout << "Do you want to truncate the vector? (y/n) ";
        cin >> yes_no;
        if (yes_no == 'y')
            total_elements = newSize;
        else
            return;
    }

    int * newVector = new int [newSize];
    if (!newVector)
    {
        cout << "\nCannot create vector.";
        return;
    }
    for (int i = 0; i < total_elements; i++)
        newVector[i] = theVector[i];
    delete [] theVector;
    theVector = newVector;
```

Listing 2-2 (Continued) Implementation of the vector manager class for a simple data type

```
    current_size = newSize;
}
```

Listing 2-2 (Continued) Implementation of the vector manager class for a simple data type

The major addition, of course, is the `resize` function. The function begins by dynamically allocating space for a new vector, based on the desired new size of the vector (supplied as an input parameter). Then the function copies elements from the current vector to the new vector, one element at a time.

> **Note:** One of the things you want to be sure to do is to check that the allocation of space for a new object or data structure has succeeded. There are several ways to do so. The quickest—in the sense that it uses the least code—is to use the C++ `assert` command, which aborts a program when the evaluation of some expression produces false. The problem with this, however, is the simple fact that it aborts the program without indicating *why*. All the poor user knows is that the program crashed and that there has been no opportunity to save preceding work to disk. The data structrures in this book take a somewhat different tack: If no space can be allocated, they display an error message and exit the current function. An application class can then give the user a chance to save work before exiting.

There is nothing to prevent a user from making a vector smaller. However, if the new vector is smaller than the original and there are valid elements in array positions higher than the new vector's size, those elements must be truncated. As you can see in Listing 2-2, in that case the user can either allow the truncation or abort the resizing.

The process finishes by deleting the old vector to avoid creating a memory leak and then copies the address of the new vector into the variable that holds a pointer to the vector's array (`theVector`).

Because a vector is essentially an array, an iterator to list the elements in a vector looks exactly like an array iterator (see Listing 2-3 and Listing 2-4).

```
#ifndef VECTOR_ITR
#define VECTOR_ITR 1

#include "VectorMgr.h"

class VectorItr
{
    private:
        VectorMgr * theVector;
        int numb_elements;
        int current_index;

    public:
        // pass in the vector manager and total elements
        VectorItr (VectorMgr *, int);
        bool getNext (int &);
};
#endif
```

Listing 2-3 The declaration of an iterator class for a vector that manages a simple data type

The application class for the example program differs primarily in the addition of the resize function (Listing 2-5).

```
#include "vectorItr.h"

VectorItr::VectorItr (VectorMgr * inVector, int iElements)
{
    theVector = inVector;
    numb_elements = iElements;
    current_index = 0;
}

bool VectorItr::getNext (int & value)
{
    bool result = false;
    if (current_index <numb_elements)
    {
        theVector->getElement (current_index, value);
        result = true;
```

Listing 2-4   The implementation of an iterator class for a vector that manages a simple data type

```
        current_index++;
    }
    return result;
}
```

Listing 2-4 (Continued) The implementation of an iterator class for a vector that manages a simple

```
void AppClass::resize()
{
    cout << "Enter a new size for the vector: ";
    int newsize;
    cin >> newsize;
    testVector->resize (newsize);
}
```

Listing 2-5 An application class function to trigger the resizing of a vector

2.2   *Managing a Vector of Objects*

The more generic way to write a vector manager class, of course, is to write it to manage objects. The class being managed is the Thing class that you first saw in Chapter 1. However, in this case it uses a mix-in class named Vectorable instead of Arrayable (see Listing 2-6 and Listing 2-7). Because Vectorable is actually the same as Arrayable, the implementation of the Thing class looks the same as it did for the version that was handled by an array manager.

```
#ifndef THING
#define THING

#include "Vectorable.h"

class Thing : public Vectorable
{
    private:
        int thing_id;
        char thing_name [20];
```

Listing 2-6   The declaration of the Thing class supporting participation in a vector

```
    public:
        Thing ();
        Thing (int, char []);
        int getID ();
        char * getName ();
        int getKey();
};

#endif
```

Listing 2-6 (Continued) The declaration of the Thing class supporting participation in a vector

```
#include "Thing.h"
#include <string.h>

Thing::Thing ()
{

}

Thing::Thing (int iID, char iName[])
{
    thing_id = iID;
    strcpy(thing_name, iName);
}

int Thing::getID ()
    { return thing_id; }

char * Thing::getName ()
    { return thing_name; }

int Thing::getKey ()
    { return thing_id; }
```

Listing 2-7 The implementation of the Thing class supporting participation in a vector

> **Note:** Although most of the mix-in classes used in this book simply require an object to implement a `getKey` function, there is no restriction on what a mix-in class can do. An object that participates in more than one type of data structure in the same program may therefore need to inherit from the mix-in classes for each type of data structure.

Under the assumption that the object being managed has implemented the necessary function(s) from the mix-in class, the vector manager (declared in Listing 2-8 and implemented in Listing 2-9) looks essentially like the version you saw earlier in this chapter, with appropriate changes made to handle objects rather than simple data types.

```
#ifndef VECTOR_MGR
#define VECTOR_MGR 1

#include "thing.h"

class VectorMgr
{
    private:
        int total_elements, current_size;
        Thing * theVector;
    public:
        VectorMgr (int); // pass in initial size
        ~VectorMgr ();
        bool addElement (Thing); // pass in a single element
        // pass in ordinal position of element
        bool getElement (int, Thing &);
        // pass in ordinal position of element to delete
        bool deleteElement (int);
        // pass in element value; return ordinal value
        bool findElement (int, int & pos);
        int getNumbElements (); // return total elements in vector
        int getSize (); // return current size
        bool isEmpty (); // true if vector is empty
        void resize (int); // pass in new size
```

Listing 2-8 Declaration of a vector manager to handle objects

```
};

#endif
```

Listing 2-8 (Continued) Declaration of a vector manager to handle objects

```
#include "vectormgr.h"

VectorMgr::VectorMgr (int size)
{
    theVector = new Thing [size];
    if (!theVector)
    {
        cout << "\nCannot create vector.";
        return;
    }
    // holds next array index as well as total elements
    total_elements = 0;
    current_size = size;
}

VectorMgr::~VectorMgr ()
    { delete [] theVector; }

bool VectorMgr::addElement (Thing theThing)
{
    if (total_elements == current_size)
       return false; // vector is full
    theVector [total_elements] = theThing;
    total_elements++;
    return true;
}

bool VectorMgr::getElement (int element, Thing & theThing)
{
    if (element >= total_elements)
       return false;
    theThing = theVector [element];
    return true;
}
```

Listing 2-9   Implementation of a vector manager to handle objects

```
bool VectorMgr::deleteElement (int element)
{
    bool result = true;
    if (element >= total_elements)
        result = false;
    else
    {
        for (int i = element; i < total_elements - 1; i++)
            theVector[i] = theVector[i+1];
        total_elements--;
    }
    return result;
}

bool VectorMgr::findElement (int searchValue, int & element)
{
    int result = true;
    int i = 0;
    while (i < total_elements)
    {
        if (theVector[i].getKey() == searchValue)
            element = i;
        i++;
    }
    if (i >= total_elements)
        result = false;
    return result;
}

int VectorMgr::getNumbElements ()
    { return total_elements; }

int VectorMgr::getSize ()
    { return current_size; }

bool VectorMgr::isEmpty ()
{
    if (total_elements == 0)
        return true;
```

Listing 2-9 (Continued) Implementation of a vector manager to handle objects

```
        return false;
}

void VectorMgr::resize (int newSize)
{
    char yes_no;
    if (newSize < total_elements)
    {
        cout <<
"\nThe new size is too small to contain all existing elements."
            << endl;
        cout << "Do you want to truncate the vector? (y/n) ";
        if (yes_no == 'y')
            total_elements = newSize;
        else
            return;
    }

    Thing * newVector = new Thing [newSize];
    if (!newVector)
    {
        cout << "\nCannot create vector.";
        return;
    }
    for (int i = 0; i < total_elements; i++)
        newVector[i] = theVector[i];
    delete [] theVector;
    theVector = newVector;
    current_size = newSize;
}
```

Listing 2-9 (Continued) Implementation of a vector manager to handle objects

The vector iterator class is identical to the array iterator class and therefore will be not repeated here.

2.3 Summary

A vector is a dynamic array, one that appears to expand or shrink as needed. In reality, changing the size of a vector requires creating a new array and copying existing data elements into the new array. Then, the program can delete the original array from main memory. In most other aspects, a vector manager class operates in the same way as an array manager class.

CHAPTER 3

Linked Lists

One of the problems with using a vector is the need to allocate and release storage each time the vector is resized, which can lead to memory fragmentation. If you cut down on the number of times you resize the vector, allocating blocks of elements and removing blocks of elements, then the vector will often occupy more space than necessary.

If you want a data structure that occupies only as much space as absolutely necessary and you don't need direct access to the objects in the structure, then you can use a linked list. A linked list chains objects together in some known order. Access begins at the first object in the list and continues to the next object. In other words, a linked list is a sequential access data structure, as opposed to the direct access provided by arrays and vectors.

3.1 The Basic Operation of a Linked List

To build a linked list, you need a list manager object that points to the first object in the list. Each object in the list then points to the next object, with the last object pointing nowhere. Because a linked list requires that an

NULL

object contain a pointer to the next object, building the list out of the objects being listed means adding a variable for the next object pointer to the object's class. If an object participates in more than one list, then it must have a separate variable to point to its neighbor in each list.

To avoid adding pointers to entity classes (classes that are most typically handled by data structures), a linked list (and other more sophisticated data structures) usually is made up of a list of *nodes*. A node is an object that contains pointers to the next node in the list and to the object that is part of the list.

To make this a bit clearer, take a look at Figure 3-1, which depicts a single-linked list (pointers only in the forward direction). The list manager object points to the first node. Each following node points to the next node in the list. Each node also points to the object it is linking.

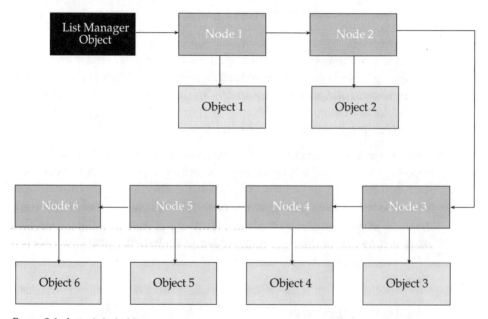

Figure 3-1 A single-linked list

By using node objects, the objects being linked do not have to be modified to include pointers. In fact, an object will be unaware if it is part of more than one list.

Access to elements in the list must follow the pointers. Therefore, access must begin by going through the list manager, which provides access to the first node. You must use this sequential access method, regardless of whether you are displaying information from all the elements or searching for a specific element. There is no fast search technique that can be used on a linked list.

Linked lists are ordered in some way. Most typically, they are sorted on some key. For example, if you had a list of people that were enrolled in a class, you would probably keep that list in alphabetical order by name. You could just as easily use chronological order or numeric order, depending on the order in which you want displays of the contents of the list to appear. When you keep a list sorted, you must able to insert new elements anywhere in the list. You will see examples of this later in this chapter.

Removing an element from a linked list causes less memory fragmentation than removing an element from an array. You simple readjust some pointers in the nodes and remove the deleted node object from memory. The object being referenced by the node can be left in memory if it is still needed by the program.

3.2   A Single-Linked List

A single-linked list like the one in Figure 3-1 is easy to maintain because there is only one pointer per node. It is also limited, because all access is in a forward direction. However, a single-linked list makes a great starting place for examining how linked lists operate.

The sample program for a single-linked list can do only three things (see Figure 3-2): add an element to the list, remove an element from the list, and display the elements in list order.

```
1. Add an element
2. Remove an element
3. View elements
9. Quit

Choice:
```

Figure 3-2 The capabilities of the single-linked list demonstration program

3.2.1 A Mix-in Class for a Linked List

The objects being linked are from the Thing class (Listing 3-1 and Listing 3-2) and are ordered on the thing_id variable. In this case, Thing inherits from a mix-in class named Listable, which once again enforces the implementation of a getKey function (Listing 3-3 and Listing 3-4).

```
#ifndef THING
#define THING

#include "listable.h"

class Thing : public Listable
{
    private:
        int thing_id;
        char thing_name [20];

    public:
        Thing ();
        Thing (int, char []);
        int getID ();
        char * getName ();
        int getKey();
};

#endif
```

Listing 3-1 Declaration of the Thing class for use in a linked list

```
#include "Thing.h"
#include <string.h>

Thing::Thing ()
{

}

Thing::Thing (int iID, char iName[])
{
    thing_id = iID;
    strncpy(thing_name, iName, strlen(thing_name));
}

int Thing::getID ()
    { return thing_id; }

char * Thing::getName ()
    { return thing_name; }

int Thing::getKey ()
    { return thing_id; }
```

Listing 3-2 Implementation of the Thing class for use in a linked list

```
#ifndef LISTABLE
#define LISTABLE 1

class Listable
{
    public:
        Listable ();
        virtual int getKey () = 0;
};

#endif
```

Listing 3-3 Declaration of the Listable class

```
#include "listable.h"

Listable::Listable ()
{
    // this does nothing
}
```

Listing 3-4 Implementation of the Listable class

3.2.2 The Node Class for a Single-Linked List

The node class for a single-linked list (Listing 3-5 and Listing 3-6) has two variables: a pointer to the next node and a pointer to a `Thing` object. The node class must be able to change the value of its next pointer (`setNext`) and retrieve the value of that pointer (`getnext`). It must also be able to retrieve the address of the object to which it points (`getThing`).

```
#ifndef NODE
#define NODE

#include "thing.h"

class Node
{
    private:
        Thing * theThing; // pointer to object being linked
        Node * next; // pointer to next node in list
    public:
        Node (Thing *);
        Node * getNext ();
        Thing * getThing ();
        void setNext (Node *);
};

#endif
```

Listing 3-5 Declaration of a node class for a single-linked list

The node does not control *when* its next pointer is changed. The linked list manager is in charge of deciding which pointers need to be modified and

```
#include "node.h"

Node::Node (Thing * theObject)
{
    theThing = theObject;
    next = 0;
}

Node * Node::getNext ()
    { return next; }

Thing * Node::getThing ()
    { return theThing; }

void Node::setNext (Node * nextNode)
    { next = nextNode; }
```

Listing 3-6 Implementation of a node class for a single-linked list

the order in which those modifications should occur. The list manager is also responsbile for saving any pointers that need to be saved as modifications are made.

Notice that there is no function to change the object to which the node points. As you will see shortly, if you need to insert or delete an element, you remove or add a node. You never modify the object to which a node points.

3.2.3 The Linked List Manager

As mentioned earlier, all access to a linked list begins with the list manager object. As you can see in Listing 3-7, the list manager class stores a pointer to the first node in the list, but nothing else. The list manager does not need to know how many elements are in the list or which element is last. The last node will simply have a "next" pointer of 0.

This list manager class does four things:

- Inserts a new node into the list.
- Locates an element by traversing the list to match the element's key.

```
#ifndef LISTMGR
#define LISTMGR

#include "thing.h"
#include "node.h"

class ListMgr
{
    private:
        Node * first;
    public:
        ListMgr ();
        void insert (Thing *);
        Thing * find (int); // traverse list to locate by ID
        int remove (int); // use ID number to locate for removal
        Node * getFirst();
};

#endif
```

Listing 3-7 Declaration of a list manager class

- Removes a node from the list.
- Returns a pointer to the first node. This function is used by a list iterator so it knows where to start its traversal.

3.2.3.1 Adding an Element to a List

You can find the code for adding an element to a linked list in Listing 3-8. The Thing objects are kept in key order (in this case, numeric order).

```
void ListMgr::insert (Thing * theThing)
{
    Node * newNode, * current, * previous;
    Thing * currentThing;

    newNode = new Node (theThing); // create a node object
    int newKey = theThing->getKey();
    if (!newNode)
```

Listing 3-8   Inserting an element into a single-linked list

```
    {
        cout << "\nCannot create node." << endl
        return;
    }

    if (first == 0) // list is empty
        first = newNode;
    else
    {
        int firstNode = true;
        current = first; // start at head of list
        while (current != 0)
        {
            currentThing = current->getThing();
            if (newKey < currentThing->getKey())
// spot found (between current and current's previous node
                break;
// save preceding because there aren't backward pointers
            previous = current;
            current = current->getNext ();
            firstNode = false; // not the first node
        }

// set previous node to point to new node except when first in list
        if (!firstNode)
            previous->setNext (newNode);
        else
            first = newNode; // have new first in list

// set new node to point to following node
        newNode->setNext (current);
    }
}
```

Listing 3-8 (Continued) Inserting an element into a single-linked list

Insertion works in the following way:

1. Create a new **Node** object, inserting a pointer to the object being managed into the node.

2. Retrieve the object's key.

3. Determine whether the list is empty by checking the contents of the `first` variable. If it contains 0, then there are no nodes in the list. In that case, set `first` equal to the newly created node and exit. Otherwise, continue with the insertion procedure.

4. Assume that the node to be inserted will become a new first node.

5. Set a pointer to the node in the list that will be processed next (the variable `current`). At the beginning of the process, the current node is the first node.

6. Enter a loop that continues until the there is no current node (`current` contains 0). If the process has reached the end of the list, continue with Step 15. Otherwise, continue with Step 7.

7. Retrieve the object linked by the current node.

8. Retrieve the object's key.

9. Compare the object's key to the key of the object being inserted.

10. If the key of the object being inserted is less than the key of the current node, then the object being inserted should go between the current node and the node preceding it. (When the current node is the first node, then the node being inserted becomes a new first node.) Exit the loop.

11. Save the current node as the previous node. This is necessary because there are no pointers to preceding nodes, but insertion between two nodes requires access to the preceding.

12. Make the current node the "next" node by retrieving the contents of the current node's next pointer.

13. Indicate that the node being inserted is not a new first node by setting `firstNode` to `false`.

14. Go back to step 6 to determine whether the process has reached the end of the list.

The actual process of inserting a new node into a linked list involves breaking the link between the nodes that will be on either side of the node being inserted and linking the two existing nodes to the new node. For example, assume that you are inserting node 7 in Figure 3-3 between nodes 4 and 5. To do so, you must make node 5 point to node 7 and node 7 point to node 4. The existing link between nodes 4 and 5 disappears.

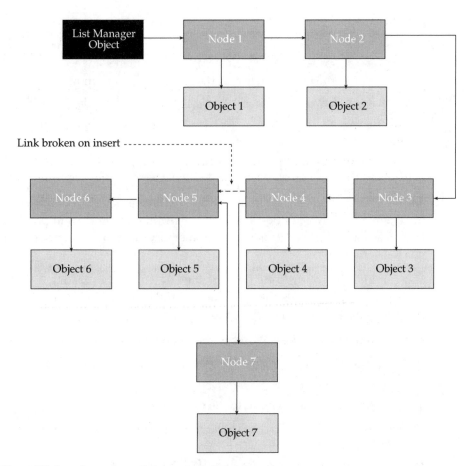

Figure 3-3 Inserting a new node into a single-linked list

15. If the node being inserted is not a new first node, set the previous node's next pointer to point to the node being inserted. Otherwise, set the list manager's `first` variable to point to the node being inserted.

16. Set the next pointer in the node being inserted to point to the current node. If the new node is going at the end of the list, this will set its next pointer to 0, since the current node is 0 at this point.

> **Note:** Although it is most common to keep elements in a linked list sorted by a key, you can also adopt an policy in which all new elements are added to the head of this list or to the tail of the list. In the latter case, you can make coding much simpler by keeping a pointer to the last node in the list as part of the list manager object.

3.2.3.2 Removing an Element from a List

Removing an element from a single-linked list is essentially the opposite of adding one. As you can see in Figure 3-4, removing node 5 requires creating a new link between node 4 and node 6. Although node 5 still points to node 6 as long as node 5 exists in main memory, the pointer in node 5 has no effect on the list.

You can find the source code for removing an element in Listing 3-9. The calling function supplies the key value of the object to be removed. The function must then traverse the list to find the correct node to remove.

The actual removal process works in the following way:

1. Determine whether the list is empty. If it is empty, exit the function.
2. Assume that the node to be removed is the first node.
3. Set the current node to point to the first node.
4. Enter a loop that continues as long as there is a current node. If there is no current node, skip to Step 11.
5. Retrieve the object linked by the current node.
6. Compare the key of the node being removed to the key of the current node. If the keys match, the node to be removed has been found. Exit the loop and continue with step 11. Otherwise, continue with step 7.
7. Save the current node as the previous node.
8. Set the current node to point to the next node in the list.
9. Indicate that the node being removed isn't the first node in the list.
10. Return to step 4.
11. If the current node is 0, the key value of the node to be removed isn't in the list. Exit the function.

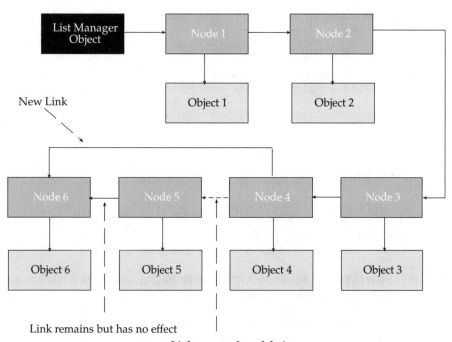

Figure 3-4 Removing a node from a single-linked list

```
int ListMgr::remove (int searchNumb)
{
    Thing * currentThing;
    Node * current, * previous, * next;

    if (first == 0)
        return false; // list is empty

    int firstNode = true;
    current = first;

    while (current != 0)
    {
        currentThing = current->getThing();
```

Listing 3-9   Removing an element from a single-linked list

```
        if (searchNumb == currentThing->getKey())
            break; // jump out of loop
        // save preceding because there aren't backward pointers
        previous = current;
        current = current->getNext ();
        firstNode = false; // not the first node
    }

    if (current == 0)
        return false; // node not found

    if (!firstNode)
    {
        // gets node after node being removed
        next = current->getNext ();
        previous->setNext (next);
    }
    else
        // sets first to node after node being removed
        first = current->getNext ();

    delete current->getThing(); // remove thing object from memory
    delete current; // remove node object from memory

    return true; // remove was successful
}
```

Listing 3-9 (Continued) Removing an element from a single-linked list

12. If the node being removed is not the first node, get the node following the node to be removed. Set the current node's next pointer to point to the node following the node to be removed. Skip to step 13.

13. If the node being removed is the first node, set the list manager's first node to point to the node after the node being removed.

14. Delete the object linked by the node being removed from main memory.

15. Delete the node being removed from main memory.

You will always want to delete a node object from main memory once the node has been removed from its list. However, it will depend on the nature of your program whether you will delete the object that was linked. If the object is participating in other data structures or will be used in some other way, then you will want to leave it in main memory.

> **Note:** One way to decide whether you want to delete an element from main memory is to give the element an integer variable that holds a *reference count*. Each time you add the element to a data structure, you increment the reference count by one. By the same token, each time you remove the element from a data structure, you decrement the reference count. When the reference count drops to 0, you can delete the element from memory.

3.2.3.3 Searching a Single-Linked List

There is only one way to search a linked list: sequentially. In the case of a single-linked list, you must start at the first element in the list and move in "next" order, checking each linked object to determine if satisfies the search criteria. There is no faster way because a linked list provides only sequential access to its members.

As an example, consider Listing 3-10. The list manager's `find` function accepts a value that is to be matched against the keys of objects stored in the list as an input parameter. The search begins by initializing the current node to the first node in the list. (That is the only node that the list manager object can reach directly!)

```
Thing * ListMgr::find (int searchNumb)
{
    Thing * currentThing;
    Node * current;
    current = first; // start at head of list

    while (current != 0)
    {
        currentThing = current->getThing();
        if (searchNumb == currentThing->getKey())
            return currentThing;
```

Listing 3-10   Searching a linked list

```
        current = current->getNext ();
    }
    return 0; // not found
}
```

Listing 3-10 (Continued) Searching a linked list

The remainder for the search proceeds in the following way:

1. Enter a loop that continues as long as there is a current node. If there is no current node, go to step 7.
2. Retrieve the object linked by the current node.
3. Compare the object's key value with the search key value.
4. If the two keys are the same, return a pointer to the object. Otherwise, continue with step 5.
5. Retrieve a pointer to the next node from the current node and make it the new current node.
6. Return to step 1.
7. Return a 0 indicating that no element in the list contains the search key.

3.2.4 Using the List Manager

The application class that uses the single-linked list manager can be found in Listing 3-11 and Listing 3-12. As with programs that used the array and vector managers, this application class's constructor creates an object of the list manager. The remainder of the class's member functions handle the user interface and basic list manipulation.

```
#ifndef APP
#define APP

#include "listmgr.h"

#define INSERT 1
#define REMOVE_THING 2
#define VIEW 3
```

Listing 3-11 Declaration of the application class for the single-linked list demonstration program

```
#define QUIT 9

class AppClass
{
    private:
        ListMgr * theList;
        int menu ();
        void addThing ();
        void removeThing ();
        void view ();
    public:
        AppClass();
        void run();
};

#endif
```

Listing 3-11 (Continued) Declaration of the application class for the single-linked list demonstration

```
#include "appclass.h"
#include "listmgr.h"
#include "listitr.h"
#include "thing.h"
#include <iostream.h>

AppClass::AppClass()
{
    theList = new ListMgr();
}

void AppClass::run()
{
    int choice = menu ();

    while (choice != QUIT)
    {
        switch (choice)
        {
            case INSERT:
                addThing();
```

Listing 3-12 Implementation of the application class for the single-linked list demonstration program

```
                break;
            case REMOVE_THING:
                removeThing();
                break;
            case VIEW:
                view ();
                break;
            case QUIT:
                break;
            default:
                cout << "Unrecognized menu option." << endl;
        }
        choice = menu ();
    }
}

int AppClass::menu ()
{
    cout << "\n1. Add an element";
    cout << "\n2. Remove an element";
    cout << "\n3. View elements";
    cout << "\n9. Quit";
    cout << "\n\nChoice: ";
    int choice;
    cin >> choice;
    return choice;
}

void AppClass::addThing()
{
    Thing * newThing;
    int ID;
    char name [26];

    cout << "\nID: ";
    cin >> ID;
    cin.get (); // eat CR in keyboard buffer
    cout << "Name: ";
    cin.getline (name,26);
    newThing = new Thing (ID, name);
```

Listing 3-12 (Continued) Implementation of the application class for the single-linked list

```
    theList->insert (newThing);
}

void AppClass::removeThing()
{
    int ID;

    cout << "ID number to remove: ";
    cin >> ID;
    int result = theList->remove (ID);
    if (result)
        cout << "Remove successful";
    else
        cout << "Remove unsuccessful";
}

void AppClass::view ()
{
    Thing * current;
    ListItr * theIterator;

    theIterator = new ListItr (theList);
    current = theIterator->getNext();
    cout << endl; // just a blank line for spacing
    while (current != 0)
    {
        cout << "ID = " << current->getID() << "; Name = "
            << current->getName() << "." << endl;
        current = theIterator->getNext();
    }
}
```

Listing 3-12 (Continued) Implementation of the application class for the single-linked list

3.2.4.1 Adding and Removing Elements

To enter an element, the application collects data for the object to be linked into the list (in this case, a Thing object), creates the object, and then calls the list manager's insert function. To remove an element, the application needs only the element's key, which is then passed to the list manager's `remove` function. The list manager takes care of all of the actual list manipulation details.

3.2.4.2 Traversing the List

Like an array and a vector, a list manager uses an iterator object to handle a traversal. A list iterator for a single-linked list (for example, Listing 3-13 and Listing 3-14) initializes itself by retrieving the first node in the list from the list manager. It then traverses the list by following the "next" pointers in each node.

```
#ifndef LISTITR
#define LISTITR

#include "node.h"
#include "listmgr.h"

class ListItr
{
    private:
        Node * current;
        ListMgr * theList;
    public:
        ListItr (ListMgr *);
        Thing * getNext ();
};

#endif
```

Listing 3-13 Declaration of an iterator class for a single-linked list

```
#include "listitr.h"

ListItr::ListItr (ListMgr * whichList)
{
    current = 0;
    theList = whichList;
}
```

Listing 3-14 Implementation of an iterator class for a single-linked list

```
Thing * ListItr::getNext ()
{
    if (current == 0)
        current = theList->getFirst ();
    else
        current = current->getNext ();

    if (current != 0)
        return current->getThing();
    else
        return 0;
}
```

Listing 3-14 (Continued) Implementation of an iterator class for a single-linked list

It is, of course, up to the function using the iterator (in our example, the application class's `view` function in Listing 3-12) to determine when the iterator has reached the end of the list (in other words, when `getNext` returns 0).

> **Note:** The code for the entire application classes for the remaining demonstration programs in this book have not been included for two reasons. First, they would add nearly 60 pages of simple I/O code to the book and second, they are available for download from the author's Web site:
> http://www.blackgryphonltd.com.

3.3   A Double-Linked List

The biggest drawback to a single-linked list is that it can be traversed in only one direction: from beginning to end. The coding of the insert and removal operations is also more difficult because there are pointers only to the next node but not to the previous node.

A double-linked list, such as that in Figure 3-5, includes both forward and backward pointers in each node. The list manager points to both the first and last node in the list. The result is a list that can be traversed in two orders: beginning to end and end to beginning. You could, for example, keep a list of checking account transactions in chronological order, with new transactions inserted at the head of the list. A first/next traversal would give you the most recent transactions first; a last/prior traversal would give you the oldest transactions first.

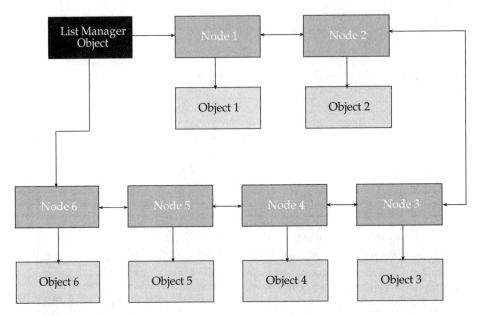

Figure 3-5 A double-linked list

Note: Theoretically, there is no limit to the number and direction of pointers that you can add to a linked list. For example, there is nothing that prevents every node from having a pointer to the list manager object. However, the more pointers you add, the more pointers you have to manipulate whenever you modify the membership of the list.

3.3.1 A Node for a Double-Linked List

The first difference between a single- and double-linked list is in the `Node` class. As you can see in Listing 3-15 and Listing 3-16, the class now includes a pointer to the prior node, along with `getPrior` and `setPrior` functions.

```
#ifndef NODE
#define NODE

#include "thing.h"

class Node
{
    private:
        Thing * theThing; // pointer to object being linked
        Node * next; // pointer to next node in list
        Node * prior; // pointer to prior node in list
    public:
        Node (Thing *);
        Node * getNext ();
        Node * getPrior ();
        Thing * getThing ();
        void setNext (Node *);
        void setPrior (Node *);
};

#endif
```

Listing 3-15 Declaration of a node class for a double-linked list

```
#include "node.h"

Node::Node (Thing * theObject)
{
    theThing = theObject;
    next = 0;
    prior = 0;
}
```

Listing 3-16 Implementation of a node class for a double-linked list

```
Node * Node::getNext ()
    { return next; }

Node * Node::getPrior ()
    { return prior; }

Thing * Node::getThing ()
    { return theThing; }

void Node::setNext (Node * nextNode)
    { next = nextNode; }

void Node::setPrior (Node * priorNode)
    { prior = priorNode; }
```

Listing 3-16 (Continued) Implementation of a node class for a double-linked list

3.3.2 A List Manager for a Double-Linked List

The list manager for a double-linked list (declared in Listing 3-17) looks very much like that of a single-linked list. There are two simple additions: a pointer to the last node in the list and a `getLast` function. The functions to add and remove elements, however, are slightly different. They can avoid saving a previous node during the traversal to find the element to be deleted, but they must also deal with the multiple pointers when modifying the list.

```
#ifndef LISTMGR
#define LISTMGR

#include "thing.h"
#include "node.h"

class ListMgr
{
    private:
        Node * first, * last;
    public:
```

Listing 3-17 Declaration of a list manager class for a double-linked list

```
    ListMgr ();
    void insert (Thing *);
    Thing * find (int); // traverse list to locate by ID
    int remove (int); // use ID number to locate for removal
    Node * getFirst();
    Node * getLast ();
};
```

#endif

Listing 3-17 (Continued) Declaration of a list manager class for a double-linked list

3.3.2.1 Adding an Element to a Double-Linked List

Assuming that a double-linked list is ordered on some key value, inserting a new element first requires that you find the location where the new element should be inserted. Then you must adjust both the forward and backward pointers (see Figure 3-6).

Code for an insert into a double-linked list can be found in Listing 3-18. The insertion works in the following way:

1. Create a Node object for the object being inserted into the list.
2. Retrieve the key value for the object being inserted.
3. Determine whether the list is empty (the list manager's first variable contains 0). If so, the list is empty. Insert the node as the first and last node in the list. Exit the function. Otherwise, continue with step 4.
4. Assume that the node being inserted is a new first node.
5. Make the first node in the list the current node.
6. Enter a loop that continues while there is a current node.
7. Retrieve the object linked by the current node.
8. Compare the key of the object being inserted into the list with the key of the object linked by the current node. If the key of the object being inserted is less than the key of the current node's object, then the place for the new object has been found. Continue with step 11.
9. Replace the current node with the current node's next pointer.
10. Return to step 6.
11. If there is no current node, insert the new node at the end of the list.

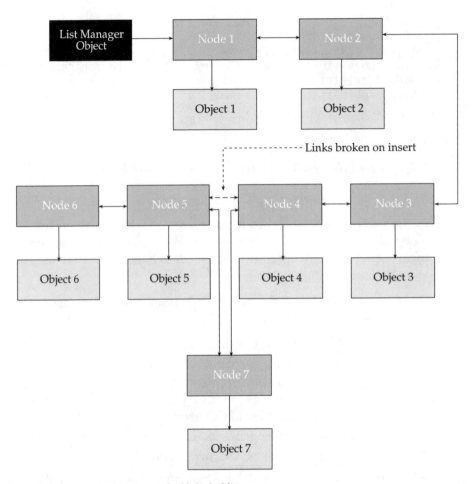

Figure 3-6 Adding an element to a double-linked list

```
void ListMgr::insert (Thing * theThing)
{
    Node * newNode, * current, * previous;
    Thing * currentThing;

    newNode = new Node (theThing); // create a node object
```

Listing 3-18 Adding an element to a double-linked list

```
if (!newNode)
{
    cout << "\nCannot create node." << endl
    return;
}

int newKey = theThing->getKey();

if (first == 0) // list is empty
{
    first = newNode;
    last = newNode;
}
else
{
    int firstNode = true;
    current = first; // start at head of list
    while (current != 0)
    {
        currentThing = current->getThing();
        if (newKey < currentThing->getKey())
// spot found (between current and current's previous node)
            break;
        current = current->getNext ();
        firstNode = false; // not the first node
    }

    if (current == 0) // insert as new last node
    {
        newNode->setPrior (last);
        last->setNext (newNode);
        last = newNode;
    }
    else if (!firstNode)  // insert in the middle of the list
    {
        previous = current->getPrior ();
        previous->setNext (newNode);
        newNode->setNext (current);
        newNode->setPrior (previous);
        current->setPrior (newNode);
```

Listing 3-18 (Continued) Adding an element to a double-linked list

```
        }
        else // have new first in list
        {
            first->setPrior (newNode);
            newNode->setNext (first);
            first = newNode;
        }
    }
}
```

Listing 3-18 (Continued) Adding an element to a double-linked list

> a. Set the new node's prior pointer to point to the current last node in the list.
>
> b. Set the last node's next pointer to point to the new node.
>
> c. Set the list manager's `last` variable to point to the new node.
>
> d. Exit the function.

12. If the new node is not a new first node, insert the new node between two existing nodes.

> a. Retrieve a pointer to the current node's previous node.
>
> b. Set the next pointer of the previous node to point to the new node.
>
> c. Set the next pointer of the new node to point to the current node.
>
> d. Set the prior pointer of the new node to point to the previous node.
>
> e. Set the prior pointer of the current node to point to the new node.
>
> f. Exit the function.

13. Insert the new node as the first node in the list.

> a. Set the prior pointer of the current first node to point to the new node.
>
> b. Set the next pointer of the new node to point the current first node.
>
> c. Set the array manager's `first` variable to point to the new node.
>
> d. Exit the function.

3.3.2.2 Removing an Element from a Double-Linked List

As you would expect, removing an element from a double-linked list is pretty much the opposite of inserting an element. You must find the element to be removed and then make the next and previous nodes point to each other, bypassing (and thus effectively removing) the node in between (see Figure 3-7).

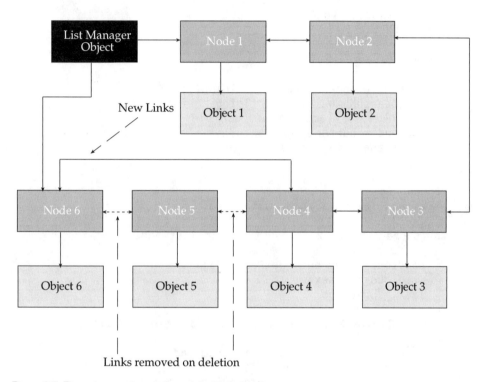

Figure 3-7 Removing an element from a double-linked list

The code for removing a node can be found in Listing 3-19. The function expects a search key value as its input parameter and returns a boolean indicating whether the removal was successful.

```
int ListMgr::remove (int searchNumb)
{
    Thing * currentThing;
    Node * current, * previous, * next;
```

Listing 3-19   Removing an element from a double-linked list

```
if (first == 0)
   return false; // list is empty

int firstNode = true;
current = first;

while (current != 0)
{
   currentThing = current->getThing();
   if (searchNumb == currentThing->getKey())
      break; // jump out of loop
   current = current->getNext ();
   firstNode = false; // not the first node
}

if (current == 0)
   return false; // node not found

if (current->getNext () == 0) // if last node
{
   previous = current->getPrior ();
   previous->setNext (0);
   last = previous;
}
else if (!firstNode) // if in the middle of the list
{
   // get node after node being removed
   next = current->getNext ();
   // get node preceding node being removed
   previous = current->getPrior ();
   previous->setNext (next);
   next->setPrior (previous);
}
else // must be first in list
   // sets first to node after node being removed
   first = current->getNext ();

delete current->getThing(); // remove thing object from memory
delete current; // remove node object from memory
```

Listing 3-19 (Continued)   Removing an element from a double-linked list

```
    return true; // remove was successful
}
```

Listing 3-19 (Continued)   Removing an element from a double-linked list

The removal works in the following way:

1. Determine whether the list is empty. If the list is empty, return `false`. Otherwise, continue with step 2.
2. Assume that the node being removed is the first node.
3. Make the current node the first node in the list.
4. Enter a loop that continues while there is a current node.
5. Retrieve the current node's object.
6. Compare the search key value to the current object's key value. If the two keys are equal, the node to be removed has been found. Exit the loop and continue with step 9.
7. Make the current node's next node the current node.
8. Continue with step 4.
9. If there is no current node, then no object with the search key value is part of the list. Return `false` indicating that the removal failed and exit the function. Otherwise, continue with step 10.
10. If the node to be removed is the last node in the list, remove it using the following procedure:
    a. Retrieve a pointer to the last node's previous node.
    b. Set the previous node's next to pointer to 0.
    c. Set the list manager's `last` variable to point to the previous node.
    d. Continue with step 13.
11. If the node to be removed is between two other nodes, remove it using the following procedure:
    a. Retrieve a pointer to the current node's next node.
    b. Retrieve a pointer to the current node's previous node.
    c. Set the previous node's next pointer to point to the next node.
    d. Set the next node's previous pointer to point to the previous node.
    e. Continue with step 13.

12. The node to be removed must be the first node in the list. Remove it by setting the list manager's `last` variable to point to the current node's next node.

13. Delete the object linked to the node being removed (optional).

14. Delete the node being removed.

15. Return `true` to indicate that the removal was successful.

3.3.2.3 Searching a Double-Linked List

Searching a double-linked list is exactly like searching a single-linked list. See Section 3.2.3.3 for details.

3.3.3 Implementing Multiple Iterators

An iterator class is designed to traverse a data structure in exactly one way. If you create multiple objects from the same iterator class, then you will be able to have multiple traversals ongoing at the same time, but each will feed you objects from the structure in precisely the same order. Therefore, if you want to support more than one traversal order on a single data structure, then you will need multiple iterator classes.

This is exactly the case with a double-linked list. One iterator (Listing 3-20 and Listing 3-21) traverses a double-linked list in ascending (first/next) order. This is the same logic used to traverse the single-linked list.

```
#ifndef LISTITR_ASC
#define LISTITR_ASC

#include "node.h"
#include "listmgr.h"

class ListItrAsc
{
    private:
        Node * current;
        ListMgr * theList;
```

Listing 3-20   Declaration of an ascending (first/next) order iterator for a double-linked list

```
    public:
        ListItrAsc (ListMgr *);
        Thing * getNext ();
};

#endif
```

Listing 3-20 (Continued) Declaration of an ascending (first/next) order iterator for a double-linked list

```
#include "listitrasc.h"

ListItrAsc::ListItrAsc (ListMgr * whichList)
{
    current = 0;
    theList = whichList;
}

Thing * ListItrAsc::getNext ()
{
    if (current == 0)
        current = theList->getFirst ();
    else
        current = current->getNext ();

    if (current != 0)
        return current->getThing();
    else
        return 0;
}
```

Listing 3-21 Implementation of an ascending (first/next) order iterator for a double-linked list

The descending (last/prior) iterator class (Listing 3-22 and Listing 3-23) uses a very similar logic. However, it uses the list manager's last variable to begin at the last node in the list. Then, rather than following a chain of next pointers, it follows the prior pointers.

The code to use the two iterators is virtually identical. For example, in Listing 3-24 you will find an application class function that uses the ascending order iterator. The only difference between that function and the function

```
#ifndef LISTITR_DESC
#define LISTITR_DESC

#include "node.h"
#include "listmgr.h"

class ListItrDesc
{
   private:
      Node * current;
      ListMgr * theList;
   public:
      ListItrDesc (ListMgr *);
      Thing * getNext ();
};

#endif
```

Listing 3-22 Declaration of a descending (last/prior) order iterator for a double-linked list

```
#include "listitrdesc.h"

ListItrDesc::ListItrDesc (ListMgr * whichList)
{
   current = 0;
   theList = whichList;
}

Thing * ListItrDesc::getNext ()
{
   if (current == 0)
      current = theList->getLast ();
   else
      current = current->getPrior ();

   if (current != 0)
      return current->getThing();
   else
      return 0;
```

Listing 3-23   Implementation of a descending (last/prior) order iterator for a double-linked list

```
}
```

Listing 3-23 (Continued) Implementation of a descending (last/prior) order iterator for a double-

in Listing 3-25, which produces the listing in descending order, is the iterator class from which an iterator object is created. This is the precise reason
to use iterator classes: Regardless of the order in which the iterator feeds
values to a function, all iterators created for use with the same data structure work in exactly the same way.

```
void AppClass::viewThingAsc()
{
    Thing * current;
    ListItrAsc * theIterator;

    theIterator = new ListItrAsc (theList);
    current = theIterator->getNext();
    cout << endl; // just a blank line for spacing
    while (current != 0)
    {
        cout << "ID = " << current->getID() << "; Name = "
            << current->getName() << "." << endl;
        current = theIterator->getNext();
    }
}
```

Listing 3-24 Using the ascending order double-linked list iterator

```
void AppClass::viewThingDesc()
{
    Thing * current;
    ListItrDesc * theIterator;

    theIterator = new ListItrDesc (theList);
    current = theIterator->getNext();
    cout << endl; // just a blank line for spacing
    while (current != 0)
    {
```

Listing 3-25 Using the descending order double-linked list iterator

```
    cout << "ID = " << current->getID() << "; Name = "
        << current->getName() << "." << endl;
    current = theIterator->getNext();
    }
}
```

Listing 3-25 (Continued) Using the descending order double-linked list iterator

3.4 *Summary*

A linked list is a linear data structure that provides sequential access to its elements through a chain of pointers. In its simplest form, a linked list contains pointers to the "next" element in the list only; for access in reverse order, the list must also contain "prior" pointers.

A linked list consists of a list manager object and a chain of node objects, each of which points to an object that is a part of the list. Use of the nodes avoids the need to place pointers within the objects being linked, making them independent of the data structures in which they participate.

CHAPTER 4

Stacks and Queues

The data structures that you have seen to this point are used frequently by both application and systems programs. In this chapter, however, you will read about two fundamental data structures—*stacks* and *queues*—that are rarely used by application programs to manage objects created from entity classes. Instead, they are used most commonly by systems programs and by other data structures. In addition, they are implemented using other data structures (arrays or linked lists). Stacks and queues are therefore logical, rather than physical, data structures.

4.1 Stacks

A stack is a list of elements that most commonly is accessed in last-in/first-out order. To make the concept clearer, consider Figure 4-1. As you can see, the stack appears as a tube with one closed end and one open end. Elements enter and leave from the top only. In this particular example, the elements are entered in the order 1, 2, 3, 4. They will leave in the reverse order: 4,3,2,1. Element 4—the last element to enter the stack—will be the first element to leave (assuming no other elements enter the stack in the meantime).

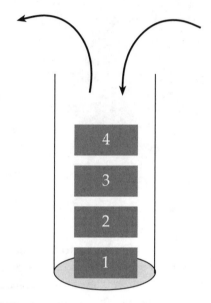

Figure 4-1 The operation of a stack

A stack requires very few operations:

- Push: Add an element to the top of the stack.
- Pop: Remove an element from the top of the stack.
- Determine whether the stack is empty.

If the idea of pushing and popping elements from a stack seems a bit strange, think of a stack like a Pez candy dispenser. You load the candy from the top and remove it in the reverse order. There is a spring at the bottom of the candy dispenser, so that when you add a piece of candy, you must push it down a bit. When you remove a piece of candy, it pops out at you as the spring uncoils to fill the space vacated by the piece you just removed.

To keep track of the location of the last element that entered the stack, a stack maintains a *stack pointer*. If the stack is implemented as an array, the stack pointer is an array index or a main memory address; if the stack is implemented as a linked list, the stack pointer is a reference to the first element in the list. The stack pointer moves as elements are pushed onto and popped off the top of the stack.

4.1.1 Uses of Stacks

Every application program that runs uses a single stack for two major purposes: to keep track of function return addresses and to pass parameters. When you launch an application program, the operating system allocates a block of main memory for the program. The program's object code and data storage begin at the lowest address in the block and grow up toward higher addresses. This range of memory is often called the *program heap*. Space for the program stack is allocated at the block's highest address and grows down toward lower addresses. In fact, one of the ways a program can run out of memory is for the heap to run into the stack. This is an unrecoverable runtime error!

4.1.1.1 Using a Stack to Handle Function Return Addresses

To understand a how a program uses a stack to handle function return addresses, you need to know a bit about how instructions are executed. The CPU uses small bits of main memory, known as *registers*, for internal storage. One of these registers, the *program counter*, stores the main memory address of the next instruction to be executed. Therefore, one of the last things the CPU does after executing an instruction is to increment the program counter. This provides for sequential instruction execution. However, if a program needs to execute a branch—either as the result of a loop, function call, or selection statement—then the CPU replaces the current contents of the program counter with the location of the statement that is the target of the branch, and does not increment the program counter.

The CPU uses the stack to store the main memory address of the statement following a statement that calls a function. As an example, consider the snippet of code in Figure 4-2. The column of numbers on the left are addresses. (This really doesn't necessarily correspond to actual object code because each high-level language statement usually generates multiple machine code instructions. Nonetheless, it will serve to illustrate the operation of the program stack.)

:	:
105	theObject->someFunction();
106	
107	
108	
109	// last executable statement }
110	void theClass::someFunction();
111	// first executable statement {
112	
113	
114	
115	
116	
117	// last executable statement }
:	

Figure 4-2 Code with a function call to demonstrate stack operation

Assume that the program counter contains 105. To execute that instruction, the CPU pushes the address of the following statement onto the stack:

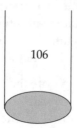

The program then replaces the contents of the program counter with 110, the address of the function being called, and continues execution at that location. Execution proceeds sequentially—in this case, there are no loops or selection statements in the function—until the program reaches 117, the last executable statement in the function. At that point, the CPU pops the 106 off the stack, places it in the program counter, and continues execution.

4.1.1.2 Using a Stack to Pass Parameters

If a function call also happens to include input parameters, the CPU also uses the stack to send those values—be they copies of data values or main memory addresses—to the called function. To illustrate this, let's add some parameters to the function in Figure 4-2, as in Figure 4-3.

```
   :        :
105        theObject->someFunction(15, "J", 27.5);
106
107
108
109        // last executable statement    }
110        void theClass::someFunction(int, char, float);
111        // first executable statement    {
112
113
114
115
116
117        // last executable statement    }
   :
```

Figure 4-3 Code with a function call to demonstrate use of a stack to pass parameters

When the CPU reaches address 105, it begins just as it did when the function had no parameters by pushing the 106 onto the stack. It then continues by pushing each parameter onto the stack, in the same order in which the parameters appear in the parameter list:

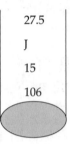

The CPU then replaces the contents of the program counter with 110 and continues execution at that location. Before entering the body of the function, however, the CPU pops the three parameters off the stack, assigning them to storage locations for the use of the function in the reverse order in which they appear in the parameter list. The return address (106) is left on the stack so that the function will return properly.

4.1.1.3 Stack Frames

Many modern compilers produce code that encapsulates function return addresses and function parameters with the values of the local variables of the calling function into a single unit known as a *stack frame*. When a function call occurs, the entire frame is pushed onto the stack.

A stack frame typically has the organization in Figure 4-4. The local variables are pushed first onto the stack, followed by the return address, and then by the called function's parameters.

Stack frames make it possible to support *recursion*, a type of programming in which a fuction calls itself. Each time the function calls itself, it creates a stack frame and pushes it onto the stack. When a function call returns, it can pop the state of its local variables off the stack and pick up execution where it left off. (You will be introduced to recursive programming in Chapter 8 and you will see a number of examples of it throughout the remainder of the book.)

Parameters
Return Address
Calling function's local variables

Figure 4-4 The organization of a stack frame

Note: Stacks are also used by binary search tree iterators to keep track of the nodes a traversal has visited on its way through the tree. (You will learn about binary search trees in Chapter 5.) The irony of this is that although a program stack is needed to implement recursion, a program can use a stack itself to avoid using recursion.

4.1.2 Implementing a Stack Using an Array

One way to implement a stack is to use an array. The advantage to this approach is that, if necessary, a function can access data in locations other than the top of the stack. Because main memory provides direct access, program stacks are arrays, at least conceptually.

On the down side, an array has a fixed size and therefore when you use an array for a stack, you run the risk of running out of space.

4.1.2.1 The Node Class

Because the order of elements in a stack is determined solely by the order in which the elements enter the stack, a stack does not use an identifying key value. Therefore, you can implement a stack without a node (using just pointers to objects) or with a simple node class such as that in Listing 4-1 and Listing 4-2.

```
#ifndef NODE
#define NODE

#include "thing.h"

class Node
{
    private:
        Thing * theThing;
    public:
        Node (Thing *);
        Thing * getThing();
};

#endif
```

Listing 4-1 Declaration of a node class for use in a stack

```
#include "node.h"
#include <string.h>

Node::Node (Thing * iThing)
{
    theThing = iThing;
}

Thing * Node::getThing()
    { return theThing; }
```

Listing 4-2 Implementation of a node class for use in a stack

4.1.2.2 The Stack Class

You can find a stack class based on an array in Listing 4-3 and Listing 4-4. This class not only provides the three capabilities described earlier (push, pop, and determining whether the stack is empty) but also supports a stack iterator just in case you need to list the elements in the stack.

```
#ifndef STACK
#define STACK

#include "node.h"

#define STACK_SIZE 25

class Stack
{
    private:
        int stackPtr;
        Node * stack [STACK_SIZE];
    public:
        Stack ();
        int is_empty ();
        bool push (Node *);
        Node * pop ();
        Node * getTop ();
        Node * getElement (int);
        int getStackPtr ();
};

#endif
```

Listing 4-3 Declaration of a stack class using an array

```
#include "stack.h"

Stack::Stack ()
    { stackPtr = -1; }

int Stack::is_empty()
    { return stackPtr >= 0; }

bool Stack::push (Node * theNode)
{
    if (stackPtr + 1 == STACK_SIZE)
        return false;
    stack[++stackPtr] = theNode;
    return true;
}
```

Listing 4-4   Implementation of a stack class using an array

```
Node * Stack::pop ()
    { return stack[stackPtr--]; }

Node * Stack::getTop ()
    { return stack[stackPtr]; }

Node * Stack::getElement (int pos)
{
    if (pos < 0 || pos > stackPtr)
        return 0;
    return stack [pos];
}

int Stack::getStackPtr ()
    { return stackPtr; }
```

Listing 4-4 (Continued) Implementation of a stack class using an array

The stack class maintains an array of pointers to the nodes in the stack as well as a stack pointer (the array index of the last used element in the stack). The class's single constructor initializes the stack pointer to –1 so that the push function can use a preincrement of the stack pointer.

To push a new element onto the stack, the stack class does the following:

1. Determine whether the stack is full. If so, return `false`. Otherwise, continue with step 2.
2. Preincrement the stack pointer and insert the new element (a `Node` object, in this case) into the stack array at the location pointed to by the stack pointer.
3. Return `true`.

Popping an element is actually quite simple. Return the element pointed to by the stack pointer and then post decrement the stack pointer. There is no need to actually delete the popped element; it will be overwritten when an element next occupies that location in the stack's array.

4.1.2.3 Traversing the Stack

If you need to access all the elements in a stack, in order, you can use a stack iterator that feeds the elements one at a time to a calling function. As you can see in Listing 4-5 and Listing 4-6, the iterator uses the stack class's `getElement` function to retrieve a single element from the stack, just as an array or vector iterator would do.

```
#ifndef STACKITR
#define STACKITR

#include "node.h"
#include "stack.h"

class StackItr
{
    private:
        int current;
        Stack * theStack;
    public:
        StackItr (Stack *);
        Node * getNext ();
};

#endif
```

Listing 4-5 *The declaration of a stack iterator class*

```
#include "stackitr.h"

StackItr::StackItr (Stack * iStack)
{
    theStack = iStack;
    current = theStack->getStackPtr();
}

Node * StackItr::getNext ()
{
    Node * theNode = theStack->getElement (current);
    current--;
    return theNode;
}
```

Listing 4-6 *The implementation of a stack iterator class*

The application class's `list` function (see Listing 4-7) uses the stack iterator just as it would an iterator for any other data structure. It initializes the iterator object with the stack object and then calls the iterator's `getNext` function repeatedly to access individual elements.

```
void AppClass::list ()
{
    StackItr * theItr = new StackItr (theStack);
    Node * theNode = theItr->getNext();
    Thing * theThing;
    while (theNode)
    {
        theThing = theNode->getThing();
        cout << "\nID = " << theThing->getID() << "; Name = "
            << theThing->getName() << "." << endl;
        theNode = theItr->getNext();
    }
}
```

Listing 4-7 Using a stack iterator

4.1.3 Implementing a Stack Using a Linked List

If you are writing a program that has no need to access elements other than at the top of the stack, you can avoid the problem of having a full stack by using a linked list rather than an array. In this case, you always insert a new element at the beginning of the list and remove an element from the beginning of the list.

The node class for a linked list implementation contains a pointer to the object being linked into the stack and a pointer to the next object, just as it does for a single-linked list (see Listing 4-8 and Listing 4-9).

The stack class (Listing 4-10 and Listing 4-11) looks very much like a class for a linked list where elements are always inserted at the beginning of the list. However, the names of the functions conform to the idea of a stack (for example, `push` and `pop` rather than `insert` and `remove`). The idea is to make the actual implementation of the stack irrelevant; the program using

```
#ifndef NODE
#define NODE

#include "thing.h"

class Node
{
    private:
        Thing * theThing;
        Node * next;
    public:
        Node (Thing *);
        Thing * getThing();
        Node * getNext ();
        void setNext (Node *);
};

#endif
```

Listing 4-8 *Declaration of a node class for a linked list implementation of a stack*

```
#include "node.h"

Node::Node (Thing * iThing)
{
    theThing = iThing;
    next = 0;
}

Thing * Node::getThing()
    { return theThing; }

Node * Node::getNext ()
    { return next; }

void Node::setNext (Node * iNode)
    { next = iNode; }
```

Listing 4-9 *Implementation of a node class for a linked list implementation of a stack*

the stack class shouldn't need to be aware of whether the stack is an array or a linked list.

```
#ifndef STACK
#define STACK

#include "node.h"
#include "thing.h"

class Stack
{
    private:
        int stackPtr;
        Node * first;
    public:
        Stack ();
        int is_empty ();
        bool push (Thing *);
        Thing * pop ();
        Node * getTop ();
};

#endif
```

Listing 4-10   Declaration of a stack class for a linked list implementation

```
#include "stack.h"

Stack::Stack ()
    { first = 0; }

int Stack::is_empty()
    { return (first == 0); }

bool Stack::push (Thing * theThing)
{
    Node * theNode = new Node (theThing);
    if (!theNode)
    {
        cout << "\nCannot create node.";
```

Listing 4-11   Implementation of a stack class for a linked list implementation

```
        return;
    }
    theNode->setNext (first);
    first = theNode;
    return true;
}

Thing * Stack::pop ()
{
    Node * theNode = first;
    Thing * theThing = theNode->getThing();
    first = theNode->getNext();
    delete theNode;
    return theThing;
}

Node * Stack::getTop ()
    { return first; }
```

Listing 4-11 (Continued) Implementation of a stack class for a linked list implementation

To push an element onto the stack, the stack class does the following:

1. Create a Node object to point to the object being added to the stack.
2. Set the new node's next pointer to point to the node that is currentlt the first node in the linked list.
3. Set the stack object's first variable to point to the new node.

To pop an element from the stack, the stack class does the following:

1. Set the current node to the first node in the list.
2. Retrieve the object pointed to by the current node.
3. Set the first node in the list to point to the current node's next node.
4. Delete the current node.
5. Return a reference to the object linked by the current node.

4.2 Queues

A queue is a first-in/first-out data structure (for example, Figure 4-5). Elements enter at the end of the queue and leave from the front of the queue. A queue is therefore a waiting list, similar to the type we all stand in at banks and retail stores. People, like the elements in a queue, are served in the order in which they arrive.

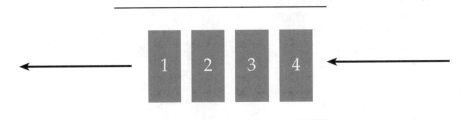

Figure 4-5 The operation of a queue

4.2.1 Use of a Queue

A queue is used by a multitasking operating system to hold processes waiting for access to the CPU. One of the most common schemes, which is used by OSs such as Linux, is known as *round-robin* scheduling.

Newly created processes enter the queue at the end. When the CPU is available, the operating system sends (*dispatches*) the process at the head of the queue to execute. The process continues to execute until either its time allocation (a *quantum*) expires, it must wait for I/O, or an interrupt occurs.

If the process relinquished control of the CPU because its quantum expired or because an interrupt occurred, it reenters the queue at the end. However, if the process is waiting for I/O, it is *blocked*, and cannot reenter the queue until its I/O completes. Only processes that are ready to run if the CPU becomes available are stored in the queue.

Using a queue for process scheduling provides a relatively fair way to give CPU time to each process. Small processes aren't unfairly penalized by being made to wait for long processes to complete. The result is acceptable throughput and end-user response time.

Nonetheless, long jobs often require many passes through the queue to complete execution. Some operating systems attempt to alleviate the discrimination against long processes by giving processes priorities. The longer a process waits in the queue, the higher its priority. The OS dispatches the process with the highest priority. In this case, the OS needs direct access to the elements in the queue.

> **Note:** It is virtually impossible for a process scheduling algorithm to be fair to processes of all lengths or to increase throughput and at the same time provide equal response time to all users. There are indeed many trade-offs in designing a process scheduling scheme.

4.2.2 Implementing a Queue Using an Array

Like a stack, a queue can be implemented as either an array or a linked list. The array implementation, which reflects the way in which an operating system uses main memory to maintain its process queue, provides direct access to elements in the queue, but is limited by the amount of space originally allocated for the array.

The node class for a queue is exactly the same as that for a stack (look back at Listing 4-1 and Listing 4-2). A queue also accesses elements by their position in the data structure rather than a key value and therefore does not require a mix-in class to force the implementation of a getKey function.

> **Note:** Like a stack, a queue is not required to use nodes because membership in a queue needs no pointers in the member objects. A queue therefore can store pointers to the objects in the queue instead. Nodes are used in these examples for consistency with the other examples in the book.

The queue class itself (Listing 4-12 and Listing 4-13) contains functions to add an element to the queue (*enqueue* an element), remove an element from the queue (*dequeue*), retrieve a single element based on its position in the queue, determine whether the queue is empty, and retrieve the current number of elements in the queue.

```
#ifndef QUEUEMGR
#define QUEUEMGR

#include "Thing.h"
#include "node.h"

#define MAX_ELEMENTS 10

class QueueMgr
{
    private:
        int queue_end;
        Node * theQueue [MAX_ELEMENTS];

    public:
        QueueMgr ();
        bool enqueue (Thing *); // pass in a single element
        // pass in ordinal position of element
        bool getElement (int, Thing * &);
        bool dequeue (Thing * &);
        bool is_empty (); // true if queue is empty
        int getSize (); // return total elements in the array
};

#endif
```

Listing 4-12 Declaration of a queue class implemented as an array

```
#include "QueueMgr.h"

QueueMgr::QueueMgr ()
{
    queue_end = 0;
}
```

Listing 4-13   Implementation of a queue class implemented as an array

```
bool QueueMgr::enqueue (Thing * newObject)
{
    bool result;
    Node * theNode = new Node (newObject);
    if (queue_end < MAX_ELEMENTS)
    {
        theQueue[queue_end] = theNode;
        queue_end++;
        result = true;
    }
    else
        result = false;
    return result;
}

bool QueueMgr::getElement (int position, Thing *  & element)
{
    int result = true;
    if (position > queue_end || queue_end == 0)
        result = false;
    else
    {
        Node * theNode = theQueue [position];
        element = theNode->getThing ();
    }
    return result;
}

bool QueueMgr::dequeue (Thing * & element)
{
    bool result = true;
    if (queue_end == 0)
        result = false;
    else
    {
        Node * theNode = theQueue [0];
        element = theNode->getThing ();
        for (int i = 0; i < queue_end - 1; i++)
            theQueue[i] = theQueue[i+1];
        queue_end--;
    }
```

Listing 4-13 (Continued) Implementation of a queue class implemented as an array

```
    return result;
}

bool QueueMgr::is_empty ()
{
    return (queue_end == 0);
}

int QueueMgr::getSize ()
    { return queue_end; }
```

Listing 4-13 (Continued) Implementation of a queue class implemented as an array

The queue manager class should theoretically maintain two pointers, one to the head of the queue and one to the end of the queue. However, when using an array, you can get away with keeping track of only the end of the queue if you always ensure that the first element of the queue is stored in array element 0.

To enqueue an element, the queue manager does the following:

1. Create a new node to link an object to the queue.
2. If there is room in the queue, insert the new node at the end of the queue and increment the end-of-queue pointer. Return `true`.
3. Otherwise, return `false`.

Dequeuing an object is a bit more complex because it requires shifting the elements in the array up one position to ensure that the first element is always in array element 0:

1. Determine whether the queue is empty. If it is empty, return `false` and exit the function.
2. Otherwise, retrieve the node at the top of the queue.
3. Retrieve the object pointed to by the node at the top of the queue.
4. Delete the node object.
5. Execute a loop that begins at array element 1 and moves each successive element into the array position above.
6. Decrement the pointer to the end of the queue.
7. Return `true`.

4.2.3 Implementing a Queue Using a Linked List

The queue class for a linked list implementation of a queue looks a bit
more as you would expect: It has both head and tail pointers to provide
access to both ends of the queue (see Listing 4-14 and Listing 4-15). This
queue class uses the same node class as the linked list implementation of a
stack (Listing 4-8 and Listing 4-9).

```
#ifndef QUEUE
#define QUEUE

#include "Thing.h"
#include "node.h"

class Queue
{
    private:
        Node * head, * tail;
    public:
        Queue ();
        int is_empty ();
        bool enqueue (Thing *);
        Thing * dequeue ();
        Node * getHead ();
};

#endif
```

Listing 4-14 Declaration of a queue class for implementation as a linked list

```
#include "queue.h"

Queue::Queue ()
    { head = 0; }

int Queue::is_empty()
    { return (head == 0); }
```

Listing 4-15 Implementation of a queue class for implementation as a linked list

```
bool Queue::enqueue (Thing * theThing)
{
    Node * theNode = new Node (theThing);
    if (!theNode)
    {
        cout << "\nCannot create node.";
        return;
    }
    if (is_empty())
    {
        head = theNode;
        tail = theNode;
    }
    else
    {
        tail->setNext (theNode);
        tail = theNode;
    }
    return true;
}

Thing * Queue::dequeue ()
{
    Node * theNode = head;
    head = theNode->getNext();
    Thing * theThing = theNode->getThing ();
    delete theNode;
    return theThing;
}

Node * Queue::getHead ()
{
    Node * theNode = head;
    return theNode;
}
```

Listing 4-15 (Continued) Implementation of a queue class for implementation as a linked list

To enqueue an object, the linked list implementation does the following:

1. Create a node to link the object to the queue.

2. If the queue is empty, set both the head and tail of the queue to point to the new node. Skip to step 5.

3. Otherwise, set the next pointer in the tail node to point to the new node.

4. Set the queue manager's `tail` variable to point to the new node.

5. Return `true`.

> **Note:** An insertion into a linked list should not fail unless the program has run out of memory, an error that can be detected by determining whether the creation of a new node succeeded.

Dequeuing an object from a linked list implementation is actually much simpler than dequeuing from an array:

1. Retrieve the node that is the head of the queue.

2. Set the queue manager's `head` variable to point to the node following the current head of the queue.

3. Retrieve the object pointed to by the current head of the queue.

4. Delete the node.

5. Return the object that was pointed to by the head of the queue.

4.3 Summary

A stack is a last-in/first-out data structure that can be implemented either as an array or a linked list. It is used by operating systems during program execution to store function return addresses and to pass parameters. It is also used by other data structures such as binary search trees during traversals.

A queue is a first-in/first-out data structure that can also be implemented either as an array or a linked list. Queues are used, for example, by operating systems to keep waiting lists of processes that are ready to execute when the CPU becomes available.

Part II: Trees

Trees are among the most widely used data structures for providing fast access to stored data. They can also be algorithmically complex. However, if you are going to be writing programs that require fast searches of large amounts of data, then you probably will find yourself turning to a tree at some time.

This part begins with the simplest type of tree: a binary search tree. You will then encounter a chapter on an enhanced type of binary tree (the AVL tree). The third type of tree—a B-Tree—provides a further enhancement of tree structures that use linked (non-continugous) storage. Finally, this part looks at a contiguous method of storing a binary tree (a heap) and its use to implement a priority queue.

CHAPTER 5

Binary Search Trees

The data structures designed to store entity objects about which you have been reading to this point have each made compromises between type of access (sequential versus random) and ease of resizing. Even vectors, which appear to be dynamically resizeable to the programmer, require allocating new storage and copying from one array to another, a possible source of memory fragmentation. If you were limited to arrays, vectors, and linked lists, you would often be faced with a trade-off between the ability to perform a fast search and the ability to resize easily and cleanly.

However, there is an alternative data structure that is both dynamic in size and easily searchable: a binary search tree, sometimes simply called a binary tree. The nodes in a binary search tree are kept in sorted order; the tree itself is constructed to support a very fast search. The drawback to a binary search tree is that it is ordered on a single key. If you need more than one search key, you must maintain one binary search tree for each key. In contrast an array or vector can be resorted on the values of different variables as needed.

> **Note:** In actuality, the biggest stumbling block to the use of binary search trees is their algorithmic complexity. Don't worry if you need to read the material in this chapter several times before what is happening becomes clear.

Because an entity object may belong to many binary search trees, each ordered on a different key, the mix-in class that provides the `getKey` function will need to be modified to support overloading of that function for differing data types. You will therefore also find a discussion of this expanded, more generic, mix-in class in this chapter.

5.1   The Structure of a Binary Search Tree

A binary search tree is constructed of linked nodes, each of which typically has four values:

- The node's key value.
- A pointer to the object belonging to the key value.
- A pointer to a right child node.
- A pointer to a left child node.

You can find the delcaration of the node in Listing 5-1 and its implementation in Listing 5-2.

```
#ifndef NODE
#define NODE

#include "thing.h"
#include "stringclass.h"

class Node
{
    private:
```

Listing 5-1   The declaration of a node class for a binary search tree

```
        int intKey;
        float floatKey;
        long longKey;
        double doubleKey;
        char charKey;
        String stringKey;
        Node * right_child, * left_child;
        Thing * theThing;
    public:
        Node (Thing *);
        void getKey (int &);
        void getKey (long &);
        void getKey (float &);
        void getKey (double &);
        void getKey (char &);
        void getKey (String &);
        Thing * getThing ();
        Node * getRight();
        Node * getLeft();
        void setRight (Node *);
        void setLeft (Node *);
};

#endif
```

Listing 5-1 (Continued) The declaration of a node class for a binary search tree

```
#include "node.h"

Node::Node (Thing * iThing)
{
    theThing = iThing;
    theThing->getKey(intKey);
    right_child = 0;
    left_child = 0;
}

void Node::getKey(int & theKey)
    { theKey = intKey; }
```

Listing 5-2 The implementation of a node class for a binary search tree

```
void Node::getKey(String & theKey)
   { theKey = stringKey; }

Thing * Node::getThing ()
   { return theThing; }

Node * Node::getRight ()
   { return right_child; }

Node * Node::getLeft ()
   { return left_child; }

void Node::setRight (Node * iNode)
   { right_child = iNode; }

void Node::setLeft (Node * iNode)
   { left_child = iNode; }
```

Listing 5-2 (Continued) The implementation of a node class for a binary search tree

We typically build binary search trees so that the right child has a key value greater than the current node and the left child has a key value less than the current node. (You could do it the other way and the tree would work just as well, as long as you were consistent with which side held the larger key and which held the smaller.) The sample tree on which the explanations in the first part of this chapter are based can be found in Figure 5-1.

The sample tree has eight nodes. The numbers on the nodes represent the order in which the nodes entered the tree. (Although the entity objects used in the sample code are ordered by an integer key, we will be using names for the discussion to make the logic easier to follow.)

The first node has a key of Jones. As the first node is stored, it automatically becomes the *root* of the tree, the only place where the tree manager (or a tree iterator) can enter the tree. Notice that the tree manager object points only to the root.

The second node stored was Smith. Because Smith is alphabetically greater than Jones, Smith becomes the right child of Jones. The third node—Abbott—has a key less than Jones and therefore becomes Jones's left child.

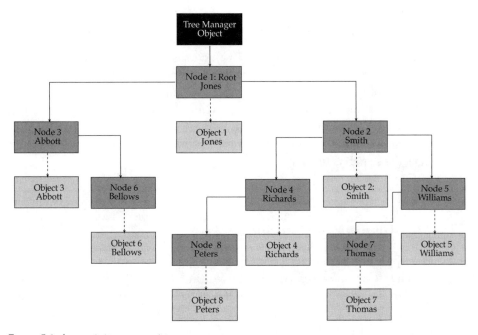

Figure 5-1 A sample binary search tree

The next node to enter is Richards. Richards is greater than Jones, so we go right. However, Jones already has a right child. Therefore, we evaluate Richards against Smith. Richards is less than Smith; we go left and discover that Smith has no left child. Richards therefore becomes Smith's left child.

When the fifth node—Williams—enters the tree, we determine that it is greater than Jones and also greater than Smith, Jones's right child. We go right and, when we discover that Smith has no right child, Williams becomes Smith's right child.

Bellows enters sixth. It is less than Jones; we go left and discover that Jones already has a left child. Bellows is greater than Abbot, so we go right. Since Abbott has no left child, Bellows becomes its left child.

Thomas, the seventh node, is greater than Jones (go right), greater than Smith (go right), but less than Williams (go left). Thomas therefore becomes the left child of Williams.

Finally, Peters is greater than Jones (go right), less than Smith (go left), and less than Richards (go left). Peters ends up as a left child of Richards.

Searching the tree for a single key value uses much the same technique as inserting a new node: Evaluate the key for which you are searching against the current node. If the search key is less than the current key, look at the left child; otherwise, look at the right child. If you haven't found the node you want, repeat the process until you either find the node you need or reach a node that has no child in the direction you need to go, in which case, the search is unsuccessful.

5.2   *The Application Program*

The application class declared in Listing 5-3 provides a test of the binary search tree about which you will be reading. In addition to storing, listing, and finding elements in the tree, the program stores and retrieves data from a text file, recreating the tree as it loads data. You will see the implementation of some of the member functions throughout this chapter. (As noted in the preface, the entire program can be downloaded from the author's Web site.)

```
#ifndef TREEAPP
#define TREEAPP

#define ADD 1
#define DELETE 2
#define FIND 3
#define LIST 4
#define QUIT 9

#include "tree.h"

class AppClass
{
    private:
```

Listing 5-3   Declaration of the application class to demonstrate the use of a binary search tree

```
        Tree * theTree;
        int simpleMenu();
        void addThing ();
        void deleteThing ();
        void findThing ();
        void listThings ();
    public:
        AppClass ();
        void run ();
};

#endif
```

Listing 5-3 (Continued) Declaration of the application class to demonstrate the use of a binary search

5.3 Modifying the Mix-In Class

As mentioned earlier, the mix-in class we have been using to enforce the implementation of a getKey function assumes that an entity object never has more than one key. However, when an entity object must belong to multiple data structures that are ordered on different keys, there must be some way to implement a getKey function for each key. The solution is a set of getKey functions that can be overloaded.

The mix-in class used for the binary search tree—and many subsequent data structures discussed in this book—can be found in Listing 5-4. Because you cannot overload functions by simply varying the return data type, the overloaded getKey functions now use a reference parameter.

```
#ifndef TREEABLE
#define TREEABLE

#include "stringclass.h"

class Treeable
{
```

Listing 5-4   Declaration of a mix-in class with overloaded getKey functions

```
    public:
        Treeable ();
        virtual void getKey (int &);
        virtual void getKey (long &);
        virtual void getKey (float &);
        virtual void getKey (double &);
        virtual void getKey (char &);
        virtual void getKey (String &);
};

#endif
```

Listing 5-4 (Continued)   Declaration of a mix-in class with overloaded getKey functions

An entity object can then redefine any of the getKey functions needed. For example, the Thing class used for the binary search tree demonstration implements an integer key and a key of a String class.

> **Note:** The class named String that is used in this example is included with the downloadable sample code and is printed in Chapter 12. You could also use the string class that is part of the C++ libraries.

> **Note:** There is one major limitation to the mix-in classes: There is no way to support multiple keys of the same data type. To provide this capability, you need to work with a pointer to a comparison function. Pointers to functions are a tricky part of C++. If you are interested in pursuing this strategy, see the last section of this chapter.

5.4 The Tree Manager Class

The container class that manages a binary search tree (declared in Listing 5-5) has `load`, `write`, `insert`, and `find` functions. The `Tree` class also has member functions to delete a node from the tree and to return the root node. Iterators will need to use the latter to gain an entry point into the tree.

```
#ifndef TREE
#define TREE

#include "node.h"
#include "thing.h"

class Tree
{
    private:
        Node * root;
        int numb_nodes; // for reading file only
        // used by deleteNode function only
        Node * find (int, Node * &, char &);
    public:
        Tree ();
        int load ();
        void write();
        void insert (Thing *, int);
        int deleteNode (int);
        Thing * find (int);
        Node * find (int, Node &, char &);
        Node * getRoot();
};

#endif
```

Listing 5-5 Declaration of a tree manager class

The private `find` function is used by `deleteNode` only, which needs to keep track of the parent node of the current node and whether the current node is the left or right child of its parent. The `Tree` class also needs to keep track of the root node so that it can provide an entry point to the tree.

As far as working with the tree itself goes, there is no reason to keep track of the number of nodes. However, it greatly simplifies reading data from a text file if the program knows how many objects to read.

5.5 *Inserting Nodes*

The Tree class member function that inserts a node into a binary search tree appears in Listing 5-6. The function requires three parameters: a pointer to the Thing object, the key used to order the tree (in this case, the ID number), and a boolean that indicates whether the source of the call to the function is the Tree class's load function or an application class function. (If the call comes from the load function, we don't want to increment the numb_nodes variable after inserting a node into the tree, given that the total number of nodes is already known.)

```
void Tree::insert (Thing * theThing, int source)
{
   Node * current, * child, * newNode;
   int key;
   theThing->getKey(key);
   if (source)
      numb_nodes++;
   if (root) // if root node exists
   {
      current = root;
      while (current) // keep going while there's a pointer
      {
         int currentKey;
         current->getKey (currentKey);
         if (currentKey < key)
         {
            // go down right side
            child = current->getRight();
            if (!child) // if no right child, insert
            {
               newNode = new Node (theThing);
```

Listing 5-6 Implementation of a function to insert a node into a binary search tree

```
            if (!newNode)
                (
                    cout << "\nCannot create node.";
                    return;
                }
            current->setRight (newNode);
            return;
        }
    }
    else
    {
        // go down left side
        child = current->getLeft();
        if (!child) // if no left child, insert
        {
            newNode = new Node (theThing);
            if (!newNode)
                (
                    cout << "\nCannot create node.";
                    return;
                }
            current->setLeft (newNode);
            return;
        }
    }
    current = child;
    }
}
else
{
    root = new Node (theThing);
    if (!root)
    (
        cout << "\nCannot create node.";
        return;
    }
    }
}
```

Listing 5-6 (Continued) Implementation of a function to insert a node into a binary search tree

The process for inserting a node—which was described for the sample tree in Figure 5-1 earlier in this lesson—works as follows:

1. Check to see if there is a root node. If not, the tree is empty and the new node becomes the root. Stop.
2. Otherwise, start at the root. Make it the current node.
3. Get the key of the current node.
4. Compare the key of the current node with the key of the new node. If the key of the current node is less than (alphabetically precedes) the key of the new node, then the new node will be in the current node's right subtree. If not, skip to step 7.
5. Check to see if the current node has a right child. If not, make the new node the current node's right child. Stop. Otherwise, continue with step 6.
6. Make the right child the current node. Go back to step 4.
7. Check to see if the current node has a left child. If not, make the new node the current node's left child. Stop. Otherwise, continue with step 8.
8. Make the left child the current node. Go back to step 4.

5.6 *Finding a Single Node*

Finding a node in a tree based on a matching key value is really just another version of the process used to insert a node. As you can see in Listing 5-7, the function returns either a pointer to the Thing object containing the search key or a 0, indicating that a node with the search key is not part of the tree.

```
Thing * Tree::find (int key)   // search by key
{
    Node * current;

    if (root) // make sure there is at least one node
    {
        current = root;
```

Listing 5-7 Implementation of a function to search a binary search tree for a node with a specific key value

```
        int currentKey;
        current->getKey (currentKey);
        while (current) // as long as there's a pointer
        {
            if (currentKey == key)
                // send back pointer to Thing object
                return current->getThing();
            // if less, go down right side
            if (currentKey < key)
                current = current->getRight();
            // if greater, go down left side
            else
                current = current->getLeft();
            if (current)
                current->getKey (currentKey);
        }
    }
    return 0; // Thing not found
}
```

Listing 5-7 (Continued) Implementation of a function to search a binary search tree for a node with a specific key value

The function uses the following search technique:

1. Make the root the current node. If there is no root node, the tree is empty. Return 0. Otherwise, continue with step 2.

2. Get the key for the current node. If the key for the current node matches the search key, get a pointer to the Family object pointed to by the node. Return the Family object pointer. Otherwise, continue with step 3.

3. If the key for the current node is less than the search key (search key is alphabetically greater than the key of the current node), get the right child of the current node and make it the current node. Otherwise, make the left child of the current node the current node.

4. If the current node is 0, the search is unsuccessful. Return 0. Otherwise, continue with step 2.

The maximum number of nodes that a search will need to examine to determine that a search key is not in the tree is equal to the number of levels in the tree. For example, in Figure 5-1, the longest possible search will need to check at most four nodes. Of course, this is a worst-case scenario; typically a search will be successful after examining fewer than the maximum number of nodes.

5.7 Deleting Nodes

Deleting a node from an array or linked list is relatively straightforward: You just plug the hole made when you remove a node. A binary search tree, however, is a totally different situation. (It's a toss-up whether tree traversals or deleting nodes is more difficult to understand and program.) There are four scenarios you must consider:

- The node is a leaf (has no children): Delete the node and set the correct pointer of its parent to 0.
- The node has a left subtree but no right subtree: Replace the node being deleted with the node's left child.
- The node has a right subtree but no left subtree: Replace the node being deleted with the node's right child.
- The node has both left and right subtrees: Replace the node being deleted with the node from the right subtree of the left child with the largest key value. (Got that on the first reading? Don't worry; you're not the only one who didn't.) If the left child has no right subtree, replace the node with the left child.

Complicating matters is that deleting the root node in any of the preceding four scenarios is a special case.

The code to delete a node appears in Listing 5-8. The process for deleting a node begins by finding the node to be deleted, using the find function in Listing 5-9. Unlike the find function in Listing 5-7, this function must return three values: a pointer to the node found, a pointer to its parent in the tree, and a character indicating whether it is the left or right child of its parent. The Node pointer is returned using a return statement. The other two values are reference parameters.

```
int Tree::deleteNode (int key)
{
    Node * previous = 0;   // use to save parent of found node
    char direction;
    Node * theNode = find (key, previous, direction);

    if (theNode == 0)
        return 0; // key not found in tree
    // needed to delete the object pointed to
    Thing * theThing = theNode->getThing ();

    // if no children, just disconnect; set parent pointer to 0
    if (theNode->getRight() == 0 && theNode->getLeft() == 0)
    {
        if (theNode == root)
            root = 0; // empty tree
        else
            if (direction == 'r')
                previous->setRight (0);
            else
                previous->setLeft (0);
    }
    // right subtree but no left subtree
    else if (theNode->getRight() != 0 && theNode->getLeft() == 0)
    {
        Node * subtree = theNode->getRight();
        if (theNode == root)
            root = subtree;
        else
        {
            if (direction == 'r')
                previous->setRight (subtree);
            else
                previous->setLeft (subtree);
        }
    }
    // left subtree but no right subtree
    else if (theNode->getRight() == 0 && theNode->getLeft() != 0)
    {
        Node * subtree = theNode->getLeft();
```

Listing 5-8 Implementation of a function to delete a node from a binary search tree

```
    if (theNode == root)
        root = subtree;
    else
    {
        if (direction == 'r')
            previous->setRight (subtree);
        else
            previous->setLeft (subtree);
    }
}
else // must have both left and right subtrees
{
    Node * next;
    Node * current = theNode->getLeft();
    // if there is a right subtree of left child...
    if (current->getRight() != 0)
    {
        next = current->getRight();
        while (next->getRight() != 0) // find last right child
        {
            current = next;
            next = current->getRight();
        }

        // replace deleted node with node found
        current->setRight (next->getLeft());
        next->setLeft (theNode->getLeft());
        next->setRight (theNode->getRight());
        // set parent pointers
        if (theNode != root)
            if (direction == 'l')
                previous->setLeft (next);
            else
                previous->setRight (next);
        else root = next;
    }
    // since no right subtree, replace with left child
    else
    {
        next = current;
```

Listing 5-8 (Continued) Implementation of a function to delete a node from a binary search tree

```
            next->setRight (theNode->getRight());
            if (theNode != root)
                if (direction == 'l')
                    previous->setLeft (next);
                else
                    previous->setRight (next);
            else root = next;
        }
    }

    // remove both the node and the family objects from memory
    delete theThing;
    delete theNode;
    numb_nodes--;
    return 1;
}
```

Listing 5-8 (Continued) Implementation of a function to delete a node from a binary search tree

```
Node * Tree::find (int key, Node * & previous, char & direction)
    // for deletion only
{
    Node * current;

    if (root) // make sure there is at least one node
    {
        current = root;
        previous = current;
        while (current) // as long as there's a pointer
        {
            int currentKey;
            current->getKey (currentKey);
            if (currentKey == key)
                return current; // send back pointer to Node object
            // if less, go down right side
            if (currentKey < key)
            {
                previous = current;
                direction = 'r';
                current = current->getRight();
```

Listing 5-9 Implementation of a function to find a node for deletion from a binary search tree

```
        }
        // if greater, go down left side
        else
        {
            previous = current;
            direction = 'l';
            current = current->getLeft();
        }
      }
   }
   return 0;
};
```

Listing 5-9 (Continued) Implementation of a function to find a node for deletion from a binary search

After finding the node to be removed, the `deleteNode` function obtains a pointer to the `Thing` object being deleted and sets it aside. The only use for this reference is so that the object can be removed from memory at the end of the deletion. (If the node could not be found, the function returns 0, indicating that the deletion failed.)

The bulk of the work comes in deleting the `Node` object from the tree. The code works in the following way:

1. If the node has no right or left child, check to see if is the root. If so, set the root variable to 0. Skip to step 8. Otherwise, set the appropriate parent pointer to 0. Skip to step 8.

2. If the node has a right subtree but no left subtree, check to see if it is the root. If so, make the node's right child the root and reset the root variable. Skip to step 8. Otherwise, connect the right child to the node's parent. Skip to step 8.

3. If the node has a left subtree but no right subtree, check to see if it is the root. If so, make the node's left child the root and reset the root variable. Skip to step 8. Otherwise, connect the left child to the node's parent. Skip to step 8.

4. The node must have both right and left subtrees. Determine whether there is a right subtree of left child. If there is, skip to step 5. If not, determine whether the node being deleted is the root. If so, make the

moved node point to the deleted node's left child and modify the root variable. Skip to step 8. Otherwise, replace node with its left child. Skip to step 8.

5. Go down the right subtree of the node's left child. When there is no longer a right child, the lowest right child has been found. This will be the node with the smallest key in the subtree.

6. Replace the node to be deleted with the node found in step 5. If the node being moved is the root, set the root variable to point that node. Otherwise, set the deleted node's parents to point to the moved node.

7. Set the moved node to point to the deleted node's children, if any.

8. Delete the `Node` and `Thing` objects from main memory.

Note: The code for a binary search tree class should not necessarily delete the object being managed from memory. If you want to be truly generic, then delete only the node and leave the decision whether to delete the managed object up to the application.

9. Decrement the number of nodes variable.

10. Return 1 indicating a successful deletion.

To help you see how this works, let's look at some examples using the sample tree in Figure 5-1. First, assume that you want to delete Bellows. The program would:

1. Find the node with the key of Bellows.

2. Since Bellows is a leaf, set Abbot's right child to 0.

3. Delete the Bellows Node and Family objects. (This step is the last step for all situations and therefore won't be repeated in the following examples.)

As a second example, assume you want to delete Abbot. In this case, where there is a right subtree but no left subtree, the program would:

1. Find the node with the key of Abbot, noting that it is the left child of Jones.

2. Set Jones's left child to point to Bellows.

When there is a left subtree but no right subtree, as in a delete of Williams, the procedure is very similar to the preceding example:

1. Find the node with the key of Williams, noting that it is the right child of Smith.
2. Set Smith's right child to point to Thomas.

Next, assume that you want to delete Smith, which has both left and right subtrees:

1. Find the node with the key of Smith, noting that it is the right child of Jones.
2. Note that Smith has a left subtree and that Richards is the top of that subtree.
3. Richards has no right subtree. Therefore, replace Smith with Richards.
4. Set Jones's right child to Richards.
5. Set Richard's left child to Williams.

Finally, let's assume that we want to delete Jones, the root node of the tree:

1. Find the node with the key of Jones.
2. Note that Jones has a left subtree and that Abbot is the top of that subtree.
3. Note that Abbot has a right subtree.
4. Find the lowest node in Abbot's right subtree (Bellows). This is the node that will be replacing Jones.
5. Set Bellows's left child to point to Abbot (Jones's left child).
6. Set Bellows's right child to point to Smith (Jones's right child).
7. Set Abbot's right child to 0, since it no longer has a right child.

5.8   Tree Traversals

A tree traversal is a procedure that visits every node in the tree in some predetermined order. The iterators that you will see in this section are used in exactly the same way, but produce different results.

5.8.1 Types of Traversals

There are three ways to traverse a binary search tree:

- In-order: An in-order traversal produces the nodes in key order. In our particular example, it will visit the nodes in numeric order by ID number. The tree demonstration program uses an in-order traversal in its `list` function.
- Pre-order: A pre-order traversal visits a node and then its children, if any. The demonstration program uses this type of traversal when it writes the contents of the tree to a text file.
- Post-order: A post-order traversal visits a node's children and then the node. The demonstration program doesn't use this type of traversal.

5.8.2 The Role of a Stack in Tree Traversals

To perform any of these traversals, a program has to keep track of the nodes it visits as it descends through the tree. The trick to doing that is to use a stack.

A stack that is used in a tree traversal has to be able to do the following:

- Keep track of how many items are in the stack by maintaining a pointer to the top of the stack (the last item entered).
- Add a new item to the stack (push).
- Remove an item from the stack (pop).
- Determine when the stack is empty.

All of these can be accomplished with either the array or linked list implementation of a stack discussed earlier in this book. The tree traversals you will see use an array implementation.

5.8.3 Writing and Performing an In-Order Traversal

An in-order traversal of the sample binary search tree should retrieve the nodes in the order shown in the circles in Figure 5-2. The actual traversal is performed by an iterator class, which can feed the nodes, in the correct order, to a calling function one at a time. You can find the declaration of the in-order iterator in Listing 5-10.

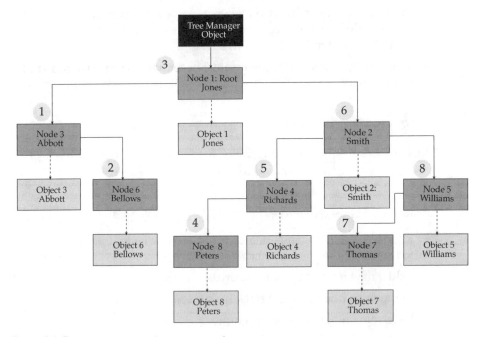

Figure 5-2 Performing an in-order tree traversal

```
#ifndef INORDER
#define INORDER

#include "node.h"
#include "tree.h"
#include "thing.h"
#include "stack.h"
```

Listing 5-10 Declaration of an in-order tree traversal iterator class

```
class InOrderItr
{
    private:
        Node * root;
        void goLeft (Node *);
        Stack * theStack;
    public:
        InOrderItr ();
        int init (Tree *);
        int operator++ (); // find node
        int operator! (); // check for end of traversal
        Thing * operator() (); // return pointer to thing pointed to
by current node
};

#endif
```

Listing 5-10 (Continued) Declaration of an in-order tree traversal iterator class

The iterator stores the root node in a variable and also maintains a `Stack` object. In addition, it has a private function (`goLeft`) that retrieves the left child of the current node. The public member functions include a constructor, an `init` function to begin a new traversal, and three overloaded operators, one to find the "next" node, one to check for the end of the traversal, and another to return the object linked to the tree by the current node. The implementation of the class can be found in Listing 5-11.

```
#include "inorderitr.h"

InOrderItr::InOrderItr()
{
    root = 0;
    theStack = new Stack ();
}

int InOrderItr::init (Tree * tree)
{
    root = tree->getRoot(); // initialize current node to root
```

Listing 5-11   Implementation of an in-order tree traversal iterator class

```
    goLeft (root); // go down left side of tree
    return theStack->is_empty(); // is stack empty?
}

int InOrderItr::operator++ ()
{
    Node * parent, * child;

    if (theStack->is_empty())
    {
        parent = theStack->pop();
        child = parent->getRight();
        if (child)
            goLeft (child);
    }
    return theStack->is_empty();
}

Thing * InOrderItr::operator() ()    // current node is top of stack
{
    Node * theNode = theStack->getTop();
    return theNode->getThing ();
}

void InOrderItr::goLeft (Node * node)
{
    while (node)
    {
        theStack->push (node);
        node = node->getLeft();
    }
}

int InOrderItr::operator! ()
    { return theStack->is_empty(); } // check for end of traversal
```

Listing 5-11 (Continued) Implementation of an in-order tree traversal iterator class

The constructor initializes the root variable and creates a **Stack** object. After that point, the function using the iterator must come into play. In Listing 5-12, you can see the application class function that uses an in-order traversal. The for loop keeps the traversal going until all nodes have been processed.

```
void AppClass::listThings()
{
    InOrderItr theItr;
    Thing * theThing;
    for (theItr.init (theTree); !theItr; ++theItr)
    {
        theThing = theItr();
        cout << "ID = " << theThing->getID() << "; Name = "
            << theThing->getName() << "." << endl;
    }
}
```

Listing 5-12 Using an in-order iterator to perform a binary search tree traversal

To perform the traversal using our sample tree, an application class object and the iterator object interact in the following way:

1. The application class function creates an iterator object. Notice that in this case, we are using static binding. This is essential for the overloaded operators to work properly.

2. The iterator class constructor initializes its root variable to 0 and creates a `Stack` object.

3. The application class function sets up a local variable to hold a pointer to an entity object.

4. The application class function initializes a for loop by calling the iterator's `init` function.

5. The iterator object retrieves the root node of the tree, giving itself an entry point into the tree. It then goes down the left side of the tree, pushing all nodes onto the stack as it encounters them. Pushing stops when all left nodes have been stored on the stack. In our particular example, the `init` function pushes Jones, then Abbot.

6. The `for` statement uses the overloaded ! operator to see if the traversal should begin. For an in-order search, the traversal is complete when the stack is empty at the top of the loop. Since the stack is not empty, the program enters the loop.

7. The overloaded () operator retrieves the "next" object in alphabetical order by returning the top object on the stack (in this case, Abbot, which was added to the stack on top of Jones). The stack pointer does not move.

8. The loop displays the object's data.

9. The program increments the control variable using the overloaded ++ operator. The ++ operator function first pops the top element off the stack (Abbot, which was just processed in the body of the loop; Jones is now at the top of the stack). The function then attempts to get the node's right child. If there is a right child, it goes down the right child's left subtree. In our example, the goLeft function pushes Abbot's right child—Bellows—onto the stack and stops because Bellows has no left subtree.

10. The for statement uses the overloaded ! operator to see if the traversal is done. Since the stack is not empty, the program re-enters the loop.

11. The program returns to the top of the loop.

12. The program retrieves Bellows from the top of the stack and displays its data.

13. The loop iterates, popping Bellows off the stack. Bellows has no right child, so goLeft does nothing more.

14. The loop processes Jones.

15. The loop iterates, popping Jones off the stack. Because Jones has a right subtree, goLeft pushes Smith, Richards, and Peters onto the stack.

16. The loop processes Peters.

17. The loop iterates, popping Peters off the stack. Peters has no right subtree, so the loop goes into its body.

18. The loop processes Richards.

19. The loop iterates, popping Richards off the stack.

20. The loop processes Smith.

21. The loop iterates, popping Smith off the stack. Smith's right child, Williams, is pushed onto the stack, followed by William's left child, Thomas.

22. The loop processes Thomas.

23. The loop iterates, popping Thomas off the stack.

24. The loop processes Williams, the last node.

25. The loop iterates, popping Williams off the stack and leaving the stack empty.

26. The check to see if the stack is not empty fails, and the for loop stops.

5.8.4 Writing and Performing a Pre-Order Traversal

As mentioned earlier, a pre-order traversal visits the current node first, followed by its children. A pre-order traversal of our sample tree would be performed in the order indicated by the circles in Figure 5-3.

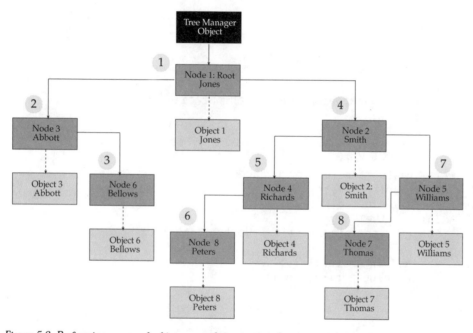

Figure 5-3 Performing a pre-order binary search tree traversal

The demonstration program uses a pre-order traversal to write data to a text file. Why not just use the existing in-order traversal? Consider what would happen if the data were in alphabetical order in the data file. When they were read in, each successive entity object would become a right child of the preceding object because it would have a greater key. The result would be equivalent to a linked list!

Instead, we want to recreate the tree so that the nodes are in the same position as they were the last time the program was run. A pre-order traversal will do this for us. (As you will see, this is traversal is actually less logically complex than the in-order traversal.)

To perform a pre-order traversal, we need an iterator that navigates the tree in a pre-order manner. However, the function using the iterator (in this case, the Tree class's write function in Listing 5-13) uses it in exactly the same way as it would use the in-order iterator.

```
void Tree::write ()
{
    ofstream fout ("things");
    if (!fout.is_open())
    {
        cout << "Problem opening output file.";
        return;
    }
    fout << numb_nodes << ' ';

    // create iterator for preorder traversal of tree
    PreOrderItr theItr;
    // traverse the tree
    Thing * theThing;
    for (theItr.init (this); !theItr; ++theItr)
    {
        theThing = theItr();
        theThing->write (fout);
    }
}
```

Listing 5-13 Using a pre-order binary search tree iterator

The pre-order iterator class also has the same functions as the in-order iterator (Listing 5-14). It also maintains a pointer to the root of the tree and a stack for storing nodes. However, as you would expect, the implementation of the functions (with the exception of getTop and the overloaded () operator) is somewhat different (see Listing 5-15).

```
#ifndef PREORDER
#define PREORDER

#include "node.h"
#include "tree.h"
#include "thing.h"
#include "stack.h"

class PreOrderItr
{
    private:
        Node * root;
        Stack * theStack;
    public:
        PreOrderItr ();
        int init (Tree *);
        int operator++ (); // find node
        int operator! (); // check for end of traversal
        // return pointer to family pointed to by current node
        Thing * operator() ();
};

#endif
```

Listing 5-14 Declaration of a pre-order iterator class for a binary search tree traversal

```
#include "preorderitr.h"

PreOrderItr::PreOrderItr()
{
    theStack = new Stack();
    root = 0;
}

int PreOrderItr::init (Tree * tree)
{
    root = tree->getRoot(); // initialize current node to root
```

Listing 5-15 Implementation of a pre-order iterator for binary search tree traversal

```
    if (root)
        theStack->push (root); // push root onto stack
    return theStack->is_empty(); // is stack empty?
}

int PreOrderItr::operator++ ()
{
    Node * current = theStack->getTop();
    Node * next = current->getLeft();

    if (next)
    {
        theStack->push (next);
        return 1;
    }

    while (theStack->is_empty()) // while stack still has elements
    {
        current = theStack->pop();
        next = current->getRight();
        if (next)
        {
            theStack->push (next);
            return 1;
        }
    }
    return 0;
}

Thing * PreOrderItr::operator() ()
{
    Node * theNode = theStack->getTop();
    return theNode->getThing ();   // current node is top of stack
}

int PreOrderItr::operator! ()
    { return theStack->is_empty(); } // check for end of traversal
```

Listing 5-15 (Continued) Implementation of a pre-order iterator for binary search tree traversal

To write the sample tree to a text file, a program would do the following:

1. Create a pre-order iterator object for use with static binding.
2. Initialize the for loop that will process the nodes by calling the iterator's `init` function. This function retrieves the root of the tree and pushes it onto the stack.
3. Check to see if the stack is empty. Since it is not, enter the loop.
4. Retrieve the current node (in this case, the root) and write it to the file.
5. he loop iterates and calls the ++ overloaded operator function to move to the next node.
6. Check to see if the current node (the root) has a left child. Since it does, push the left child (Abbot) onto the stack and return. (We need to leave the root on the stack because we haven't checked for its right child yet.)
7. Check to see if the stack is empty. Since it is not, enter the loop.
8. Process the node at the top of the stack (Abbot).
9. Move to the next node. This time, the ++ function determines that Abbot has no left child. Therefore, it pops Abbot off the stack (we're done with it) and checks to see if it has a right child. Since there is a right child (Bellows), push it onto the stack and return.
10. The loop processes Bellows.
11. The loop iterates. Since Bellows has no left child, the ++ function pops it off the stack and checks to see if it has a left child. Since there is no left child, the function looks to see if there is a right child. Since there is no right child, it pops Bellows off the stack; the root node (Jones) is now at the top of the stack. Jones has a right child (Smith). Therefore, the function pops Jones off the stack and pushes Smith.
12. The loop processes Smith.
13. The loop iterates. Smith has a left child (Richards), which is pushed onto the stack.
14. The loop processes Richard.
15. The loop iterates. Richards has a left child (Peters), which is pushed onto the stack.
16. The loop processes Peters.

17. The loop iterates. Peters has no left child. The ++ function pops it off the stack and checks to see if it has a right child. There is no right child. The function therefore pops Richards off the stack and checks for a right child. There is no right child. The function pops Smith off the stack. Smith's right child—Williams—gets pushed onto the stack.

18. The loop processes Williams.

19. The loop iterates. Williams has a left child—Thomas—that is pushed onto the stack.

20. The loop processes Thomas.

21. The loop iterates. Thomas has no left child. The ++ function pops it off the stack and determines that it has no right child. There, the function pops Williams off the stack. Williams has no right child. The stack is now empty, so the ++ function returns.

22. The loop stops because the stack is empty.

5.9 Using a Compare Function

As noted earlier in this chapter, the mix-in classes we have be using support only a single key of any given data type. If you have a situation where you need multiple keys of the same data type, then a mix-in class won't do what you need. The solution is to provide a pointer to a comparison function that compares a key value of some specific type to a data value in an object. You can then define as many comparison functions as needed, one for each key.

As an example, let's look at a modified version of the binary search tree demonstration program. In this case, the tree will be initialized with a pointer to the comparison function that is to be used for that specific tree.

The first modification that needs to be made is to the Thing class, which must include at least one comparison function (see Listing 5-16). This particular function is named compare, but there is no limitation to the number of comparison functions a class might include and there are no restrictions on how the function should be named. The function must, however, return 0 if the keys are equal, > 0 if the object's key is greater than the key to which it is being compared, and < 0 if the object's key is less than the key to which it is being compared. Other return schemes are certainly possible, but the Tree class has been modified to interpret these return values.

```
int Thing::compare (int key)
{
    int result;
    if (thing_id == key)
        result = 0;
    else if (thing_id > key)
        result = 1;
    else
        result = -1;
    return result;
}
```

Listing 5-16 A comparison function for the Thing class

In addition to the compare function, the *thing.cpp* file contains a typedef for a pointer to a function of the Thing class:

```
typedef int(Thing::*functionPtr) (int);
```

The typedef is certainly optional, but it simplifies the rest of the code and makes it easier to modify the definition if necessary.

Two changes are required to the Tree class:

- The constructor must accept a functionPtr as an argument whose value is stored in one of the classes's variables (see Listing 5-17).

```
Tree::Tree(functionPtr iPtr)
{
    root = 0;
    numb_nodes = 0;
    compareFunction = iPtr;
}
```

Listing 5-17 The modified Tree class constructor

- All comparisons of a key to the key stored in an object must be made using the pointer to the function. As an example, look at the modified find function in Listing 5-18.

```
Thing * Tree::find (int key)   // search by key
{
    Node * current;
    Thing * currentThing;

    if (root) // make sure there is at least one node
    {
        current = root;
        while (current) // as long as there's a pointer
        {
            currentThing = current->getThing();
            if ((currentThing->*compareFunction)(key) == 0)
                // send back pointer to Thing object
                return current->getThing();
            // if less, go down right side
            if ((currentThing->*compareFunction) (key) < 0)
                current = current->getRight();
            // if greater, go down left side
            else
                current = current->getLeft();
        }
    }
    return 0; // Thing not found
}
```

Listing 5-18 The Tree class's modified find function that uses a call to a stored function pointer

The syntax for calling a function referenced by a function pointer is very specific, as in:

```
(currentThing->*compareFunction)(key)
```

Assuming that the calling object is referenced by a pointer (as it is in this case), then you must dereference the function pointer. You must also enclose the object name, the arrow operator, the contents of operator, and the function pointer variable in a single set of parentheses. The input parameters to the called function follow in their own set of parentheses.

Finally, the application class must obtain the pointer to the comparison function when space for the tree is allocated and its constructor called (see Listing 5-19). It is this constructor that gives you the opportunity to choose which comparison function (and thus, which key) will be used for any given tree. All you need to do is supply the address of the comparison function you want to use when the tree is created.

```
AppClass::AppClass ()
{
    theTree = new Tree(&Thing::compare);// create tree
}
```

Listing 5-19   The modified application class constructor

5.10 Summary

A binary search tree is a data structure that maintains objects in order by a single key. It is dynamic in size and supports very fast searches on its key. However, it does not provide direct access to its nodes; access is only through the single root node.

CHAPTER 6

AVL Trees

The binary tree used as an example in Chapter 5 was a relatively *balanced* tree, where the height of both subtrees of the root are of approximately the same height. When nodes enter the tree with keys in more or less random order, then the result will be a more-or-less balanced tree. However, if the keys of the nodes enter the tree in order, then the result will be the equivalent of a linked list. (As you may remember, we wrote the data from the tree to a text file using a pre-order traversal to avoid this problem when reloading the tree.)

The maximum number of nodes that a search will need to visit to determine that a search key isn't part of the tree is roughly equivalent to the number of levels in the tree (the height of the tallest subtree of the root plus 1). Therefore, searches of a binary tree will be most efficient if the tree is balanced.

Note: To be precise, if a binary tree has n nodes, then the longest path through the tree will be *log n*.

If there is a good chance that keys will not enter a tree in random order, then you may want to use a variation on a binary tree—called an *AVL tree* (named after the Russian mathematicians that devised it, G. M. Adelson-Velskii and E. M. Landis)—that readjusts the tree each time a new node is stored to maintain the balance. Using an AVL tree adds considerable algorithmic complexity to the tree manipulation. In addition, the time to readjust the balance will slow the process of adding to and deleting from the tree. AVL trees therefore represent a trade-off between the time required to maintain the balanced tree and search time.

6.1   The Operation of an AVL Tree

The nodes in an AVL tree are far busier than the nodes in the traditional binary tree. First, they must keep track of the heights of their subtrees to determine whether the tree is balanced. Second, when the tree is unbalanced, they must move the nodes in their subtrees until balance is restored.

6.1.1 Balance Factors

An AVL tree is considered to be balanced if the difference between the heights of the right and left subtrees of any given node is no more than 1. Rather than storing the actual heights of the subtrees, a node stores what is known as a *balance factor*, computed by subtracting the height of the left subtree from the right subtree:

```
Balance Factor =
    right_subtree_height - left_subtree_height
```

There are therefore only three possible values for the balance factor in a balanced tree:

- 1: The right subtree is taller than the left subtree.
- 0: The right and left subtrees are of the same height.
- −1: The left subtree is taller than the right subtree.

For example, assume that the first key value to enter a new tree is Jones. Initially, this node will have a balance factor of 0 because it has no subtrees. When we add Smith, the tree remains balanced. The Smith node has a balance factor of 0—it has no subtrees—and the Jones node now has a balance factor of 1 because its right subtree has a height of 1 and its left subtree has a height of 0. (The value following the colon (:) in the illustration is the balance factor.)

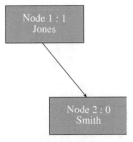

But what happens when we add a node with a key of Thomas to the tree? Because Thomas is greater than both Jones and Smith, it becomes Smith's right child. Thomas has a balance factor of 0 and Smith of 1, but Jones has a balance factor of 2. The tree is no longer acceptably balanced and therefore must be manipulated in some way that will make it conform to the rule that the difference in the heights of subtrees of the same node can be no greater than 1.

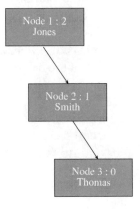

The solution is what is known as a *rotation*, through which the root of a subtree is literally rotated either right or left, producing a new root and changing the height of the right and left subtrees by 1. For example, a left rotation of the three node tree makes Smith the root:

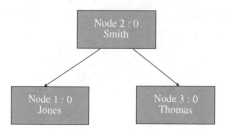

All of the balance factors are now 0 and the tree is once more in balance.

Most of the time when an AVL tree becomes unbalanced—either through addition or removal of a node—only one rotation left or right is required to rebalance the tree. On rare occasions, however, two rotations will be needed. The code that inserts and deletes nodes must therefore not assume that a single rotation will fix a problem, but must recompute the balance factors after an insertion, deletion, or rotation and then check to determine whether further rotation is necessary.

What makes an AVL tree so algorithmically complex is the need to recompute the balance factors after adding or deleting a node so that the program can determine whether a rotation is necessary. If mathematical logic makes you uncomfortable (or if you don't really care about the underlying details), you can certainly skip the rest of this section and take the formulas as they appear in the sample code. Otherwise, you can read the rest of this section to see the derivation of the balance factor computations.

Note: Don't be surprised if you find that you must read the description of the derivation of the formulas several times. They are algorithmically (although not mathematically) complex and do take a considerable amount of time and persistence to understand fully.

6.1.2 Maintaining Balance When Modifying an AVL Tree

As an example, let's start with the sample binary tree first introduced in Chapter 5 (Figure 6-1). As in the previous illustrations, the node number indicates the order in which the node was added to the tree. The node number is separated from the balance factor by a colon.

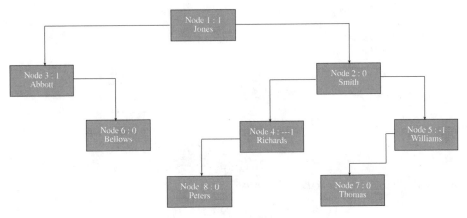

Figure 6-1 A sample AVL tree to which a node will be added

Assume that a node with a key of Summers is added to the tree. The result, found in Figure 6-2, places Summers as the left child of Thomas: Summers is greater than Jones (go right), greater than Smith (go right), less than Williams (go left), and less than Thomas (go left). Adding Summers therefore affects the balance factors of Jones, Smith, Williams, and Thomas. By simply examining the result of the added node, we can determine that the resulting balance factors are those found in Figure 6-3.

Because two nodes—Jones and Williams—have balance factors of 2, the tree is now out of balance. A rotation will be needed. The rotation will be made at the lowest level possible. In this example, that means performing a right rotation on Williams' left subtree, making Thomas the root of the subtree and Williams its right child, as in Figure 6-4. A visual inspection of the tree indicates that it is now balanced and no further rotations will be necessary.

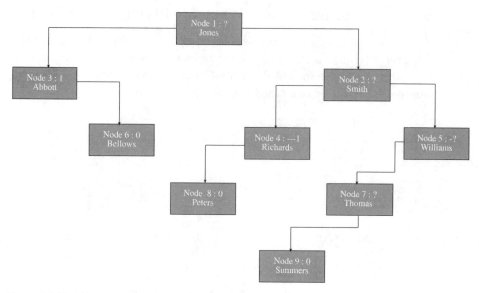

Figure 6-2 The AVL tree after adding a new node

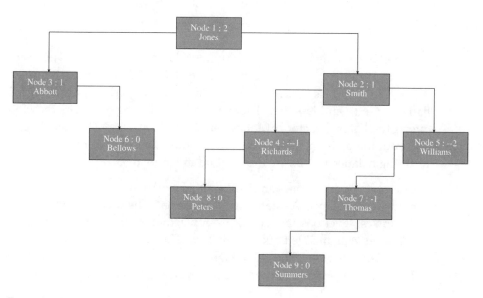

Figure 6-3 Balance factors after adding a new node

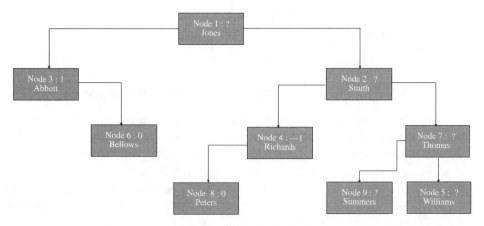

Figure 6-4 The AVL tree after a rotation

The remaining step is to recompute the balance factors, producing the result in Figure 6-5. When the program examines the new balance factors, it will be able to determine that all balance factors are correct and that the tree requires no further manipulation.

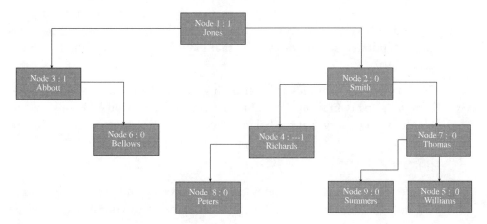

Figure 6-5 The final AVL tree with its added node

It's fairly easy to recompute balance factors when you have a picture to look at, but unfortunately your code doesn't have that luxury. Therefore, we have to find some mathematical way of deriving new balance factors from existing ones, both after adding/removing a node and rotating a subtree.

6.1.3 New Balance Factors After Adding/Removing a Node

When you add a node to an AVL tree, the balance factor of each node in the path to the new node's location is increased by 1 for a right child and decreased by 1 for a left child. (To see this in action, compare Figure 6-1 and Figure 6-3.) Conversely, when you remove a node from an AVL tree, the balance factor of each node in the path to the location from where the node was removed is decreased by 1 if a right child is removed and increased by 1 if a left child is removed. That's the easy part!

6.1.4 Computing New Balance Factors After a Right Rotation

But how do you determine the balance factors after a rotation? Notice in Figure 6-4 that the rotation affects the balance factors all the way up the tree to the root, even though nodes that were rotated are two levels removed from the root. This means that the computation must be performed on every node in the path to reach the node whose subtree was rotated. In our particular example, that includes Williams, Thomas, Smith, and Jones.

To develop the formulas for computing new balance factors after a rotation, let's focus first on the right rotation performed on Williams and its children. You know that the balance factor for any node is given by the formula

RH − LH

where RH is the height of the node's right subtree and LH is the height of the node's left subtree. (The height is the same as the number of levels in the tree.)

Now assume that the height of a node's right subtree is n. If the node's balance factor is BF, then the height of the left subtree must be n − BF

because of the formula used to compute the balance factor.

In the sample tree in Figure 6-3, Smith's right subtree has a height of 3; its left subtree has a height of 2. Therefore, the resulting balance factor should be 1. It also holds that given the right subtree height of 3, the left subtree's height is 2.

The height's of William's subtrees are represented by William's balance factor. Because William's balance factor is negative, the height of its left subtree is greater than its right, and is equal to

n − 1

where n is the height of Smith's right subtree. In this case, the height of William's left subtree is therefore 3 − 1. The height of the right subtree is therefore

(n − 1) − BF

For this example, we get (3 − 1) − 2, which gives the correct height of 0 for the right subtree.

If the balance factor is positive, then the formula n − 1 gives the height of the right subtree, and (n − 1) − BF is the height of the left subtree.

The tree in Figure 6-3 represents the balance factors after the new node has been added. As mentioned earlier, you adjust the balance factors of the nodes in the path to the new node based on whether the new node is part of an existing node's left or right subtree. The formulas you have just seen are part of computations applied after determining that a rotation is needed. That being the case, look again at Figure 6-5, which contains the balance factors *after* a rotation has been made. This is where we should end up after the balance factor computations.

The process begins at the lowest level affected by the rotation. In this example, that means Williams, which has been rotated to become a subtree of Thomas. Because the nodes don't store the exact heights of their subtrees, the computations must be based on the previous balance factors.

To understand exactly what will happen and to make it easier to develop the formulas for the new balance factors, let's take a short side step to look at a more generic example. Assume that Thomas has two subtrees with unknown specific heights. Williams also has two subtrees, also with unknown specific heights, as in Figure 6-6. You apply a right rotation, lifting Thomas into the spot formerly occupied by Williams. The result can be found in Figure 6-7.

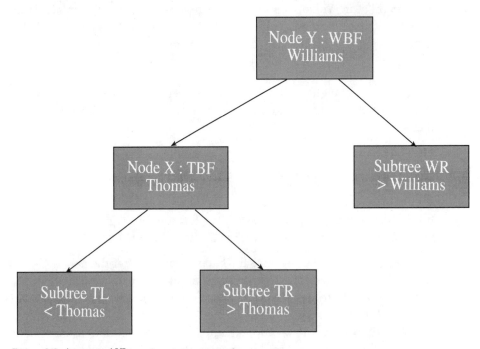

Figure 6-6 A generic AVL tree for rotation example

First notice what has happened to the three subtrees. Williams has kept its right subtree to handle nodes with keys greater than Williams. Thomas has kept its left subtree for nodes with keys less than Thomas. However, Thomas's right subtree, with keys greater than Thomas but less than Williams, has now migrated to become Williams's left subtree. In its new position, this subtree will continue to hold nodes with keys greater than Thomas but less than Williams.

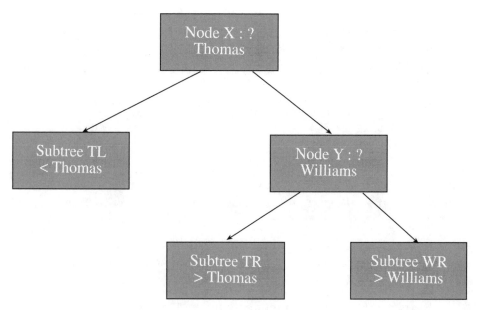

Figure 6-7 The generic AVL tree after a right rotation

The problem is that you must figure out the balance factors for Williams and Thomas, without being given the precise heights of the three subtrees. The only information you have is the previous balance factors for Williams and Thomas and the preceding formula for the heights of subtrees in a balanced AVL tree.

The process begins by calculating Williams's new balance factor. There are two possibilities, each of which generates a different formula: Subtree TL could be taller than Subtree TR, giving Thomas a negative balance factor, or Subtree TR could be taller than Subtree TL, giving Thomas a positive balance factor. In both cases, however, the new balance factor computation uses the formulas for computing the heights of subtrees that you saw earlier in this discussion.

If Thomas has a negative balance factor (meaning Subtree TL is the heavier), then Williams's new balance factor is

```
Height_of_SubtreeWR - Height_of_SubtreeTR =
(n - WilliamsBF)- ((n-1)-ThomasBF) =
1 + WilliamsBF - ThomasBF
```

Conversely, if Thomas has a positive balance factor, then Williams's new balance factor is

```
Height_of_SubtreeWR - Height_of_SubtreeTR =
(n - WilliamsBF) - (n - 1) =
1 + WilliamsBF
```

Note: If the subtrees have the same height, producing a balance factor of 0, then you can use either formula to figure out the new balance factor.

Now we need to develop formulas for figuring out Thomas's new balance factor. To do this, we need to know the height of the subtree now anchored by Williams because Thomas's balance factor will be

```
Height_of_Subtree_anchored_by_Williams -
    Height_of_SubtreeTL
```

To start, let's figure out the heights of the three subtrees, beginning with the computations in Figure 6-8. The heights at the bottom of the figure are expressed relative to the total height of the parent (either Williams or Thomas, as appropriate). To perform the balance factor computations, however, the heights of the subtrees need to be expressed in terms of the overall height of the tree. In other words, they must be expressed in terms of Wn in the illustration, or simply n, the height of the tree.

Combining the possible values for Williams's balance factor and Thomas's balance factor gives us four possibilities. These combinations and the translation of the heights of SubtreeTR and SubtreeTL can be found in Table 6-1. The major substitution that was made to go from heights expressed in terms of Thomas's subtree (Tn) to the overall height of the tree (Wn) was Tn = Wn - 1.

Notice that in Figure 6-8 we were only considering whether WBF was positive or negative. However, to determine the relative heights of subtrees TL,

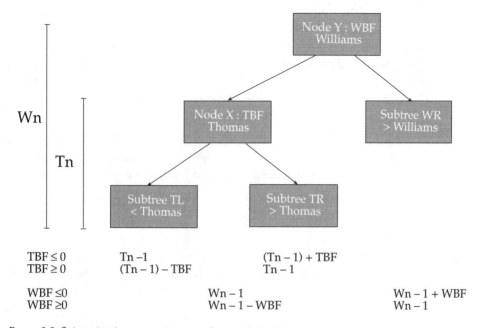

$$TBF \leq 0 \qquad Tn - 1 \qquad (Tn - 1) + TBF$$
$$TBF \geq 0 \qquad (Tn - 1) - TBF \qquad Tn - 1$$

$$WBF \leq 0 \qquad Wn - 1 \qquad Wn - 1 + WBF$$
$$WBF \geq 0 \qquad Wn - 1 - WBF \qquad Wn - 1$$

Figure 6-8 Subtree heights express in terms of parent balance factors

TR, and WR after the rotation, you need to look at the relationship of Williams's balance factor to Thomas's balance factor.

Table 6-1 Heights of AVLTree Subtrees for a Right Rotation

TBF	WBF	Height of TL	Height of TR	Height of WR
≤0	< TBF	$(n - 1) - 1 =$ $n - 2$	$(n - 1) - 1 + TBF =$ $n - 2 + TBF$	$n - 1 - WBF$
≤ 0	> TBF	$(n - 1 - WBF) - 1 =$ $n - WBF - 2$	$(n - 1 - WBF) - 1 - TBF =$ $n - WBF - TBF - 2$	$n - 1$
> 0	< -1	$(n-1) - 1 - TBF =$ $n - TBF - 2$	$(n-1) - 1 =$ $n - 2$	$n - 1 - WBF$
> 0	≥ 0	$(n - 1 - WBF) - 1 - TBF =$ $n - WBF - TBF - 2$	$(n - 1 - WBF) - 1 =$ $n - 2 - WBF$	$n - 1$

Why are the relative heights of TL, TR, and WR important? Because the trick is to determine in each case whether SubtreeTR is taller than SubtreeWR. This tells you which of the two determines the overall height of Williams's subtree after the rotation. (If you look back at Figure 6-7, you'll notice that both of those subtrees are connected to Williams.) Once you know which is taller, you can add 1 to the height of the appropriate subtree to get the total height of the subtree anchored by Williams and then subtract the corresponding height of SubtreeTL from it to obtain Thomas's new balance factor. The four computations, which use the expressions from Table 6-1, are as follows:

- If Thomas's original balance factor is less than or equal to zero and Thomas's original balance factor is greater than Williams's original balance factor, then TR is heavier than WR and Thomas's new balance factor is

```
(Height_of_SubtreeTR + 1) - Height_of_SubtreeTL
(n - 2 + ThomasBF + 1) - (n - 2)
ThomasBF + 1
```

- If Thomas's original balance factor is less than or equal to zero and Thomas's original factor is less than or equal to Williams's original balance factor, then SubtreeWR is taller than SubtreeTR and Thomas's new balance factor is therefore

```
(Height_of_SubtreeWR + 1) - Height_of_SubtreeTL
(n - 1 + 1) - (n - WilliamsBF - 2)
WilliamsBF + 2
```

- If Thomas's original balance factor is greater than zero and Williams's original balance factor is less than or equal to −1, then SubtreeTR is heavier than WR and the computation becomes

```
(Height_of_SubtreeTR + 1) - Height_of_SubtreeTL
(n - 2 + 1) - (n - ThomasBF - 2)
ThomasBF + 1
```

- If Thomas's original balance factor is greater than zero and Williams's original balance factor is greater than or equal to 0, then SubtreeWR is heavier than Subtree TR and the computation is

```
(Height_of_SubtreeWR + 1) - Height_of_Subtree_TL
(n - 1 + 1) - (n - WilliamsBF - ThomasBF - 2)
WilliamsBF + ThomasBF + 2
```

With the formulas for computing the new balance factors after a right rotation in place, we can apply them to the tree with which we started (Figure 6-3 after a node is added and Figure 6-4 after the tree is rebalanced with a right rotation).

First, compute the new balance factor for Williams. Because Thomas has a negative balance factor before the rotation, you use the formula

```
1 + WilliamsBF — ThomasBF
```

Therefore, Williams's new balance factor is

```
1 + −2 − (−1) = 0
```

To determine Thomas's new balance factor, first determine which of the four conditions you are facing. In this case, Thomas's original balance factor is negative and also less than Williams's original balance factor. You therefore use the second of the four formulas:

```
WilliamsBF + 2
```

The computation then becomes

```
−2 + 2 = 0
```

6.1.5 Computing New Balance Factors After a Left Rotation

The computations for balance factors after a left rotation are the mirror image of those for a right rotation. Because you are familiar with the process used to obtain the formulas, the left rotation formulas aren't presented in quite as much detail.

To start, take a look at the modified generic tree in Figure 6-9. After a left rotation, Williams will become the root and Thomas gains Williams's left subtree as its right subtree (see Figure 6-10).

To compute Williams's new balance factor as the new root of the tree, you use the formulas in Table 6-2. As with the formulas for the new root after a right rotation, the expressions are based on the definition of the balance factor ($RH − LH$) and the knowledge that in a balanced AVL tree, the difference between the right and left subtrees can be no more than 1.

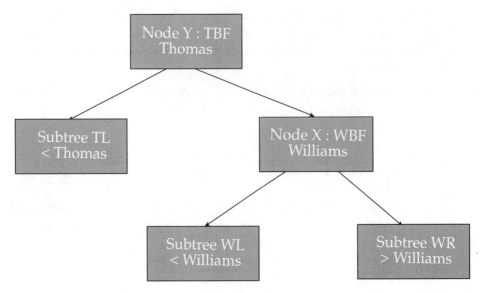

Figure 6-9 A generic AVL tree for demonstrating balance factor computations for a left rotation

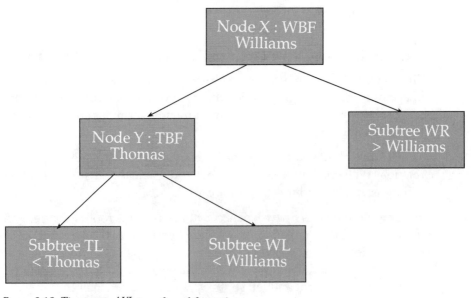

Figure 6-10 The generic AVL tree after a left rotation

Table 6-2 Balance Factor Formulas for New Root Node After a Left
Rotation

TBF	Formula

≤ 0	`Height_of_SubtreeTL - Height_of_SubtreeWR =`
	 `(n - 1) - (n - WBF) =`
	 `WBF - 1`

≥ 0	`Height_of_SubtreeTR - Height_of_SubtreeWR =`
	 `(n - 1 - TBF) - (n - WBF) =`
	 `TBF = WBF - 1`

The computations for Thomas's new balance factor begin with the heights of the subtrees in terms of their parent nodes, which can be found in Figure 6-11. From those, you can derive the formulas for the heights of the three subtrees in terms of the overall height of the table, as in Table 6-3, just as was done for the right rotation. In this case, the translation from the heights of Williams's subtree (Wn) to the height of the overall tree (Tn) was based on the fact that Wn = Tn − 1.

You will find the resulting formulas for the four conditions that are the mirror images of those for the right rotation in Table 6-4. As you examine the table, keep in mind that you need to add 1 to the height of the left subtree to account for the additional height of its parent node (Thomas). Also notice that in this case, the right subtree is always WR; to calculate the new balance factor, you need to know whether TL or WL is heavier to determine the height of the subtree anchored by Thomas.

6.2 AVL Tree Classes

Believe it or not, the hard part of working with an AVL tree is done! Once you know the formulas for recomputing balance factors, all you need to do is use those formulas in the appropriate places.

After inserting or removing a node and rebalancing the tree, an AVL tree is no different than a regular binary tree. It can use the same search technique and the same iterators. Therefore, it makes sense to derive the AVL tree

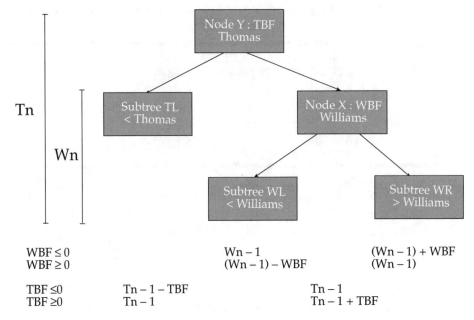

Figure 6-11 Subtree heights in terms of parent balance factors

Table 6-3 Heights of AVLTree Subtrees for a Left Rotation

WBF	TBF	Height of TL	Height of WL	Height of WR
≤0	<1	(n − 1) − TBF	(n − 1) − 1 = n − 2	(n − 1) − 1 + WBF = n + WBF − 2
≤ 0	≥1	(n − 1)	(n − 1) − 1 = n − 2	(n − 1) − 1 + WBF = n − 2 + WBF
> 0	≤ WBF	(n − 1) − TBF	(n−1) − 1 − WBF = n − WBF − 2	(n − 1) − 1 = n − 2
> 0	> WBF	(n − 1)	(n−1) − 1 − WBF = n − WBF − 2	(n − 1) − 1 = n − 2

classes from the binary tree classes so you can avoid duplicating code. The only change required to the `Tree` class from what you saw in Chapter 5 is that its `private` elements have been changed to `protected` to give the `AVLTree` class access to them. The same is true of the `Node` class.

Table 6-4 Formulas for Computing the Balance Factor of a Root Node After a Left Rotation

WBF	TBF	Formula

≤ 0	< 1	`Height_of_SubtreeWR — (Height_of_SubtreeTL + 1) =`
		 `(n + WBF — 2) — ((n — 1) — TBF + 1)`
		 `TBF + WBF — 2`

≤ 0	≥ 1	`Height_of_SubtreeWR — (Height_of_SubtreeWL + 1) =`
		 `(n + WBF — 2) — (n — 2 + 1)`
		 `WBF — 1`

> 0	$\leq$ WBF	`Height_of_SubtreeWR — (Height_of_SubtreeTL + 1) =`
		 `(n — 2) — (n — 1 — TBF + 1)=`
		 `TBF — 2`

> 0	$>$ WBF	`Height_of_SubtreeWR — (Height_of_SubtreeWL + 1) =`
		 `(n — 2) — (n — WBF — 2 + 1) =`
		 `WBF — 1`

6.2.1 The AVL Tree Manager Class

You can find the declaration of the AVLTree class in Listing 6-1. Because the process for inserting and deleting nodes is quite different from that of the basic binary tree, AVLTree overrides the `insert` and `deleteNode` functions. Otherwise, it inherits everything from Tree.

```
#ifndef AVLTREE
#define AVLTREE

#include "tree.h"
#include "avlnode.h"
#include "thing.h"

class AVLTree : public Tree
{
    public:
        AVLTree ();
        void insert (Thing *);
        bool deleteNode (int);
};

#endif
```

Listing 6-1 Declaration of the AVLTree class

> **Note:** To simplify the AVLTree demonstration program, the constructor that reads from a file and the write function have been commented out from the Tree class used as a base class for AVLTree. The application program therefore also excludes code for file I/O.

As mentioned at the beginning of this chapter, a node in an AVL tree is much busier than a node in a basic binary tree. The declaration of the AVL-Node (Listing 6-2) uses the `right` and `left` child pointers from the Node class, but overrides the `setLeft`, `setRight`, `getLeft`, and `getRight` functions so they handle pointers to AVLNode objects rather than Node objects. In addition, the AVLNode class stores the node's balance factor and includes functions to modify and retrieve that value.

```
#ifndef AVLNODE
#define AVLNODE

#include "node.h"
#include "thing.h"

class AVLNode : public Node
{
   private:
      int balanceFactor;
      AVLNode * singleRotateLeft ();
      AVLNode * singleRotateRight ();
      AVLNode * restoreLeftBalance (int);
      AVLNode * restoreRightBalance (int);
      AVLNode * balance ();
      AVLNode * removeLeftChild (AVLNode * &);
   public:
      AVLNode (Thing *);
      void setLeft (AVLNode *);
      void setRight (AVLNode *);
      AVLNode * getLeft ();
      AVLNode * getRight ();
      int getBalanceFactor ();
```

Listing 6-2 Declaration of the AVLNode class

```
      void setBalanceFactor (int);
      AVLNode * insert (Thing *);
      AVLNode * deleteNode (int, AVLNode * &);
};

#endif
```

Listing 6-2 Declaration of the AVLNode class

The remainder of the functions are used when inserting and/or removing nodes. You will be introduced to them in the remaining sections of this chapter.

6.3 *Adding Nodes to an AVL Tree*

In Chapter 5, you saw that the Tree class was in charge of the entire process of adding a node. With the AVL tree, the AVLTree class and the Node class share the responsibility. The process begins with the AVLTree class's `insert` function (Listing 6-3).

```
void AVLTree::insert (Thing * theThing)
{
    AVLNode * theRoot = (AVLNode *) root;
    if (theRoot)
        root = theRoot->insert (theThing);
    else
        root = new AVLNode (theThing);
}
```

Listing 6-3 Implementation of the AVLTree function to insert a new node

If there is no existing root node (the tree is empty), then `insert` creates a new AVLNode object and makes it the root. However, if there is at least one node in the tree, the `insert` function turns the responsibility over to the root node, which executes its own `insert` function (Listing 6-4). This function returns the root of the subtree into which the new node was inserted.

```
AVLNode * AVLNode::insert (Thing * theThing)
{
    // handle keys this way to make it type independent when
    // implemented as a template
    int newKey, currentKey;
    theThing->getKey (newKey);
    getKey (currentKey);

    AVLNode * left = (AVLNode *) left_child;
    AVLNode * right = (AVLNode *) right_child;

    if (newKey < currentKey) // insert into left subtree
    {
        if (left) // if there is a left child
        {
            int oldBF = left->getBalanceFactor ();
            setLeft (left->insert (theThing));
            // determine whether tree is larger
            if ((left->getBalanceFactor () != oldBF)
                && left->getBalanceFactor())
                balanceFactor--;
        }
        else
        {
            setLeft (new AVLNode (theThing));
            balanceFactor--;
        }
    }
    else  // insert into right subtree
    {
        if (right) // if there is a right child
        {
            int oldBF = right->getBalanceFactor ();
            setRight (right->insert (theThing));
            // determine whether tree is larger
            if ((right->getBalanceFactor () != oldBF)
                && right->getBalanceFactor())
                balanceFactor++;
        }
        else
```

Listing 6-4 Implementation of the AVLNode class's insert function

172

```
    {
        setRight (new AVLNode (theThing));
        balanceFactor++;
    }
}

//determine whether tree is balanced
if (balanceFactor < -1 || balanceFactor > 1)
    return balance ();
return this;
}
```

Listing 6-4 Implementation of the AVLNode class's insert function

The insertion proceeds in the following way:

1. If the key for the node being inserted (newKey) is less than the key of the current node (currentKey), the new node will be inserted into the current node's left subtree. Otherwise, the new node will be inserted into the right subtree. In that case, continue with step 10.

2. If the current node has no left child, continue with step 7.

3. Retrieve the left child node's balance factor (oldBF).

4. Set the current node's left pointer to point to the root of its left subtree after the new node is inserted into the left subtree. (This may be the same left child or it may be a new left child created by a rotation.) Notice that the insertion into the left subtree is accomplished by calling insert for the current node's left subtree. This repeated calling of insert for each node down a subtree will continue until the function reaches a node where there is no child and the new node can be inserted.

5. Adjust the balance factor for the current node.

6. Skip to step 17.

7. Insert the new node as the current node's left child.

8. Adjust the balance factor for the current node.

9. Skip to step 17.

10. If the current node has no right child, skip to step 15.

11. Retrieve the right child node's balance factor (oldBF).

12. Set the current node's right pointer to point to the root of its right sub-tree after the new node is inserted into the right subtree. As with an insertion into the left subtree, this is handled by calling `insert` for the right child node.

13. Adjust the balance factor for the current node.

14. Skip to step 17.

15. Insert the new node as the current node's right child.

16. Adjust the balance factor for the current node.

17. If the subtree anchored by the current node is not balanced, call the `balance` function to rebalance it. Return the new root of the subtree.

18. Otherwise, return the current node.

Rebalancing of a subtree is handled by the `balance` function (Listing 6-5). If the current balance factor is negative (left subtree tree heavier than right), the function performs a single right rotation if the left subtree's balance factor is less than or equal to 0. Otherwise, it performs a left rotation followed by a right rotation.

```
AVLNode * AVLNode::balance ()
{
    AVLNode * left = (AVLNode *) left_child;
    AVLNode * right = (AVLNode *) right_child;
    if (balanceFactor < 0)
    {
        if (left->getBalanceFactor() <= 0)
            return singleRotateRight ();
        else
        {
            setLeft (left->singleRotateLeft());
            return singleRotateRight();
        }
    }
    else
    {
        if (right->getBalanceFactor() >= 0)
            return singleRotateLeft();
        else
```

Listing 6-5 Implementation of the function that balances a subtree in an AVL tree

```
        {
            setRight (right->singleRotateRight());
            return singleRotateLeft();
        }
    }
}
```

Listing 6-5 Implementation of the function that balances a subtree in an AVL tree

On the other hand, if the current node's balance factor is greater than or equal to 0 (right subtree heavier than left), then the function performs a single left rotation if the right subtree's balance factor is greater than or equal to 0. Otherwise, it performs a single right rotation followed by a single left rotation.

To perform a right rotation, the balance function calls the function `singleRotateRight` (Listing 6-6). The actual rotation takes only two steps: Set the current node's left pointer to its left child's right node; set the left child's right pointer to the current node. Then, the `singleRotateRight` function recomputes the balance factors for the current node and its left child, using the formulas developed earlier in this chapter.

```
AVLNode * AVLNode::singleRotateRight ()
{
    AVLNode * current = this;
    AVLNode * child = (AVLNode *) left_child;

    //perform the rotation
    current->setLeft (child->getRight());
    child->setRight (current);

    //recompute balance factors
    int currentBF = current->balanceFactor;
    int childBF = child->getBalanceFactor();
    if (childBF <= 0)
    {
        if (childBF > currentBF)
            child->setBalanceFactor (childBF + 1);
```

Listing 6-6 Performing a single right rotation on an AVL subtree

```
            else
                child->setBalanceFactor (currentBF + 2);
            current->balanceFactor = 1 + currentBF - childBF;
        }
        else
        {
            if (currentBF <= -1)
                child->setBalanceFactor (childBF + 1);
            else
                child->setBalanceFactor (currentBF + childBF + 2);
            current->balanceFactor = 1 + currentBF;
        }
        return child;
}
```

Listing 6-6 Performing a single right rotation on an AVL subtree

The left rotation is handled by `singleRotateLeft` (Listing 6-7). The rotation itself involves setting the current node's right child pointer to its right child's left child pointer and setting the right child's left node to point to the current node. The function then completes its work by recomputing the balance factors.

```
AVLNode * AVLNode::singleRotateLeft ()
{
    AVLNode * current = this;
    AVLNode * child = (AVLNode *) right_child;

    // perform the rotation
    current->setRight (child->getLeft());
    child->setLeft (current);

    // recompute balance factors
    int currentBF = current->balanceFactor;
    int childBF = child->getBalanceFactor();
    if (childBF <= 0)
    {
        if (currentBF >= 1)
            child->setBalanceFactor (childBF - 1);
```

Listing 6-7 Performing a single right rotation on an AVL subtree

```
        else
            child->setBalanceFactor (currentBF + childBF - 2);
        current->balanceFactor = currentBF - 1;
    }
    else
    {
        if (currentBF <= childBF)
            child->setBalanceFactor (currentBF - 2);
        else
            child->setBalanceFactor (childBF - 1);
        current->balanceFactor = (currentBF - childBF) - 1;
    }
    return child;
}
```

Listing 6-7 Performing a single right rotation on an AVL subtree

6.4   *Removing Nodes from an AVL Tree*

As with adding a node, removing a node from an AVL tree is controlled by the AVLTree class's `deleteNode` function (Listing 6-8). The deletion begins by determining if there is a root node. If there is no root node, the tree is empty and the function returns `false`. Otherwise, the function calls the root node's `deleteNode` function, which returns the root node of the tree. This will be the same as the current root unless the deletion causes a rotation of the entire tree.

```
bool AVLTree::deleteNode (int key)
{
    AVLNode * deletedNode = 0;
    AVLNode * theRoot = (AVLNode *) root;

    if (theRoot)
        root = theRoot->deleteNode (key, deletedNode);
    if (deletedNode)
    {
```

Listing 6-8 Implementation of the AVLTree function to remove a node

```
        delete deletedNode;
        return true;
    }
    else
        return false;
}
```

Listing 6-8 Implementation of the AVL Tree function to remove a node

As with adding a node, most of the work is done by the nodes. The node's `deleteNode` function (Listing 6-9) works much like that of the Tree class. It finds the node to be deleted and then determines which node should replace it. Once it has found the replacement node—the lowest left child of the right subtree, if there is one—it reconnects the replacement node, recomputes balance factors, and then completes any needed rotations to restore the tree's balance.

```
AVLNode * AVLNode::deleteNode (int key, AVLNode * & deletedNode)
{
    AVLNode * right = (AVLNode *) right_child;
    AVLNode * left = (AVLNode *) left_child;

    if (key == intKey)  // this is where the deletion occurs
    {
        deletedNode = this;
        if (!right)
            return left;

        int oldBF = right->getBalanceFactor();
        AVLNode * newRoot;
        setRight (right->removeLeftChild (newRoot));
        newRoot->setLeft ((AVLNode *) left_child);
        newRoot->setRight ((AVLNode *) right_child);
        newRoot->setBalanceFactor (balanceFactor);
        return newRoot->restoreRightBalance (oldBF);
    }
    else if (key < intKey)
    {
        if (!left)
```

Listing 6-9   Implementation of the AVLNode function to remove a node

```
            return this;

        int oldBF = left->getBalanceFactor();
        setLeft (left->deleteNode (key, deletedNode));
        return restoreLeftBalance (oldBF);
    }
    else
    {
        if (!right)
            return this;

        int oldBF = right->getBalanceFactor();
        setRight (right->deleteNode (key, deletedNode));
        return restoreRightBalance (oldBF);
    }
}
```

Listing 6-9   Implementation of the AVLNode function to remove a node

Specifically, the process works in the following way:

1. If the key of the node to be deleted is equal to the key of the current node, then the node to be deleted has been found. Otherwise, continue with Step 11.

2. Store a pointer to the deleted node (the current node).

3. If the current node has no right child, exit the function, returning the current node's left child.

4. Otherwise, store the right child's balance factor.

5. Set the current node's right child to the lowest left child by calling removeLeftChild (Listing 6-10). This function returns the node that will be the new right child in the newRoot reference parameter. It works by continuing to call itself for each successive left child until the lowest left child is found.

```
AVLNode * AVLNode::removeLeftChild (AVLNode * & childNode)
{
    AVLNode * left = (AVLNode *) left_child;
```

Listing 6-10 Implementation of the AVLNode function to remove the lowest left child

```
if (!left)
{
    childNode = this;
    return (AVLNode *) right_child;
}

int oldBF = left->getBalanceFactor();
setLeft (left->removeLeftChild (childNode));
return restoreLeftBalance (oldBF);
}
```

Listing 6-10 Implementation of the AVLNode function to remove the lowest left child

6. Set the new root's left child to the current node's left child.

7. Set the new root's right child to the current node's right child.

8. Set the new root's balance factor to the current node's balance factor.

9. Adjust the balance factor to account for the removal of a node from the right subtree by calling `restoreRightBalance` (Listing 6-11).

```
AVLNode * AVLNode::restoreRightBalance (int oldBF)
{
    AVLNode * right = (AVLNode *) right_child;

    if (!right)
        balanceFactor--;
    else
        if ((right->getBalanceFactor() != oldBF) &&
            (right->getBalanceFactor() == 0))
            balanceFactor--;

    if (balanceFactor < -1)
        return balance();
    return this;
}
```

Listing 6-11 Implementation of the AVLNode function to restore the balance of a right subtree after removing a node

10. Exit the function.

11. If the key of the node to be removed is less than the key of the current node, the node to be deleted must be in the left subtree. Otherwise, continue with step 17.

12. If there is no left child, return the current node.

13. Otherwise, store the current node's balance factor.

14. Set the current node's left child to the node returned by calling `deleteNode` on the left child.

15. Restore the balance of the left subtree by calling `restoreLeftBalance` (Listing 6-12).

```
AVLNode * AVLNode::restoreLeftBalance (int oldBF)
{
    AVLNode * left = (AVLNode *) left_child;

    if (!left)
        balanceFactor++;
    else
        if ((left->getBalanceFactor() != oldBF) &&
            (left->getBalanceFactor() == 0))
            balanceFactor++;

    if (balanceFactor > 1)
        return balance();
    return this;
}
```

Listing 6-12 Implementation of the AVLNode function to restore the balance of a left subtree after removing a node

16. Exit the function.

17. The deleted node must be in the right subtree.

18. If there is no right child, return the current node.

19. Otherwise, store the current node's balance factor.

20. Set the current node's right child to the node returned by calling `deleteNode` on the right child.

21. Restore the balance of the right subtree by calling `restoreRightBalance`.

6.5   Summary

An AVL tree is a binary tree in which the difference between the heights of the right and left subtrees of any node is never more than one. Each node maintains a balance factor that indicates whether the right subtree is heavier (1), the left subtree is heavier (–1), or the heights are equal (0).

Whenever a node is added to or removed from an AVL tree, the program must first recompute the balance factors after the modification. It must rebalance the tree if necessary by rotating a subtree and then recomputing the balance factors once more.

An AVL tree ensures that most searches take the minimum amount of time. However, the algorithmic complexity of maintaining the tree and the time necessary to maintain balance may offset the gains in search efficiency. (As long as the keys of nodes enter the tree in relatively random order, a simple binary tree will remain fairly well balanced without the AVL tree manipuations.)

CHAPTER 7   *B-Trees*

Disk access time has more impact on the performance of many applications than CPU, system bus, or main memory speed. This is particularly true for programs such as DBMSs that store vast amounts of data on disk, only bringing it into memory as needed. Even the indexes to databases must be stored on disk; they are simply too large to keep main-memory resident.

To minimize retrieval speed, a DBMS attempts to move entire disk pages at once. However, data structures such as binary trees, indexes, arrays, and vectors are designed to handle only a single key and associated information at one time. If the element stored in a data structure is a key and a disk file location, then it likely takes up far less space than a whole disk page. These therefore are not efficient data structures for use in a disk-based environment. What is needed is a node that is about the size of a disk page and that can handle multiple keys and values at the same time so they can all be retrieved with one disk access. (The fewer the disk accesses, the faster the program will run.) The typical data structure used to provide indexes to stored database data is a B-Tree (from Balanced Tree).

7.1 B-Tree Concepts

This conceptually simple, but algorithmically complex, data structure stores multiple elements and pointers in a single node. To see how this works, let's build a B-Tree that uses an integer as a key. We won't worry initially about pointers to data value, but just look at how the keys and pointers to other nodes create the structure of the true.

For this first example, let's assume that all nodes except the root must have a minimum of two keys and can have a maximum of four keys (a B-Tree of *order four*). If there are less than two keys, the two nodes must be combined; if there are more than four keys, then the node must be split.

> **Note:** There is no fixed rule about the maximum or minimum number of elements that can be stored in a B-Tree node. You adjust those values depending on the size of the data being stored and the size of a disk page. However, in theory, a tree of order n should have a minimum of $n/2$ entries in each node and a maximum of n.

A B-Tree node has the logical structure you can see in Figure 7-1. The top row of squares, numbered 1 through 4, represent the elements stored by the node. The elements are in key order, with location 1 holding the element with the smallest key. The bottom row holds pointers to nodes in the next level of the tree. Conceptually, each element in the top row has one right subtree, the tree whose root node has the corresponding number. Subtree 0, which is technically a left subtree of element 1, is handled separate in most cases.

In addition to the preceding, all leaves of the tree must be on the same level. In other words, the tree must be balanced, even more so than an AVL tree, which at least allows a difference of one between the height of right and left subtrees.

Let's begin by adding four keys to the node, as in Figure 7-2. Because there is room for four elements in the node, all a program has to do to add a new node in key order is to perform the equivalent of an insertion sort.

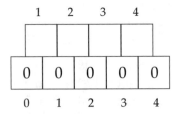

Figure 7-1 *The structure of a B-Tree node of order four*

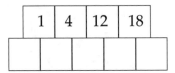

Figure 7-2 *A B-Tree with a full root node*

However, what happens when we attempt to add an element with a key of 15? There isn't room in this node for a fifth element. Therefore, the current root node has to be split. The root node can be left with a single element. The split can therefore place two elements in each of two new nodes, as in Figure 7-3.

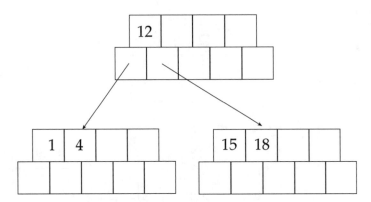

Figure 7-3 *A B-Tree after the full root node has been split*

Notice that the root node now has two of its pointers (called *branches*) in use. Branch 0 points to a node with key values less than element 1; branch 1 points to a node with key values greater than element 1.

Now let's add an element with a key of 30, which is larger than 20. Will it cause a split of the right subtree? Yes, it does (see Figure 7-4). The insert function recognizes that 30 is greater than 12 and that there are no other elements in the root node. It therefore takes branch 1, which leads to elements with keys greater than 12.

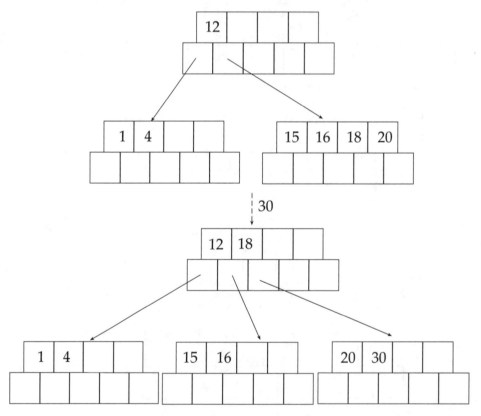

Figure 7-4 Adding a new high value to the B-Tree

The function searches for the position in which the new element should be stored, which in this case is to the right of 20. However, there is no room in the node to store the element. Instead, the node must be split, but the function can't simply add a new subtree: the tree must remain balanced. The solution is to split the node and promote the median note (in this example, 18) back up one level.

As a result, the root node now has three branches. Branch 0 points to a node containing elements with keys less than element 1; branch 1 points to a node containing elements with keys greater than element 1 and less than element 2; branch 2 points to a node with elements greater than element 2.

The tree will continue to split sideways until the root node is full, at which point it will introduce a third level into the tree. The result is a tree that is broader than it is deep. As you may remember from our previous discussion of binary search trees, the maximum number of nodes a search needs to visit to determine that a desired element isn't in the tree is equal to the number of levels in the tree. A B-Tree therefore minimizes the number of levels and also minimizes the number of disk accesses necessary to bring parts of the tree into main memory for manipulation.

To search a B-Tree, you begin at the root, performing a sequential search on the keys of the elements it contains. (If the node contained a large number of elements, then a binary search would be faster.) If you find the right element, you stop. Otherwise, you find the branch that leads to elements with keys in the range of the one for which you are searching. You repeat the search of the node, taking the appropriate branch until you find either the correct element, or reach a leaf node (one with no branches), at which point it is clear that the desired element isn't in the tree.

7.2   The B-Tree Node Class

Because the structure of a B-Tree node is so different from that of a binary tree node, it doesn't buy you anything to attempt to derive a B-Tree node from the binary tree node. The B-Tree node is therefore a standalone class (see Listing 7-1).

```
#ifndef B_NODE
#define B_NODE

#include "thing.h"

#define MAX 4   // maximum keys per node
#define MIN 2   // minimum keys per new subtree

class BNode
{
    private:
        int numbElements;
        BNode * branches [MAX+1];
        // elements[0] is not used
        Thing * elements [MAX+1]; // use getKey() to retrieve keys
    public:
        BNode ();
        int getNumbElements ();
        int getKey (int); // gets key for a specified Thing object
        Thing * getElement (int);
        BNode * getBranch (int);
        void setNumbElements (int);
        void setBranch (int, BNode *);
        void setElement (int, Thing *);
};

#endif
```

Listing 7-1 Declaration of a B-Tree node class

Notice that the elements and branches are stored in two matched arrays. (A structure or class pairing an element and a branch really doesn't make sense here because the two are relatively independent.) The numbering of the elements does present a small problem for C++, given that C++ arrays are 0 based. The logic of the code for the B-Tree becomes much simpler if the element array begins with array index 1; therefore, array index 0 will remain unused in the sample code you see in this book. The elements array in this example contains room for five elements just as the branches array stores five branches. (There will always be one more branch than element.)

The implementation of the node class in Listing 7-2 is straightforward. The constructor initializes both the `branches` and `elements` arrays to 0. The remaining functions get and set private data items.

```
#include "bnode.h"

BNode::BNode ()
{
    for (int i = 0; i <= MAX; i++)
        branches[i] = 0;
    for (int i = 0; i < MAX; i++)
        elements[i] = 0;
    numbElements = 0;
}

int BNode::getNumbElements ()
    { return numbElements; }

int BNode::getKey (int index)
{
    int key;
    elements[index]->getKey(key);
    return key;
}

Thing * BNode::getElement (int index)
    { return elements[index]; }

BNode * BNode::getBranch (int index)
    { return branches[index]; }

void BNode::setNumbElements (int value)
    { numbElements = value; }

void BNode::setBranch (int index, BNode * theNode)
    { branches[index] = theNode; }

void BNode::setElement (int index, Thing * theThing)
    { elements[index] = theThing; }
```

Listing 7-2 Implementation of a B-Tree node class

7.3   The B-Tree Class

In Listing 7-3 you can find the declaration of the B-Tree class. Like the binary tree, the only data value it maintains is the address of the root node of the tree. The class includes public functions to insert an element, find an element by its keys, determine whether the tree is empty, and delete an element. The private functions are used by the find, insert, and delete functions.

```
#ifndef B_TREE
#define B_TREE

#include "bnode.h"
#include "thing.h"

class BTree
{
    private:
        BNode * root;
        // used by find function
        bool search (int, BNode *, BNode * &, int &);
        bool searchNode (int, BNode *, int &);
        // used by insert function
        bool pushDown (Thing *, BNode *, Thing * &, BNode * &);
        void pushIn (Thing *, BNode *, BNode *, int);
        void split (Thing *, BNode *, BNode *, int, Thing * &,
            BNode * &);
        // used by deleteElement function
        bool recursiveDelete (int, BNode *);
        void remove (BNode *, int);
        void successor (BNode *, int);
        void restore (BNode *, int);
        void moveRight (BNode *, int);
        void moveLeft (BNode *, int);
        void combine (BNode *, int);
    public:
        BTree ();
        void insert (Thing *); // initiate an insertion
        Thing * find (int); // initiate a search
```

Listing 7-3   Declaration of a B-Tree class

```
    bool isEmpty ();
    bool deleteElement (int); // initiate a deletion
};

#endif
```

Listing 7-3 (Continued) Declaration of a B-Tree class

7.4   *Finding an Element*

Although it may seem backwards to talk about searching for an element before examining element insertion, it is important to understand the search code because it is used by the insertion code. Therefore, as we examine the search code, assume that elements already have been inserted properly into the tree.

Like the search of a binary tree, the search of a B-Tree traverses the tree, taking branches as necessary. The B-Tree search must search within each node that it reaches as well. The search stops when either the correct node is found or the search reaches a leaf node without finding the desired element.

The functions that provide the B-Tree search can be found in Listing 7-4. The search is triggered by the `find` function, providing the public interface to the search functionality. The `find` function triggers the first call to search, which handles traversing the nodes. Searching within a single node is handled by the `searchNode` function.

```
Thing * BTree::find (int key)
{
    // start search
    BNode * foundNode = 0;
    int position;
    bool found = search (key, root, foundNode, position);
    // handle result
    if (found)
```

Listing 7-4   Searching a B-Tree

```
            return foundNode->getElement (position);
        else
            return 0;
}

bool BTree::search (int key, BNode * currentNode,
        BNode * & foundNode, int & position)
{
    bool found;
    if (currentNode == 0)
        found = false;
    else
    {
        found = searchNode (key, currentNode, position);
        if (found)
            foundNode = currentNode;
        else
            found = search (key, currentNode->getBranch(position),
                foundNode, position) ;
    }
    return found;
}

// sequential search of a single node
bool BTree::searchNode (int key, BNode * currentNode,
        int & position)
{
    bool found = false;
    if (key < currentNode->getKey(1))
        position = 0;
    else
    {
        position = currentNode->getNumbElements();
        while (key < currentNode->getKey(position) && position > 1)
            position--;
        found = (key == currentNode->getKey(position));
    }
    return found;
}
```

Listing 7-4 (Continued) Searching a B-Tree

The algorithms for working with a B-Tree can be coded using a stack or a technique known as *recursion.* Recursion refers to a function that calls itself. When a recursive call returns, the program restores the state of the function at the time the recursive call was issued and continues execution. You will see several examples of recursion in this chapter and in some of the sort routines in Chapter 9 as well.

> **Note:** B-Tree manipulations can be either stack-based or recursive. The implementation you will be reading about is recursive. There is no specific reason to prefer one strategy over the other. Some programmers find recursion difficult to follow and therefore prefer to use a stack; yet others believe that recursion produces clearer code.

The code for manipulating the B-Tree can be difficult to follow. Therefore, as you are reading the code, you may wish to refer back to Table 7-1, which provides a directory of the major variable and macro names used throughout the program.

Table 7-1 Variable and Macro Usage in the B-Tree Class Implementation

Variable Name	Use
currentNode	The node being examined at any given time.
foundNode	A pointer to a B-Tree node object that has been found by a search.
insertedThing	A pointer to a Thing object that is to be inserted into the tree.
key	The key value of an element. In this example, it is the integer ID of a Thing object.
MAX	The maximum number of elements that can be stored in a node.
MIN	The minimum number of elements that can appear in a node other than the root.
newNode	A new node that has been created and that needs to be linked into the tree.
newRightSubtree	A pointer to a node that is created when a node is split and that must be linked into the tree as a branch.
newThing	A pointer to a Thing object that is to be inserted into the tree.
position	The position within a node (1 through 4) representing the location of an element within a node.
rightSubtree	A pointer to a node that is the right subtree of a given element in the tree.

To see how a search is performed, assume that the B-Tree appears as in Figure 7-5. The keys were added in the following order: 1, 4, 12, 15, 16, 18, 20, 30, 22, 5, 27, 40, 11, 3, 50, 60, 45, 47, 13, 6, 10. (Keep in mind that the way in which a tree is built depends on the order in which keys enter the tree. Therefore, if you want to try these examples yourself, be certain that you follow the preceding key order.)

To find the element with a key of 10, a program would *logically* do the following:

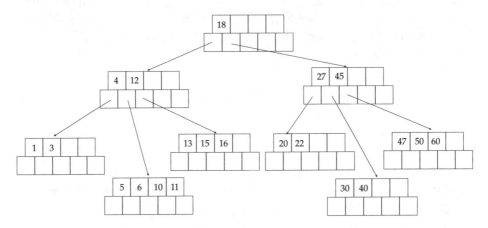

Figure 7-5 A sample B-Tree to use for querying

1. Enter the tree at the root.
2. Search the root node and determine that there is no match for the key.
3. Because the key is less than the single key value in the root node, take branch 0.
4. Search the node at branch 0 and determine that there is no match for the key.
5. Because the value of the key is between the two keys in the node, take branch 1.
6. Search the node at branch one for a match. Since a match for the key is found within the node, the search is successful.

The program code follows the same procedure, but in what appears to be a less straightforward way:

1. Enter the `find` function. Notice that the only information supplied to that function is the key of the element to be found.

2. Allocate space for a pointer to a node (the variable `foundNode`) and for the position of the found element within the node (`position`).

3. Call `search`, passing in the key value, the root of the tree, and references to node and position storage. The root `node` enters search as the current node.

4. If the current node does not exist, then the search is unsuccessful. This can occur when the tree is empty or when a search has taken a branch that does not exist. In our particular example, the current node does exist.

5. Therefore, call `searchNode` to determine if the element with a key of 10 is within the current node or which branch should be taken.

6. Because 10 is less than the single key value in the root node (18), the search is not complete (`found = false`) and the position of the branch to be taken is 0. Return to the `search` function.

7. Because the node has not been found and there is still a valid branch that can be taken, place a recursive call to `search`, this time passing in the key, branch 0 of the root node, and the two reference parameters.

8. If the current node does not exist, then the search is unsuccessful. Exit the function and return `false`. For this particular example, there is still a current node.

9. Call `searchNode` to begin a sequential search of the node.

10. The key of 10 is greater than the first key in the node (4). Therefore, the search should not take branch 0.

11. Set `position` equal to the number of elements in the node (2).

12. Compare 10 to the last key in the node (12). Because 10 is less than 12, enter the while loop and decrement `position` (1). The loop stops at this point because `position` is equal to 1. This will be the number of the branch that will be taken for the next call to `search`.

13. Set `found` to `false` because the search key (10) is not equal to the key at position 1 (4). Exit the function and return `false`.

14. Since the desired node has not been found, call `search` a third time, now passing in the key, branch 1 from the previous node, and the two reference parameters.

15. If the current node does not exist, then the search is unsuccessful. However, in this case there is a node at branch 1 of the previous current node.

16. Call `searchNode` to search the current node. This time, the function finds the desired node in position three. Exit the function and return `true`.

17. Because found is `true`, set `foundNode` to the current node. Exit from the third recursive call to `search` and return `true`.

18. Return from the second recursive call to `search`, returning `true`.

19. Exit from the first call to `search`, returning `true`. The program is now back in the `find` function.

20. Because the search was successful, retrieve the element at the found position in the found node. Return a pointer to the element.

If the program was searching for 9, which is not in the tree, there would be a fourth call to `search`, using the nonexistent branch 3 in the node containing 5, 6, 10, and 11. The `search` function would immediately detect that the current node was 0 and therefore would report an unsuccessful search.

7.5   Inserting an Element

Inserting a new node is logically complex because there are a number of situations that the code must handle:

- If there is room in a node for an insertion, the new element can simply be added to the node, moving existing elements as needed to make room for it. This is a simple insertion sort and would occur, for example, if you inserted 21 into the tree in Figure 7-5.

- The node is full but the parent node above has room. For example, if you wanted to insert 7 into Figure 7-5, it would go between 6 and 10. In this case, the program would split the node, placing 5, 6, and 7 in the existing node, moving 10 into the parent node, putting 11 and 12 into a new node, and moving 13 into the parent node; the node that previously contained 13 would retain 15 and 16. The parent node would then contain 4, 10, and 13 and there would be four branches. If the parent node is full, then the process recursively moves a level up the tree, continuing until there is a node that isn't full.

- The recursive splitting and insertions provide a single element for a new root. The program must then insert the element into the new root and connect it to the rest of the tree.

Keep in mind that whenever a node is split, the tree must remain balanced: All leaf nodes must be on the same level. Adding a level to the tree requires modifying at least all nodes on the previous level. The tree maintenance algorithm therefore splits horizontally if at all possible before going to a new level.

The code for adding a new node requires the four functions in Listing 7-5 as well as searchNode. The insert function triggers the process. As you can see, its public interface requires only a pointer to the element being inserted.

```
void BTree::insert (Thing * newThing)
{
    BNode * rightSubtree;
    Thing * insertedThing;
    bool pushUp = pushDown (newThing, root, insertedThing,
        rightSubtree);
    if (pushUp)
    {
        BNode * newNode = new BNode ();
        newNode->setNumbElements (1);
        newNode->setElement (1, insertedThing);
        newNode->setBranch (0, root);
        newNode->setBranch (1, rightSubtree);
        root = newNode;
    }
}
```

Listing 7-5   Functions used to insert a new element into a B-Tree

```
bool BTree::pushDown (Thing * newThing, BNode * currentNode,
    Thing * & insertedThing, BNode * & rightSubtree)
{
    int position;
    bool found, pushUp;
    if (currentNode == 0)
    {
        pushUp = true;
        insertedThing = newThing;
        rightSubtree = 0;
    }
    else
    {
        int key;
        newThing->getKey(key);
        found = searchNode (key, currentNode, position);
        if (found)
            cout << "\nWarning: Inserting duplicate key.";
        pushUp = pushDown (newThing,
            currentNode->getBranch(position), insertedThing,
            rightSubtree);
        if (pushUp)
        {
            if (currentNode->getNumbElements() < MAX)
            {
                pushUp = false;
                pushIn (insertedThing, rightSubtree, currentNode,
                    position);
            }
            else
            {
                pushUp = true;
                split (newThing, rightSubtree, currentNode,
                    position, insertedThing, rightSubtree);
            }
        }
    }
    return pushUp;
}
```

Listing 7-5 (Continued) Functions used to insert a new element into a B-Tree

```
void BTree::pushIn (Thing * newThing, BNode * rightSubtree,
    BNode * currentNode, int position)
{
   int elements = currentNode->getNumbElements();
   int i;
   for (i = elements; i >= position + 1; i--)
   {
      currentNode->setElement (i + 1,
         currentNode->getElement (i));
      currentNode->setBranch (i + 1, currentNode->getBranch (i));
   }
   currentNode->setElement (position + 1, newThing);
   currentNode->setBranch (position + 1, rightSubtree);
   currentNode->setNumbElements (elements + 1);
}

void BTree::split (Thing * newThing, BNode * rightSubtree,
    BNode * currentNode, int position,
   Thing * & medianThing, BNode * & newRightSubtree)
{
   int median;

   if (position <= MIN)
      median = MIN;
   else
      median = MIN + 1;
   newRightSubtree = new BNode ();
   for (int i = median + 1; i <= MAX; i++)
   {
      newRightSubtree->
         setElement (i - median, currentNode->getElement (i));
      newRightSubtree->
         setBranch (i - median, currentNode->getBranch (i));
   }
   newRightSubtree->setNumbElements (MAX - median);
   currentNode->setNumbElements (median);
   if (position <= MIN)
      pushIn (newThing, rightSubtree, currentNode, position);
   else
```

Listing 7-5 (Continued) Functions used to insert a new element into a B-Tree

```
      pushIn (newThing, rightSubtree, newRightSubtree,
         position - median);
   int elements = currentNode->getNumbElements();
   medianThing = currentNode->getElement (elements);
   newRightSubtree->setBranch (0,
      currentNode->getBranch (elements));
   currentNode->setNumbElements (elements - 1);
}
```

Listing 7-5 (Continued) Functions used to insert a new element into a B-Tree

Most of the work is done by the pushDown function. Rather than try to discuss the action of this function abstractly, let's look at two examples, one in which we insert 21 (the node has space for the element) and one in which we insert 7 (the node does not have space and will need to be split) in the tree from Figure 7-5.

7.5.1 Inserting an Element into a Node with Space

Using the code in Listing 7-5, a program would do the following when inserting a 21 into the tree in Figure 7-5:

1. Collect the data for the element to be inserted and create an object for the element. In our example, the object is from the Thing class.
2. Call the insert function, passing in a pointer to the element to be inserted.
3. Set aside storage for a B-Tree node and a pointer to an element that is inserted.
4. Call the pushDown function, passing in the pointer to the new element and the root of the tree as the current node. Also pass in references to the storage locations declared in step 3.

In general, the purpose of the pushDown function is to determine whether the new element can be placed in the current node or if the code must "push down" to a level below. If the new element belongs in the current node, then pushDown will either insert it (the pushIn function) or split the node (the split function). If the new element belongs in a node below the current node, pusdhdown calls itself to move to a lower level.

5. Allocate storage for two booleans, one to hold the result of a search for the element in the tree (found) and one to indicate whether the element being handled needs to be pushed up into a higher level of the tree (pushUp).

6. If the current node is undefined, then set pushUp to true, set the inserted element (insertedThing) to the new element (newThing), and the right subtree to 0. Return pushUp. Upon returning to insert, the program will create a new node and insert insertedThing into it. In the example we are tracing, the root node is a valid node. Therefore, the program enters the else block.

7. Declare storage to hold the new element's key and retrieve the key value from the new element.

8. Call searchNode to determine whether the new key is present in the current node. If the key exists, then the position variable contains the location of the element with that key. Otherwise, it indicates the branch to be taken to locate the key.

9. If an element with key is already in the current node, display a warning to that effect.

> **Note:** The implementation you are seeing allows duplicate key values. To ensure that keys are unique, you can modify the code to return if found is true after the call to searchNode. Before returning, do something, such as setting insertedThing to 0, that can be detected by recursive calls to pushDown and insert to indicate that the insertion has failed.

10. Place a recursive call to pushDown, passing in the new element and the branch at the position returned by searchNode. In this example, it will be branch 1, which points to the node containing 27 and 45.

11. Get the key of the new element, which is still 21.

12. Call searchNode to determine whether the key is present and if not, which branch to take. This time, searchNode returns false in branch 0, which points to the node containing 20 and 22.

13. Place another recursive call to pushDown, passing in the new element and the branch at the position returned by searchNode (branch 0).

14. Get the key of the new element, which is still 21.

15. Call searchNode to determine whether the key is present and if not, which branch to take. The search fails again and returns branch 1, which is undefined.

16. Place yet another recursive call to pushDown, passing in the new element and the branch at the position returned by searchNode (branch 1, which is 0).

17. Now when the program enters pushDown, the current node is 0. Therefore the pushUp boolean becomes true, insertedThing becomes the new element, and its right subtree will be set to 0.

18. The last (fourth) call to pushDown returns true. At this point, the current node reverts to the node containing 20 and 22.

19. Because the current node has fewer than the maximum number of elements, the new element can be inserted into that node. Set pushUp to false to prevent further insertions as the other recursive calls to pushDown return. Then call pushIn to insert the new element into the node, passing in the element to be inserted, a pointer to its right subtree, a pointer to the current node, and the position where the new element is to be inserted.

20. Enter a for loop that moves elements and branches to make space for the new element.

21. Insert the new element and the branch to its right subtree.

22. Increment the number of elements.

23. Return to pushDown.

24. Return from the third call to pushDown, returning false. At this point, the current node becomes the node containing 27 and 45.

25. Because pushUp is false, skip the rest of the else construct.

26. Return from the second call to pushDown. The current node is now the root node.

27. Because pushUp is false, skip the rest of the else construct and return to insert.

28. Because pushUp is false, skip the if construct and exit.

7.5.2 Inserting an Element into a Full Node

Now let's turn to inserting a 7 into the tree. In this case, the program will need to split the node containing 5, 6, 10, and 11 and move some elements around to make space. The discussion assumes that you are familiar with the actions of insert, pushDown, and pushIn and therefore does not discuss their actions in detail except where they affect the splitting of the node.

To insert an element that requires splitting a node—in particular, an element with a key of 7—a program would do the following:

1. Enter insert with a pointer to the new element.
2. Call pushDown for the first time.
3. Determine that the key of the new element is not in the root node.
4. Call pushDown for the second time. The current node becomes the node containing 4 and 12 (branch 0 of the root node).
5. Determine that the key of the new element is not in the current node.
6. Call pushDown for the third time. The current node becomes the node containing 5, 6, 10, and 11 (branch 1 of the node containing 4 and 12).
7. Determine that the key of the new element is not in the current node.
8. Call pushDown for the fourth time. The current node becomes 0 (branch 2 of the node containing 5, 6, 10, and 11).
9. Set pushUp to true. (Element goes into the node on the level above.) The inserted element becomes the new element with an associated branch (right subtree) of 0.
10. Return from the fourth call to pushDown. The current node becomes the node containing 5, 6, 10, and 11.
11. Because pushUp is true and the number of elements in the node is equal to the maximum, call split. (pushUp remains true.)

The split function breaks a full into two pieces and promotes the median node up one level in the tree. In our particular example, the tree will appear as in Figure 7-6. Because the element with a key of 7 would go in the middle of the node that originally contained 5, 6, 10, and 11, it ends up in the node one level above.

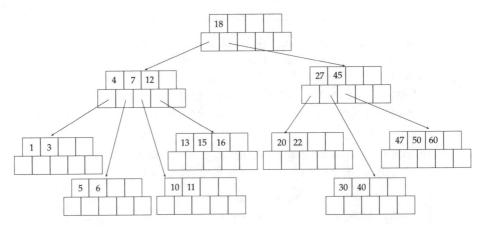

Figure 7-6 The B-Tree from Figure 7-5 after inserting an element with a key of 7

When thinking about the action of the `split` function, keep in mind that `split` is pursuing two goals: keep the tree balanced and wherever possible, leave one or two empty spaces in each node after the split. This means that the function creates a new node on the same level unless it absolutely has no choice but to add a new level to the tree. Adding a new level means rearranging the entire tree rather than just a few nodes and therefore is to be avoided at all costs.

When the insertion enters `split` in our example, the position of the new element is 2. The right subtree pointer is 0 because position 2 has no branch. The current node is the node containing 5, 6, 10, and 11.

12. Because position is equal to the minimum number of nodes, the median position is set to 2.

13. Create a new node that will become a new right subtree of the current node's parent node.

14. Copy the elements that are above the median (in this case, the elements with the keys 10 and 11) into the new node.

15. Set the number of elements in the new node (2).

16. Set the number of elements in the current node.

> **Note:** When you split a node, the elements moved into another node aren't actually removed from their original location. However, when you decrease the value in the number of elements variable, you make the invalid elements inaccessible, which is just as effective as setting their pointers to 0.

17. Because position is equal to the minimum number of nodes, call `pushIn` to add the new element to the current node (the node that now contains just 5 and 6). This temporarily adds 7 to that node, but as you will see, the element with 7 as its key doesn't stay there long!

18. Retrieve the number of elements in the current node (3).

19. Set the median element to point to the element with the highest key in the current node (7). This variable (`medianThing`) is a reference parameter and therefore the pointer to this variable will be available to the calling function in the variable `insertedThing`.

20. Set branch 0 in the new node created in Step 13 to point to the element with the highest key in the current node. Since the element with a key of 7 has no branch, then this value is 0.

21. Decrement the number of elements in the current node, effectively removing the element with 7 as its key.

22. Return to `pushDown`.

23. Return from the third call to `pushDown`. The current node is now the node containing 4 and 12.

24. Because `pushUp` is `true` and the current node has room, set `pushUp` to `false` and call `pushIn` to insert the element with a key of 7 into the current node.

25. Return from the second call to `pushDown`. The current node is the root node.

26. Return from the first call to `pushDown`, ending up in the `insert` function.

27. Return from the call to `insert`.

> **Note:** One way to see how a B-Tree is built is to run the demonstration program that accompanies the BTree class using a debugger. Put a breakpoint at the end of the `insert` function. Then you can look at the state of the tree after each insertion.

7.6 Deleting an Element

Like the binary search tree, deleting an element is more complex than inserting one. The coder must handle the following situations:

- Deleting an element in a leaf when the deletion leaves more than the minimum number of elements in the node. This is the easiest situation because all that is necessary is the removal of the element from the leaf node. The only elements and branches that possibly need to be moved are those in the leaf node itself.

- Deleting an element that is not in a leaf node when the deletion leaves less than the minimum number of elements in the node. In this case, once the deletion is performed, the node will need to be combined with another node, which, of course, may affect any number of other nodes in the tree.

- Deleting an element that is not in a leaf node. The strategy in this case is to find the key's immediate predecessor or successor in the tree—which will be in a leaf—and swap it up into the place occupied by the element to be deleted. Then the moved element can be deleted from the leaf using either of the preceding strategies.

The functions used to support deletion from a B-Tree are found in Listing 7-6. The `deleteElement` function triggers the process by calling `recursiveDelete` with the key of the element to be deleted and the root of the tree as the initial current node.

```
bool BTree::deleteElement (int key)
{
    bool found;
    found = recursiveDelete (key, root);
    if (found && root->getNumbElements() == 0)
        root = root->getBranch(0);
    return found;
}

bool BTree::recursiveDelete (int key, BNode * currentNode)
{
    int position;
    bool found;

    if (currentNode == 0)
        found = false;
    else
    {
        found = searchNode (key, currentNode, position);
        if (found)
        {
            if (currentNode->getBranch (position - 1) == 0)
                remove (currentNode, position);
            else
            {
                successor (currentNode, position);
                found = recursiveDelete
                    (currentNode->getKey (position),
                    currentNode->getBranch (position));
            }
        }
        else
        {
            found = recursiveDelete
                (key, currentNode->getBranch (position));
        }
        BNode * branchNode = currentNode->getBranch (position);
        if (branchNode != 0 && branchNode->getNumbElements () < MIN)
            restore (currentNode, position);
    }
}
```

Listing 7-6   Functions to delete an element from a B-Tree

207

```
    return found;
}

void BTree::remove (BNode * currentNode, int position)
{
    for (int i = position + 1; i <= currentNode->getNumbElements();
        i++)
    {
        currentNode->setElement (i-1, currentNode->getElement (i));
        currentNode->setBranch (i-1, currentNode->getBranch (i));
    }
    currentNode->setNumbElements
        (currentNode->getNumbElements() - 1);
}

void BTree::successor (BNode * currentNode, int position)
{
    BNode * branchNode = currentNode->getBranch (position);
    while (branchNode->getBranch (0) != 0)
        branchNode = branchNode->getBranch (0);
    currentNode->setElement (position, branchNode->getElement (1));
}

void BTree::restore (BNode * currentNode, int position)
{
    if (position == 0) // leftmost element
    {
        BNode * branchNode = currentNode->getBranch (1);
        if (branchNode->getNumbElements() > MIN)
            moveLeft (currentNode, 1);
        else
            combine (currentNode, 1);
    }
    // rightmost element
    else if (position == currentNode->getNumbElements())
    {
        BNode * branchNode = currentNode->getBranch (position - 1);
        if (branchNode->getNumbElements() > MIN)
            moveRight (currentNode, position);
        else
```

Listing 7-6 (Continued) Functions to delete an element from a B-Tree

208

```
            combine (currentNode, position);
    }
    else // middle elements
    {
        BNode * branchNode = currentNode->getBranch (position - 1);
        if (branchNode->getNumbElements() > MIN)
            moveRight (currentNode, position);
        else
        {
            branchNode = currentNode->getBranch (position + 1);
            if (branchNode->getNumbElements () > MIN)
                moveLeft (currentNode, position + 1);
            else
                combine (currentNode, position);
        }
    }
}

void BTree::moveRight (BNode * currentNode, int position)
{
    BNode * branchNode = currentNode->getBranch (position);
    for (int i = branchNode->getNumbElements(); i >= 1; i--)
    {
        branchNode->setElement (i + 1, branchNode->getElement (i));
        branchNode->setBranch (i +  1, branchNode->getBranch (i));
    }
    branchNode->setBranch (1, branchNode->getBranch (0));
    branchNode->setNumbElements
        (branchNode->getNumbElements() + 1);
    branchNode->setElement (1, currentNode->getElement (position));

    BNode * branchNode2 = currentNode->getBranch (position - 1);
    currentNode->setElement (position,
        branchNode2->getElement (branchNode2->getNumbElements()));

    branchNode->setBranch
        (0,
        branchNode2->getBranch(branchNode2->getNumbElements()));
    branchNode2->setNumbElements
        (branchNode2->getNumbElements() - 1);
```

Listing 7-6 (Continued) Functions to delete an element from a B-Tree

```
}

void BTree::moveLeft (BNode * currentNode, int position)
{
    BNode * branchNode = currentNode->getBranch (position - 1);
    branchNode->setNumbElements
        (branchNode->getNumbElements() + 1);
    branchNode->setElement (branchNode->getNumbElements(),
        currentNode->getElement (position));
    BNode * branchNode2 = currentNode->getBranch (position);
    branchNode->setBranch (branchNode->getNumbElements(),
        branchNode2->getBranch (0));

    currentNode->setElement (position,
        branchNode2->getElement (1));
    branchNode2->setBranch (0, branchNode2->getBranch (1));
    branchNode2->setNumbElements
        (branchNode2->getNumbElements() - 1);

    for (int i = 1; i <= branchNode2->getNumbElements(); i++)
    {
        branchNode2->setElement
            (i, branchNode2->getElement (i + 1));
        branchNode2->setBranch (i, branchNode2->getBranch (i + 1));
    }
}

void BTree::combine (BNode * currentNode, int position)
{
    BNode * branchNode = currentNode->getBranch (position);
    BNode * branchNode2 = currentNode->getBranch (position - 1);

    branchNode2->setNumbElements
        (branchNode2->getNumbElements() + 1);
    branchNode2->setElement (branchNode2->getNumbElements(),
        currentNode->getElement (position));
    branchNode2->setBranch
        (branchNode2->getNumbElements (),
        branchNode->getBranch (0));
    for (int i = 1; i <= branchNode->getNumbElements (); i++)
```

Listing 7-6 (Continued) Functions to delete an element from a B-Tree

210

```
{
    branchNode2->setNumbElements
        (branchNode2->getNumbElements() + 1);
    branchNode2->setElement (branchNode2->getNumbElements(),
        branchNode->getElement (i));
    branchNode2->setBranch (branchNode2->getNumbElements(),
        branchNode->getBranch (i));
}
for (int i = position;
    i <= currentNode->getNumbElements () - 1; i++)
{
    currentNode->setElement
        (i, currentNode->getElement (i + 1));
    currentNode->setBranch (i, currentNode->getBranch (i + 1));
}
currentNode->setNumbElements
    (currentNode->getNumbElements() - 1);
}
```

Listing 7-6 (Continued) Functions to delete an element from a B-Tree

The purposes of the remaining functions are as follows:

- remove: Remove an element from a node by sliding elements to its right one position to the left and decrement the number of elements in the node.
- successor: Replace an element with its immediate successor in key order.
- restore: Restores the minimum number of keys in a node by finding an element to insert and performing the insertion.
- moveRight: Move an element into the node on the right by rotating elements through the parent node.
- moveLeft: Move an element into the node on the left by rotating elements through the parent node.
- combine: Combine two nodes into one.

The last four functions are all used in restoring the minimum number of elements in a node and maintaining the balance of the tree. Deletion also uses searchNode to search within a node to find the element to be deleted.

To illustrate the actions of the code, let's look at several examples of deleting elements from the tree in Figure 7-5.

7.6.1 Deleting an Element from a Leaf Leaving Enough Elements

For this first example, assume that you want to delete the element with the key of 11. Doing so will leave more than the minimum number of elements in the node. The program will do the following:

1. Call `deleteElement` passing in the key of the element to be deleted.

2. Call `recursiveDelete`, passing in the key of the element to be deleted and the root node as the current node.

3. If the current node is undefined, the element with the specified key is not in the tree. Exit the function, returning `false`. (If a node with the desired key is not in the tree, the deletion will fail at this point.) In this case, however, the current node is defined.

4. Call `searchNode` to determine whether the element to be deleted is in the current node.

5. In this case, the element is not in the current node. Therefore, place a second call to `recursiveDelete`, passing in the key (11) and, as the new current node, the correct branch (branch 0 of the root node, the node containing 4 and 12) to locate the element with the desired key.

6. Because the current node is defined, call `searchNode` to determine whether the element to be deleted is in the current node.

7. The element is not in the current node. Therefore, place a third recursive call to `recursiveDelete`, passing in the key and, as the new current node, the correct branch (branch 1 of the node containing 4 and 12) to locate the element with the desired key.

8. Because the current node is defined, call `searchNode` to determine whether the element to be deleted is in the current node.

9. The element to be deleted is in the fourth position of the current node.

10. Determine whether there is a valid branch to the left of the current node. Because there is not, the node is a leaf node.

11. Call `remove` to delete the element.

12. If necessary, enter a `for` loop to move elements to cover the "hole" left when the element being deleted is removed. In this example, the element being deleted is in position 4. Therefore, no elements need to be moved.

13. Decrement the number of elements in the current node.

14. Return to `recursiveDelete`.

15. Determine whether a node at the branch previously taken exists and has at least the minimum number of elements. Because the current node is a leaf and has no branches, no further action needs to occur.

16. Return from the third call to `recursiveDelete`, returning `found` as `true`. The current node returns to the node containing 4 and 12.

17. Determine whether the node at the branch previously taken (the node containing 5, 6, and 10) exists and has at least the minimum number of elements. Since it does, there is no need to move any additional elements.

18. Return from the second call to `recursiveDelete`. The `found` variable continues to contain `true`. The current node is now the root node.

19. Determine whether the node at the branch previously taken (the node containing 4 and 12) exists and has at least the minimum number of elements. Because it does, there is no need to move any additional elements.

20. Return from the first call to `recursiveDelete`, ending up in the `deleteElement` function.

21. Return `found` to indicate the success or failure of the deletion.

7.6.2 Deleting an Element from a Leaf Leaving Too Few Elements

For the next example, assume that we want to delete an element with a key of 20 from the tree. Doing so will leave its node with only one element, forcing the program to move elements to maintain the minimum number of elements in a node. The discussion assumes that you understand the operation of the `remove` and `deleteElement` functions, and have a basic understanding of `recursiveDelete` from the previous example.

To delete the element with a key of 20, the program would do the following:

1. Call `deleteElement`.

2. Place the first call to `recursiveDelete`. (The current node is the root of the tree.)

3. Because the element to be deleted is not in the current node, place a second call to `recursiveDelete`. (The current node is the node containing 27 and 45.)

4. Because the element to be deleted is not in the current node, place a third call to `recursiveDelete`. (The current node becomes the node containing 20 and 22.)

5. The current node contains the element to be deleted. Because the current node is a leaf, call `remove` to delete the element, leaving the element with the key of 22 in position 1. The number of elements in the current node is now 1.

6. Determine that the current node is a leaf (there is no branch at the position where the element was removed) and therefore no restore is necessary at this point.

7. Return from the third call to `recursiveDelete`.

8. Determine that the previously visited node (the node now containing 22) has only 1 element. Because this is less than the minimum number of nodes that can be in a node, call `restore`, passing in the current node (the node containing 27 and 45) and the value of `position` (0).

9. Retrieve a pointer to the node at the current node's branch 1 (the node containing 30 and 40), storing it in the variable `branchNode`.

If `branchNode` had more than the minimum number of elements, then it would be possible to move one up into its parent node and shift a node from the parent down to join 22 (the action of the `moveLeft` function). However, in this case, `branchNode` has only two elements and can't afford to lose one. Therefore, two nodes will need to be combined.

10. Call `combine`, passing in the current node (the node containing 27 and 45) and a position of 1.

11. Retrieve a pointer to the node at the current node's branch 1 (the node containing 30 and 40) and store it as `branchNode`.

12. Retrieve a pointer to the node at the current node's branch 0 (the node containing 22) and store it as `branchNode2`.

13. Increment the number of elements in `branchNode2`.

14. Move the element and branch at `position` from the current node down into `branchNode2`. In this case, 27 joins 22.

15. Execute the `for` loop that copies elements and branches from `branchNode` to `branchNode2`. This adds 30 and 40 to the 22 and 27.

16. Execute the `for` loop that moves elements and branches in the current node to cover the "hole" left when an element was moved down.

17. Decrement the number of elements in the current node.

At this point, the tree appears as in Figure 7-7. Notice that there is now a node that is not the root containing a single element (45). This situation must be handled before the deletion can be completed.

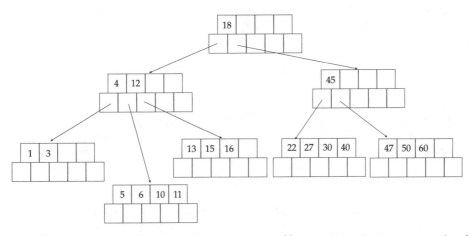

Figure 7-7   The B-Tree after deleting an element with a key of 20 and restoring the minimum number of elements in the leaf node

18. Return from `restore`.

19. Return from the second call to `recursiveDelete`. The current node is now the root node.

20. The node at the previously taken branch (the node now containing only 45) has less than the minimum number of elements. Therefore, call `restore` (current node is the root; position of branch is 1).

21. Because the we are dealing with the rightmost branch of the root node, execute the `else if` block.

22. Store the pointer to the branch to the right of `position` as `branch-Node`. This is the node at branch 0, which contains 4 and 12.

23. Because it is not possible to move an element from `branchNode` up to the root so an element from the root can be moved down to join the node containing 45, the only solution is to combine nodes. Therefore, call `combine`.

The call to `combine` moves 18 and 45 into `branchNode` (along with their associated branches), leaving the root node empty. At this point, the tree looks like Figure 7-8.

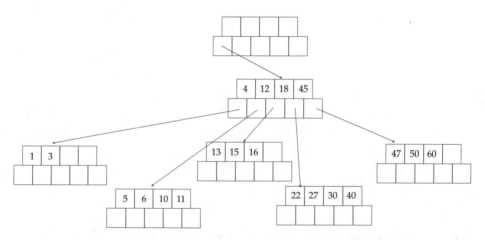

Figure 7-8 The B-Tree after combining nodes at the second level, leaving an empty root

24. Return to `deleteElement` from the first call to `recursiveDelete`.

25. Because the root node has 0 elements, reset the root to the current root's branch 0 (the node containing 4, 12, 18, and 45).

The result of the deletion produces the tree in Figure 7-9.

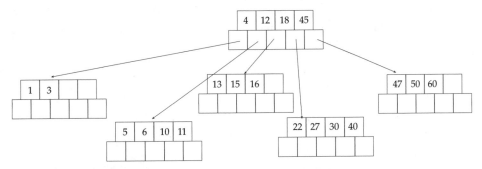

Figure 7-9   The B-Tree after the element with a key of 20 has been deleted

7.6.3 Deleting an Element from a Node That is Not a Leaf

As a final example, let's return to the original tree in Figure 7-5 and trace the deletion of the element with a key of 12. This element isn't a leaf node, which makes removing it from the tree a bit more complicated.

The deletion will proceed in the following way:

1. Call `deleteElement`.
2. Call `recursiveDelete` with the root node as the current node.
3. Because the element to be deleted is not in the root node, place a second call to `recursiveDelete`. The current node is now the node containing 4 and 12.
4. Because the current node is not a leaf, call `successor`, passing in the node containing 4 and 12 as the current node and the position as 2.
5. Retrieve a pointer to the branch at `position` (branch 2) of the current node and store it as `branchNode`. In this case, `branchNode` is the node containing 13, 15, and 16.
6. Because `branchNode` is a leaf, there is no need to go further down the tree. The `while` loop does not execute.
7. Copy the first element from `branchNode` into the current node, overlaying the element to be deleted.
8. Return from `successor` to the second call to `recursiveDelete`.

At this point, the tree appears as in Figure 7-10. Notice that the element with the key of 13 is in the tree twice. The next step is therefore to delete it from its original location.

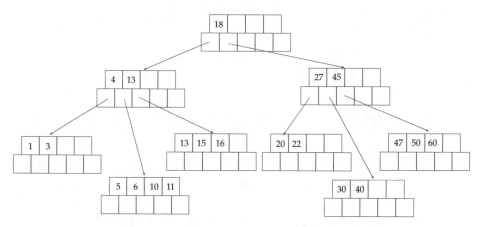

Figure 7-10 The B-Tree after moving up an element to overwrite an element that is not in a leaf node

9. Call `recursiveDelete` for the third time, in this case passing in the key of the element that was added to this node (13) and the branch to the element's original node (the node containing 13, 15, 16) as the current node.

10. Because the key (13) is present in the current node and the node is a leaf, call `remove` to delete the element.

11. Because the node is a leaf, there is no need to restore the number of elements in a child node.

12. Return from the third call to `recursiveDelete`. The current node is the node containing 4 and 14.

13. Because the previous current node has at least the minimum number of elements, a restore is unnecessary.

14. Return from the second call to `recursiveDelete`, making the current node the root node.

15. Because the previous current node has at least the minimum number of elements, a restore is unnecessary.

16. Return to `deleteElement` from the first call to `recursiveDelete`.

17. Because the root node contains at least one element, no further action is necessary. Exit the function, returning true indicating that the deletion was successful.

The final state of the tree after the deletion can be found in Figure 7-11.

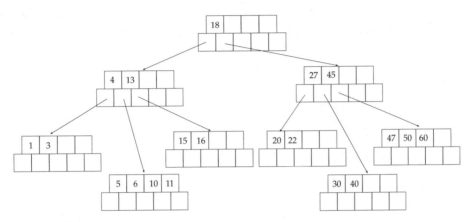

Figure 7-11 The B-Tree after deleting the element with a key of 12

7.7 Summary

A B-Tree is a tree in which each node stores more than one element along with pointers to multiple child nodes. The elements are kept in key order. The child nodes represent key values that are between adjacent elements in any given node. The leftmost child contains elements with keys less than all elements in a node; the rightmost child contains elements with keys greater than all elements in a node.

B-Trees are typically used as indexes to large sets of stored data and are particularly well suited to indexing data files and database files. They are often stored on disk rather than in main memory because they become too large for practical main memory storage.

A B-Tree has a specified maximum number of elements per node and a minimum number that is usually maximum/2. As elements are added and deleted, elements are moved and nodes combined and split to maintain this property.

In addition, all leaf nodes in a B-Tree must be on the same level. Therefore, insertion and deletion must maintain this property as well.

The size of a node is often chosen so that an entire node (or multiple of nodes) can be retrieved in a single disk access. This minimizes the number of disk accesses required to perform a search and thus makes a B-Tree more suitable for indexing large amounts of data than other data structures.

CHAPTER 8

Binary Heaps and Priority Queues

The trees that you have seen to this point use a linked organization in discontiguous memory to represent a tree structure. However, there is not reason that a tree can't be represented in contiguous storage as an array or vector. A binary tree that meets some specific properties is known as a *binary heap*. It typically is stored as an array or vector. One common use of a binary heap is to implement a *priority queue,* a queue from which you always remove the largest (or smallest) value. (A priority queue is a use of a binary heap. You therefore can have a binary heap that's not a priority queue and you can have a priority queue that is implemented using another data structure, such as a linked list.)

Note: This use of the word "heap" is not the same as the way in which we have used the term before. An application or system heap is main memory allocated while a program is running. The heaps we will be discussing in this chapter are a type of data structure.

Priority queues have many uses, especially for operating systems. For example, many operating systems use priority queues to store processes waiting for CPU time. Some processes, such as interrupt handlers, have higher priority values than others and therefore should run first. In addition, an operating system might use a priority queue to decide which spooled print job should run first. Priority queues are also used in simulations of events such as aircraft departures at airports and servicing customers at retail establishments.

A binary heap can also be used for sorting a contiguous list (vector or array). Although most sorting is discussed in Chapter 9, because the binary heap sort uses code that is introduced in this chapter, you will find the discussion of the binary heap sort here.

8.1 Characteristics of a Binary Heap

To be considered a binary heap, a binary tree must have the following characteristics:

- The key of the element in the root of any subtree must be greater than (or less than) the keys of the elements in its child nodes.

Note: A binary heap can be ordered to return the highest key or the lowest key, but not both. Which you choose will depend, of course, on the use to which you are putting the binary heap.

- The only level that is not completely full of elements is the lowest level. This means that the leaves are either on the lowest level or the level above.
- The incomplete level, if there is one, is filled from the left.

For example, the binary tree in Figure 8-1 is a binary heap. Unlike the binary search trees discussed in Chapter 5, a binary heap does not follow the insertion rule that states that elements with higher keys go to the right and lower keys go to the left. (You will be introduced to the insertion rule later in this chapter.)

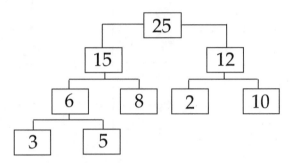

Figure 8-1 A binary tree that is a binary heap

A binary heap is not stored using the linked structure used with other trees. Instead, its nodes are stored contiguously, in an array or vector. The placement of the nodes in the tree determines the placement of the nodes in the array. As you can see in Figure 8-2, the nodes are numbered from top to bottom and left to right. Given the tree in Figure 8-2, an array used to store this binary heap would appear as in Figure 8-3.

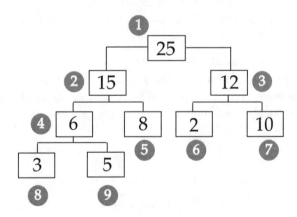

Figure 8-2 The order of placement of nodes into binary heap storage

Figure 8-3 An array representation of the binary heap in Figure 8-2

If you look carefully at the position of elements in Figure 8-3, you'll notice that if the root of a subtree is at position i, then the root of its left subtree is at position $2i$, and that the root of its right subtree is at $2i + 1$. This property makes it possible to locate related elements within the tree.

If a tree does not adhere to the restriction that all levels except the last are full and that the last level be filled from the left, then the contiguous storage representation of the tree will have unused elements, as in Figure 8-4. The result is an inefficient use of storage, given the amount of wasted space.

8.2 *Declaring a Priority Queue Class*

Assume that you enter elements with integer keys for a priority queue in the following order: 1, 4, 12, 18, 5, 3, 16, 20, 60, 22, 32, 40, 45, 47. A program that stores the elements as a binary heap will produce an array or vector

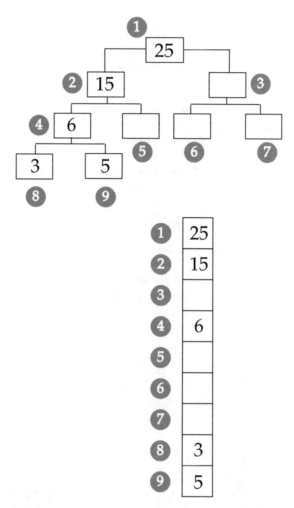

Figure 8-4 A binary tree that is not a binary heap and the resulting contiguous storage

like Figure 8-5. In this example, the leftmost digit is the array index, the second value from the left is the key, and the rightmost word is the name of the element.

```
0: 60 sixty
1: 32 thirty-two
2: 47 forty-seven
3: 18 eighteen
4: 22 twenty-two
5: 40 forty
6: 45 forty-five
7: 1 one
8: 12 twelve
9: 5 five
10: 20 twenty
11: 3 three
12: 16 sixteen
13: 4 four
```

Figure 8-5 A priority queue stored as a binary heap

To prove to yourself that this is indeed a binary heap, all you have to do is copy it into a binary tree structure such as that in Figure 8-6. Notice that this tree meets all the requirements of a binary heap.

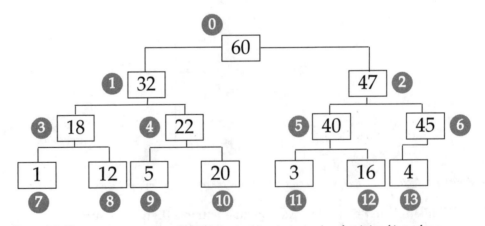

Figure 8-6 The priority queue restored to a binary tree structure, proving that it is a binary heap

The priority queue class that maintains the binary heap you have just seen is based on a vector. Although it could certainly use an array, the ability to expand the vector makes it a better choice for a structure for which you can't easily predict the size.

The declaration of the priority queue class can be found in Listing 8-1. A priority queue has only two public functions: `insert` and `remove`. (Ignore the `heapSort` function for now. It has been included for demonstration purposes and will be discussed in the last section of this chapter.) The `buildHeap` function is used by `remove`.

```
#ifndef PRIORITY_QUEUE
#define PRIORITY_QUEUE

#include "vectormgr.h"
#include "thing.h"

#define INITIAL_SIZE 25
#define SIZE_INCREMENT 10

class PQueue
{
    private:
        VectorMgr<Thing, int> * theVector; // implement as a vector
        void buildHeap (int, int, VectorMgr<Thing, int> *);
    public:
        PQueue ();
        PQueue (int); // pass in initial size
        ~PQueue ();
        void insert (Thing);
        bool remove (Thing &);
        void heapSort (); // for demonstration purposes only
        VectorMgr<Thing, int> * getVector (); // used by iterator
};

#endif
```

Listing 8-1   Declaration of a priority queue class

The `insert` function adds a new element to the binary heap, placing it in the correct order so that the largest element is in position 0 and all other elements are placed so the tree retains its properties as a binary heap. The remove function returns the element in position 0 and then restores the binary heap, moving the next largest element into position 0.

8.3 The Vector Storage Class

As you can see from Listing 8-1, the vector that stores the binary heap is a template class (see Listing 8-2). This is essentially the same class to which you were introduced in Chapter 2, with a few additional functions that are needed by the priority queue.

```
#ifndef VECTOR_MGR
#define VECTOR_MGR 1

#include "thing.h"

template <class E, class K>
class VectorMgr
{
    private:
        int total_elements, current_size;
        E * theVector;
    public:
        VectorMgr (int); // pass in initial size
        VectorMgr (VectorMgr *); // copy constructor
        ~VectorMgr ();
        bool addElement (E); // pass in a single element
        bool addElement (E, int); // pass in element and index
        bool setElement (E, int);// pass in element and index
        // pass in ordinal position of element
        bool getElement (int, E &);
        // pass in ordinal position of element to delete
        bool deleteElement (int);
        // pass in key value; return ordinal value
        bool findElement (K, int & pos);
        int getNumbElements (); // return total elements in vector
        void decrementNumbElements ();
        int getSize (); // return current size
```

Listing 8-2   A vector template class

```cpp
      bool isEmpty (); // true if vector is empty
      void resize (int); // pass in new size
};

template <class E, class K>
VectorMgr<E, K>::VectorMgr (int size)
{
   theVector = new E[size];
   // holds next array index as well as total elements
   total_elements = 0;
   current_size = size;
}

template <class E, class K>
VectorMgr<E, K>::VectorMgr (VectorMgr * iVector)
{
   current_size = iVector->getSize();
   theVector = new E[current_size];
   total_elements = iVector->getNumbElements();
   for (int i = 0; i < total_elements; i++)
      iVector->getElement (i, theVector[i]);
}

template <class E, class K>
VectorMgr<E, K>::~VectorMgr ()
   { delete [] theVector; }

template <class E, class K>
bool VectorMgr<E, K>::addElement (E theElement)
{
   bool result = true;
   if (total_elements == current_size)
      result = false; // vector is full
   else
   {
      theVector [total_elements] = theElement;
      total_elements++;
   }
   return result;
}
```

Listing 8-2 (Continued) A vector template class

```
template <class E, class K>
bool VectorMgr<E, K>::addElement (E theElement, int index)
{
    bool result = true;
    if (index <= total_elements)
    {
        theVector [index] = theElement;
        total_elements++;
    }
    else
        result = false;
    return result;
}

template <class E, class K>
bool VectorMgr<E, K>::setElement (E theElement, int index)
{
    bool result = true;
    if (index <= total_elements)
        theVector [index] = theElement;
    else
        result = false;
    return result;
}

template <class E, class K>
bool VectorMgr<E, K>::getElement (int index, E & theElement)
{
    bool result = true;
    if (index >= total_elements)
        result = false;
    else
        theElement = theVector [index];
    return result;
}

template <class E, class K>
bool VectorMgr<E, K>::deleteElement (int element)
{
    bool result = true;
```

Listing 8-2 (Continued) A vector template class

```
    if (element >= total_elements)
        result = false;
    else
    {
        for (int i = element; i < total_elements - 1; i++)
            theVector[i] = theVector[i+1];
        total_elements--;
    }
    return result;
}

template <class E, class K>
bool VectorMgr<E, K>::findElement (K searchValue, int & element)
{
    int result = true;
    int i = 0;
    while (i < total_elements)
    {
        if (theVector[i].getKey() == searchValue)
            element = i;
        i++;
    }
    if (i >= total_elements)
        result = false;
    return result;
}

template <class E, class K>
int VectorMgr<E, K>::getNumbElements ()
    { return total_elements; }

template <class E, class K>
void VectorMgr<E, K>::decrementNumbElements ()
    { total_elements--; }

template <class E, class K>
int VectorMgr<E, K>::getSize ()
    { return current_size; }

template <class E, class K>
```

Listing 8-2 (Continued) A vector template class

```
bool VectorMgr<E, K>::isEmpty ()
{
    if (total_elements == 0)
        return true;
    return false;
}

template <class E, class K>
void VectorMgr<E, K>::resize (int newSize)
{
    char yes_no;
    if (newsize < total_elements)
    (
        cout <<
    "\nThe new size is too small to contain all existing elements."
            << endl;
        cout << "Do you want to truncate the vector? (y/n) ";
        cin >> yes_no;
        if (yes_no == 'y')
            total_elements = newSize;
        else
            return;
    }

    E * newVector = new E [newSize];
    if (!newVector)
    {
        cout << "\nCannot create vector.";
        return;
    }
    for (int i = 0; i < total_elements; i++)
        newVector[i] = theVector[i];
    delete [] theVector;
    theVector = newVector;
    current_size = newSize;
}

#endif
```

Listing 8-2 (Continued) A vector template class

The new functions include the following:

- A copy constructor: This function is used only by the heap sort to create a copy of the vector to be sorted. There is no reason not to leave it as part of the class, although the copy of the vector is purely for demonstration purposes.

- An overloaded addElement function: The original addElement function adds one element at the end of the vector and increments the total number of elements. The new function adds an element at a specific position and increments the number of elements.

- A setElement function: This function inserts an element at a specified position, overwriting the element currently at that position, without increasing the number of elements in the vector.

- A decrementNumbElements function: This function is used by remove when the element in position 0 is removed.

The priority queue also needs to make use of the vector iterator, which has also been turned into a template (see Listing 8-3).

```
#ifndef VECTOR_ITR
#define VECTOR_ITR

#include "VectorMgr.h"

template <class A, class B>
class VectorItr
{
    private:
        VectorMgr<A, B> * theVector;
        int numb_elements;
        int current_index;

    public:
        // pass in the array manager and total elements
        VectorItr (VectorMgr<A, B> *, int);
        bool getNext (A &);
};
```

Listing 8-3 A vector iterator template class

```
template <class A, class B>
VectorItr<A, B>::VectorItr (VectorMgr<A, B> * inVector,
     int iElements)
{
    theVector = inVector;
    numb_elements = iElements;
    current_index = 0;
}

template <class A, class B>
bool VectorItr<A, B>::getNext (A & nextObject)
{
    bool result = false;
    if (current_index < numb_elements)
    {
        theVector->getElement (current_index, nextObject);
        result = true;
        current_index++;
    }
    return result;
}

#endif
```

Listing 8-3 (Continued) A vector iterator template class

8.4   Inserting Elements into the Priority Queue

The logic behind the insert function in Listing 8-4 is based on two facts: The binary heap is already in the correct order when a new element is inserted and an element's left child will be stored at the element's position * 2 and its right child at position * 2 + 1. Like any other algorithm for inserting into the middle of an array, it must find the correct place to insert the new element and then move existing elements to make room for it.

```
void PQueue::insert (Thing newThing)
{
    int newKey;
    newThing.getKey (newKey);
    Thing theThing;

    int numbElements = theVector->getNumbElements();

    // Add elements if vector is full
    if (numbElements + 1 >= theVector->getSize ())
        theVector->resize (theVector->getSize() + SIZE_INCREMENT);

    int position = numbElements++;
    int storedKey;
    theVector->getElement ((position-1)/2, theThing);
    theThing.getKey (storedKey);
    while (position > 0 && newKey >= storedKey)
    {
        theVector->setElement (theThing, position);
        position = (position - 1)/2;
        theVector->getElement ((position-1)/2, theThing);
        theThing.getKey (storedKey);
    }

    theVector->addElement (newThing, position);
}
```

Listing 8-4 Inserting an element into a priority queue

Assume that you have the binary heap in Figure 8-5. If you want to insert an element with a key of 30, the `insert` function would proceeded as follows:

1. Retrieve the key for the element to be inserted into the priority queue (30).

2. Retrieve the current number of elements in the vector (14).

3. Determine whether the vector is full. If it is, add elements. In this case, the vector is not full.

4. Set the initial `position` to the number of elements (14) and increment the number of elements locally (15). Note that this does not change the count of the number of elements stored in the vector. That occurs at the very end of the function with the call to `addElement`.

5. Retrieve the element that is stored at (`position` – 1)/ 2 (position 6, the element with the key of 45).

6. Retrieve the element's key.

7. Attempt to enter a `while` loop that continues as long as `position` is greater than 0 and the key of the new element (30) is greater than or equal to the key of the element at `position` / 2. In this case, the stored key (45) is greater than the new key. Therefore, the loop does not execute.

Note: If you want to create a priority queue that puts the largest element at the top, switch the key comparisons from >= to < throughout the `insert` and `buildHeap` functions.

8. Add the element to the vector at `position`. The call to `addElement` increments the number of elements stored by the vector as well as inserting the element. The vector now appears like Figure 8-7, representing the tree in Figure 8-8

As a second example, let's now add an element with a key of 50:

1. Retrieve the key of the new element (50).

2. Retrieve the number of elements (15).

3. Determine that the vector is not full so that no resizing is necessary.

4. Set `position` to 15 and the local number of elements to 16.

5. Retrieve the element at (`position` – 1)/2 and get its key (1).

6. Because the key of the new element (50) is greater than the key of the stored element (1), enter the `while` loop. (We can't simply add the element with a key of 50 as a left child of the element in position 7 because that would violate the restriction that the keys of all children be less than that of their parents.)

7. Move the element at position 7 into position 15.

8. Set `position` to (`position` – 1)/2 (7).

```
0: 60 sixty
1: 32 thirty-two
2: 47 forty-seven
3: 18 eighteen
4: 22 twenty-two
5: 40 forty
6: 45 forty-five
7: 1 one
8: 12 twelve
9: 5 five
10: 20 twenty
11: 3 three
12: 16 sixteen
13: 4 four
14: 30 thirty
```

Figure 8-7 The priority queue's vector after adding an element with a key of 30

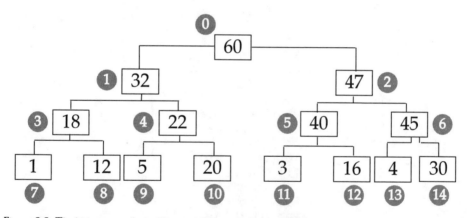

Figure 8-8 The binary tree after adding an element with a key of 30

9. Retrieve the element at $(\text{position} - 1)/2$ (position 3, with a key of 18).

10. Retrieve the key of the element at position 3.

11. The key at position 3 (18) is still less than the key of the new element (50). Therefore, enter the `while` loop again.

12. Move the element at position 3 into position 7.

13. Set `position` to (`position` − 1)/2 (3).

14. Retrieve the element at (`position` − 1)/2 (position 1, with a key of 32).

15. Retrieve the key from the element at position 1.

16. The key at position 1 (32) is still less than the key of the new element (50). Therefore, enter the `while` loop again.

17. Move the element at position 3 into position 1.

18. Set `position` to (`position` − 1)/2 (1).

19. Retrieve the element at (`position` − 1)/2 (position 0, with a key of 60).

20. Retrieve the key of the element at position 0.

21. In this case, the key of the stored element (60) is greater than the key of the new element. Therefore, do no enter the `while` loop again.

22. Store the new element in position 1, producing a vector like Figure 8-9 and a tree like Figure 8-10.

```
 0: 60 sixty
 1: 50 fifty
 2: 47 forty-seven
 3: 32 thirty-two
 4: 22 twenty-two
 5: 40 forty
 6: 45 forty-five
 7: 18 eighteen
 8: 12 twelve
 9: 5 five
10: 20 twenty
11: 3 three
12: 16 sixteen
13: 4 four
14: 30 thirty
15: 1 one
```

Figure 8-9 The priority queue's vector after adding an element with a key of 50

As you can see from the preceding examples, the insert routine moves elements down the tree until it finds the first "hole" into which a new element can be placed and still maintain the properties of the binary heap.

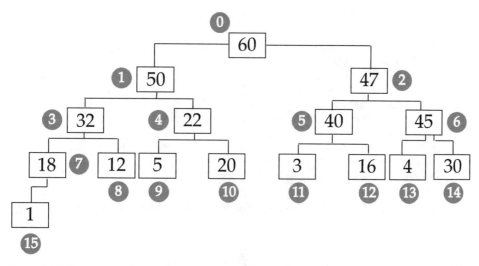

Figure 8-10 *The binary tree after adding an element with a key of 50*

8.5 Removing Elements from the Priority Queue

When you remove an element from a priority queue, you remove the first element off the top, much like popping an element off a stack. However, a stack is not ordered. In contrast, removing an element from the top of a priority queue may destroy the queue's heap properties. Therefore, once the element is removed, the binary heap may need to be rearranged.

The code that takes care of removing the element at the top of the queue and rebuilding the binary heap can be found in Listing 8-5. As an example, assume that we are working with the binary heap in Figure 8-9. The element at the top, with a key of 60, i s returned by the `remove` function. The calling function can either process the returned element or ignore it.

The removal results in the vector in Figure 8-11 and the tree in Figure 8-12. Notice that while insertion pushed elements down in the tree, removal has pushed them back up.

```
bool PQueue::remove (Thing & removedThing)
{
    bool result = theVector->isEmpty();
    if (result)
        return false;

    theVector->getElement (0, removedThing);
    int lastIndex = theVector->getNumbElements() - 1;
    Thing lastElement;
    theVector->getElement (lastIndex, lastElement);
    theVector->setElement (lastElement, 0);
    theVector->decrementNumbElements ();

    buildHeap (0, theVector->getNumbElements(), theVector);
    return true;
}

void PQueue::buildHeap (int position, int size,
        VectorMgr<Thing, int> * buildVector)
{
    int key = 0, key0 = 0, key1 = 0;

    Thing theThing, theThing1, theThing0;
    buildVector->getElement (position, theThing);
    theThing.getKey (key);

    int childPosition;
    while (position < size)
    {
        childPosition = position * 2 + 1;
        if (childPosition < size)
        {
            buildVector->getElement (childPosition, theThing0);
            theThing0.getKey (key0);
            buildVector->getElement (childPosition + 1, theThing1);
            if (theThing1)
                theThing1.getKey (key1);
            if ((childPosition + 1 < size) && key1 > key0)
                childPosition += 1;
```

Listing 8-5   Removing an element from a priority queue

```
        if (key > key0 && key < key1)
        {
           buildVector->setElement (theThing, position);
           return;
        }
        else
        {
           Thing childThing;
           buildVector->getElement (childPosition, childThing);
           buildVector->setElement (childThing, position);
           position = childPosition;
        }
     }
     else
     {
           buildVector->setElement (theThing, position);
           return;
     }
   }
}
```

Listing 8-5 (Continued) Removing an element from a priority queue

```
              0: 50 fifty
              1: 32 thirty-two
              2: 47 forty-seven
              3: 18 eighteen
              4: 22 twenty-two
              5: 40 forty
              6: 45 forty-five
              7: 1 one
              8: 12 twelve
              9: 5 five
             10: 20 twenty
             11: 3 three
             12: 16 sixteen
             13: 4 four
             14: 30 thirty
```

Figure 8-11 The priority queue's vector after removing the element with the highest key

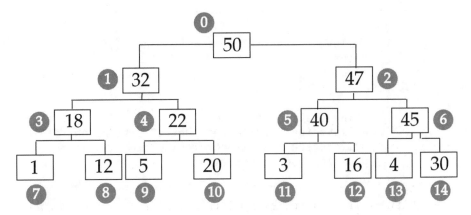

Figure 8-12 The binary tree after moving the element with the highest key

To see exactly how this works, let's trace through the code, starting with the call to `remove`:

1. If the vector is empty, return `false`, indicating that the removal failed. In this case, the vector contains elements so the function continues.

2. Retrieve the element at position 0 (the element with a key of 0) and store it in a reference parameter so that it will be accessible to the calling function.

3. Retrieve the index of the last element in the vector (15).

4. Move the last element in the vector to position 0.

5. Decrement the number of elements in the vector. This ensures that the `buildHeap` function will ignore what was previously the last element.

6. Call `buildHeap`, passing in 0 as the starting position, the size of the vector, and a pointer to the vector.

> **Note:** When called from the `remove` function, `buildHeap` does have access to both the size of the vector and the vector itself. However, `buildHeap` needs to be generic so that it can be used by the `heapSort` function. Its parameter list therefore needs to include all three pieces of data.

7. Retrieve and store the element in position 0. For purposes of this discussion, this is the current element.

8. Retrieve the key of the element in position 0 (1).

9. Enter a `while` loop that continues as long as position (currently 0) is less than the size of the vector (15).

10. Compute the position of the of the current element's left child (1).

11. if the left child's position is less than the size of the vector, which it is, enter the first block of the `if`/`else` construct.

12. Retrieve the left child element and get its key (50).

13. Retrieve the right child element and get its key (47).

14. If the position of the right child is less than the size of the vector and the right child key is greater than the left child key, increment the child position. In this case, the child position is not incremented (47 !> 50).

15. If the key of the current element is greater than the key of its left child, enter the `if` block of the nested `if`/`else` structure. In this case, however, the key of the current element (1) is less than the key of its left child (50). Therefore, we enter the `else` block.

16. Move the left child into the position occupied by the current element. In our example, this moves the element with the key of 50 into position 0.

Note: The element that was originally at position 0 is not lost. It was stored in a local variable in step 7.

17. Set `position` equal to the position of the current element's left child (1).

18. Return to the top of the `while` loop.

19. Compute the position of the left child (3).

20. Because the left child position is less than the size of the vector, retrieve the left child element and get its key (32).

21. Retrieve the right child and get its key (22).

22. Because the right child key is not greater than the left child key, do not increment the child position value.

23. Move the left child into the position occupied by the current element. In our example, this moves the element with a key of 32 into position 1.

24. Set `position` equal to the position of the current element's left child (3).

25. Return to the top of the `while` loop.

26. Compute the position of the left child (7).

27. Because the left child position is less than the size of the vector, retrieve the left child element and get its key (18).

28. Retrieve the right child and get its key (12).

29. Because the right child key is not greater than the left child key, do not increment the child position value.

30. Move the left child into the position occupied by the current element. In our example, this moves the element with a key of 18 into position 3.

31. Set `position` equal to the position of the current child's left child (7).

32. return to the top of the `while` loop.

33. Compute the position of the left child (15).

34. Because the position of the left child (15) represents an element that is not in the vector, insert the element that was in position 0 after the deletion into the current position (7).

35. Return to `remove`.

36. Exit the function, returning `true`.

8.6 Using a Binary Heap for Sorting

A binary heap keeps the element with the largest (or smallest) key at the top. If you continually shorten the size of the binary heap and rebuild it, you will eventually end up with a sorted vector. This is the simple principle behind a heap sort. The sort will be in ascending order if `buildHeap` pushes the largest keys to the bottom and in descending order if it pushes the smallest keys to the bottom. Because most sorts, including those in Chapter 9, by default sort in ascending order, the example you will see does the same.

Note: You will be introduced to the way in which sort routine efficiency is measured in Chapter 9, at which time you will see where the heap sort fits.

The code for the heap sort can be found in Listing 8-6. Like the sort routines you will see in Chapter 9, it includes some code for demonstration purposes that will not be present in the templates in Appendix A. In particular, the demonstration code makes a copy of the vector and sorts the copy. The demonstration code also includes output code to print the result of the sort.

```
void PQueue::heapSort()
{
    // for demonstration purposes only
    // sorts a copy and displays the sorted copy
    VectorMgr<Thing, int> * copyVector =
        new VectorMgr<Thing, int> (theVector);

    int numbElements = copyVector->getNumbElements();

    for (int i = numbElements - 1; i > 0; i--)
    {
        Thing tempThing, iThing, firstThing;
        copyVector->getElement (i, iThing);
        copyVector->getElement (0, firstThing);
        tempThing = firstThing;
        copyVector->setElement (iThing, 0);
        copyVector->setElement (tempThing, i);

        buildHeap (0, i, copyVector);
    }

    Thing theThing;
    cout << endl;
    for (int i = 0; i < numbElements;i++)
    {
        copyVector->getElement (i, theThing);
```

Listing 8-6   The heap sort

```
        cout << i << ": " << theThing.getID() << " "
            << theThing.getName() << endl;
    }
}
```

Listing 8-6 (Continued) The heap sort

The sort works in the following way:

1. Make a copy of the vector using the copy constructor from the Vec-torMgr class.

2. Retrieve the number of elements in the vector. (Keep in mind that this is a count of the elements and is therefore one greater than the last array index used.)

3. Enter a for loop that processes the elements in the vector one at a time, beginning at the last element. Notice that each time the loop index is decremented, it effectively shortens the vector by 1 from the bottom.

4. Retrieve the last element in the vector.

5. Retrieve the first element in the vector.

6. Store a copy of the first element.

7. Copy the last element into position 0.

8. Copy the first element from the stored copy into the location held by the last element. This and the preceding two steps swap the positions of the two elements.

9. Call buildHeap to restore the binary heap.

10. Return to step 3 to repeat the swap, this time using the next element up from the bottom.

As an example, assume that we are working with the small binary heap in Figure 8-13. Notice that the elements are in descending order, the exact opposite of the way in which they are to be sorted.

You can find the progress of the sort in Figure 8-14. As you can see, at the end of each pass through the for loop, the largest key has dropped to the bottom of the list. The call to buildHeap restores the binary heap characteristics of those elements in the unsorted portion of the vector. Because the for loop shortens the vector each pass, buildHeap ignores those elements already in order.

```
0: 50 fifty
1: 12 twelve
2: 4 four
3: 1 one
```

Figure 8-13 A small binary heap that needs to be sorted

```
Pass: 1
0: 12
1: 1
2: 4
3: 50

Pass: 2
0: 4
1: 1
2: 12
3: 50

Pass: 3
0: 1
1: 4
2: 12
3: 50
```

Figure 8-14 The progress of the heap sort

There is one more important thing to mention about this heap sort: It assumes that the vector it is given is already a binary heap. If it is not, then the sort routine needs to turn the vector into a binary heap by inserting the following code prior to entering the for loop currently in the `heapSort` function:

```
for (int i = numbElements/2; i >= 0; i--)
   buildHeap (i, numbElements, theVector);
```

8.7 Summary

A binary heap is an array or vector that represents the contents of a binary tree that meets the following criteria:

- The children of any given element have keys smaller than the keys of the parent element.
- All levels of the tree except for the lowest must be full.
- When the lowest level is not full, it is filled from the left.

One common use of a binary heap is to represent a priority queue, a data structure in which the element with either the lowest or highest key is always at the top. (The priority queue can do either highest or lowest, but not both). A priority queue supports two operations: insert a new element and remove the element at the top.

Binary heaps can also be used to sort the contents of arrays and vectors by key value. The general strategy is to move the highest (or lowest) element to the bottom of the array or vector and then shorten the size of the array or vector and rebuild the binary heap so that the next highest (or lowest) element goes to the top. Repeat the process until the array or vector size is 1. At that point, the elements are in key order.

Part III: Ordering, Accessing, and Searching

Part III considers a variety of techniques for ordering, accessing, and searching data. In Chapter 9, you will read about techniques for sorting arrays and vectors and a fast search technique (the binary search) that can be used on ordered contiguous storage.

Chapter 10 focuses on the hash table, a method for determining a physical storage location in an array or data file based on the value of a data element's key. Chapter 11 looks at dictionaries, which provide access to some data value also based on a key.

CHAPTER 9

Sorting and Searching

Many business applications include the ability to provide the end user with sorted output, such as reports organized chronologically or alphabetically. Programs that must search sets of data to find one or more specific pieces of data can search significantly faster if the data being searched are ordered on the search key.

For these reasons, among others, computer scientists have performed a considerable amount of work developing efficient sorting algorithms. In this chapter you will read about ten sorting methods (three of which have been presented in this book already) and the situations for which each is appropriate. You will also be introduced to a very fast search technique known as a binary search.

The examples in this chapter are based on an array of six objects of the Thing class (see Figure 9-1). Notice that the names of the objects indicate the order in which the objects were entered. However, all sorting is based on object ID numbers.

The program that demonstrates the sorting and searching methods is a version of the array manager program from Chapter 1 that has been modified to include a main menu option for sorting (Figure 9-2) and a sort menu to let you choose the sort method you want to explore (Figure 9-3).

```
1: ID = 20 Name = one
2: ID = 5 Name = two
3: ID = 18 Name = three
4: ID = 85 Name = four
5: ID = 4 Name = five
6: ID = 29 Name = six
```

Figure 9-1   Test data

```
You can:
   0. Add an item
   1. Delete an item
   2. Retrieve an item by its position in the structure
   3. Find ordinal position of element
   4. Find an element by its key
   5. List all items
   6. Get size of structure
   7. Examine sort methods
   8. Reset the array
   9. Exit
```

Figure 9-2 The demonstration program's main menu

```
Choose a sort method:
   1. Bubble
   2. Insertion into new array
   3. Insertion into current array
   4. Selection
   5. Shell
   6. Quick (recursive)
   7. Quick (non-recursive)
   8. Merge (recursive)
   9. Radix

  99. Exit
```

Figure 9-3 The demonstration program's sort menu

The main menu also includes an option to reset the array. The reset function deletes the current array manager and creates a new one, effectively giving you a clean array into which you can place data. You can therefore test the sort routines using a variety of sample data without exiting the program.

9.1 What You Know Already

In Chapter 8 you were introduced to the heap sort, which uses the process of building a heap to largest (or smallest) elements to the bottom of an array or vector. Although you may not have thought about them in these terms, you also know two additional ways to sort values.

Both a binary search tree and an ordered linked list sort values by a key as objects are inserted. To use these data structures to sort data, you would do the following:

1. Create a new container class for a binary search tree or an ordered linked list.
2. Insert objects from the set of data to be sorted into the data structure. A binary search tree automatically maintains its nodes in key order; an ordered linked list does the same.
3. Perform a traversal of the data structure. For the linked list, a first–next traversal order will produce the elements in key order. For the binary search tree, use an in-order traversal iterator. The traversal might, for example, be used to display data from the objects in key order or to copy object data into a file, database, array, or other data structure.

9.2 What Can Be Sorted

Not every data structure is amenable to sorting. For example, it is infeasible in terms of system resources to sort a linked list after items have been inserted. Sorting requires the ability to move nodes from one position to the other in the data structure. To be efficient, it also requires direct access to the nodes in the structure. A linked list—once built—provides only sequential access. In fact, if you have an unordered linked list, it will be more efficient to either insert the nodes one by one into an ordered linked list or to copy the nodes into an array, sort the array, and copy the sorted nodes back to the original list, in order, than it would be to attempt to sort the original list in place.

This does not mean that linked lists cannot be sorted. In fact, there are implementations for most of the sort routines discussed in this chapter for linked lists. However, even the most efficient techniques—the quicksort and merge sort—involve moving many elements around in main memory and therefore cannot approach the performance of sorting a data structure that provides direct access.

If you need the nodes in a binary tree ordered by a key other than that used in the binary tree, then you will need to use another data structure: either an array (which can be sorted), an ordered linked list into which you insert the binary tree nodes, or a second binary tree ordered on the desired key. Because its structure is maintained through pointers, a binary tree does not allow direct access to any of its nodes, other than the root. In addition, moving nodes in the tree destroys the ordering on the tree's initial key.

Any data structure that is based on an array or vector can be sorted efficiently in a variety of ways. Arrays and vectors provide direct access to their nodes based on the array index. This direct access makes it possible to move an array element (a node, any other object, or a pointer to a node or other object) from one position to another without having to modify the contents of the element itself. Assuming that your array contains pointers, to exchange the position of two elements, you do the following:

1. Copy the pointer to the first element into a temporary variable.
2. Copy the pointer to the second element into the position currently occupied by the first element.
3. Copy the element pointer stored in the temporary variable into the position that was occupied by the second element.

You will see this swapping technique used extensively throughout the sort methods presented in this chapter.

Note: You will find the word array used to describe the data structure that is being sorted throughout this chapter. In such situations, it means any data structure (for example, a vector, stack, or queue) that is implemented as an array.

9.3 Measuring Sort Algorithm Efficiency

One of the things on which computer scientists have spent a great deal of time is measuring the efficiency of sort algorithms. Most of the measurements of efficiency center on the amount of resources used as the number of elements being sorted increase. Because the amount of memory used by an implementation of a given sort application varies with the platform and compiler, memory use generally isn't included in efficiency measures. This also means that any measure of algorithm efficiency is only an approximation. Nonetheless, such measures can at least provide comparisons of sort efficiency.

One way to measure the efficiency of a sort algorithm is to count the number of comparisons of key values that the algorithm makes for a data set of size n. Assume, for example, that you write a program that provides you with a table of the number of comparisons made as the size of the data set increases. An analysis of that table tells you that the average number of comparisons is $n / 2$.

In addition to the number of comparisons, there will be some constant factors in the performance measure that you cannot identify. These, for example, include the program overhead, the speed of the CPU, and so on. To account for such factors, computer scientists express the performance of a sort algorithm using what is known as *Big Oh notation*. For the example we have been discussing, you would write

```
O(n/2)
```

The letter O represents some constant c such that the actual performance of the algorithm is actually less than

```
c * n / 2
```

More formally, computer scientists express the performance of a sort algorithm as

```
f(n)
```

where n is the number of items being sorted. In that case,

```
f(n) = O(g(n))
```

where

```
f(n) ≤ c * g(n)
```

and c is some constant.

Big Oh functions typically take the following general forms:

- *O (1)*, which indicates that the performance of an algorithm depends only on some constant and is unrelated to n.
- *O(n)*, indicating that performance depends only on n.
- *O(n^2)*, indicating that performance depends on the square of n.
- *O(n^3)*, indicating that performance depends on the cube of n.
- *O(2^n)*, indicating that performance is expressed by 2 raised to the n power.
- *O(log n)*, indicating that performance depends on the log of n.
- *O(n log n)*, indicating that performance is expressed by n times the log of n.

In addition to these, Big Oh functions can take other forms as necessary.

You will see Big Oh notation used to express the performance of sort algorithms throughout this chapter.

The heap sort, which you read about in Chapter 8, has an average performance of *O(n log n)*. It is relatively good for large data sets. However, sorting by insertion into a binary tree is actually faster.

Big Oh notation represents *average* performance for a sort method. That does not mean that each time you run a sort you will obtain that performance: Actual performance may be better or worse, depending primarily on the state of the data set when the sort starts and the sort method being used. Some sort methods perform best when the data set is almost sorted (a *best-case scenario*) and worst when the data are in relatively random order (a *worst-case scenario*). Others have their best-case performance when the data are in relatively random order and their worst-case performance when the data are nearly in order.

9.4 Structure of the Sample Sort Routines

The demonstration program that you will see in this chapter has been written to make it easy for you to examine and compare sort routines. Each sort routine therefore does two things that the templates in Appendix A do not:

- There is code to display the contents of the array at strategic places during the sort process.
- The sorts modify a copy of the array rather than the original array. It is up to you when you implement sort routines whether you want to modify the original array or return a sorted copy. For purposes of the demonstration program, it was important to leave the original array intact so you could test multiple sort routines without needing to reenter test data.

Each sort routine in this chapter is a member function of the `ArrayMgr` class. As templates, however, each sort routine is a class with a constructor and a `sort` function. You pass in the array to be sorted to the constructor when creating a sorting object. Then you call the `sort` function to perform the sort. For more details, see Appendix A.

9.5 Bubble Sort

The bubble sort is a conceptually simple sort that works by comparing the keys of pairs of adjacent objects in an array. If the keys are in the wrong order, the program swaps the elements. Each pass through the array examines all possible pairs of adjacent objects. For example, in the sample array of six elements, one pass compares the keys of elements 0 and 1, 1 and 2, 2 and 3, 3 and 4, and 4 and 5.

You can see the progress of a bubble sort on the sample array in Figure 9-4. Notice first that the array becomes ordered from the bottom up. If you are sorting in ascending order (low to high)—as we are in this case—then each pass causes the object with the highest key that is out of order to move into order at the bottom of the array.

Also notice that the array is actually properly ordered at the end of the fourth pass. However, the sort routine makes one additional pass through the array. This is the only way the code can detect that the sorting is complete: It makes a pass without swapping any elements.

A function to perform a bubble sort can be found in Listing 9-1. The bubble sort code contains two loops. The outer `while` loop controls the repeated passes through the array. It continues until a pass is made in which no swaps of elements occur.

The inner `for` loop makes a single pass through the array. It begins at element 0 and continues to element $n - 1$, where n is the last element in the array. This prevents the final iteration of the `for` loop from consulting element $n + 1$, which is not a valid member of the array.

If the key of element n is greater than the key of element $n + 1$, then the bubble sort swaps the two elements, using the swapping technique described in Section 9.2. The function also sets a boolean to `true`, indicating that at least one swap was made during that pass through the array. As you can see, if all the keys are ordered properly, the function will never enter the code following the `if` and the value of the `swap_made` variable will remain `false`, stopping the sort when it next reaches the top of the `while` loop.

Because a bubble sort makes sequential passes through an array and because it must make one extra pass after the array is completely sorted, this technique is efficient only if the array is relatively small and nearly sorted (a minimal number of elements are out of order). In such a case, only a few passes will be needed to complete the sorting and the sort time will be relatively short. However, if the array is large and/or the elements are in random order, then the bubble sort is one of the least efficient sort methods in terms of processing time.

```
Pass # 1
    ID: 5    Name: two
    ID: 18   Name: three
    ID: 20   Name: one
    ID: 4    Name: five
    ID: 29   Name: six
    ID: 85   Name: four
Pass # 2
    ID: 5    Name: two
    ID: 18   Name: three
    ID: 4    Name: five
    ID: 20   Name: one
    ID: 29   Name: six
    ID: 85   Name: four
Pass # 3
    ID: 5    Name: two
    ID: 4    Name: five
    ID: 18   Name: three
    ID: 20   Name: one
    ID: 29   Name: six
    ID: 85   Name: four
Pass # 4
    ID: 4    Name: five
    ID: 5    Name: two
    ID: 18   Name: three
    ID: 20   Name: one
    ID: 29   Name: six
    ID: 85   Name: four
Pass # 5
    ID: 4    Name: five
    ID: 5    Name: two
    ID: 18   Name: three
    ID: 20   Name: one
    ID: 29   Name: six
    ID: 85   Name: four
```

Figure 9-4   The progress of a bubble sort

In the worst case scenario—where the array is in inverse order—a bubble sort will need to make n passes through the array. Since each pass requires $n - 1$ key comparison, the entire sort will take $n * (n - 1)$ comparisons and

```
void ArrayMgr::bubble ()
{
    Thing * sortArray [MAX_ELEMENTS], * tempThing;
    for (int i = 0; i < total_elements; i++) // sort a copy
        sortArray[i] = theArray[i];

    bool swap_made = true;
    int count = 0; // count number of passes through array
    while (swap_made)
    {
        swap_made = false;
        count++;
        for (int i = 0; i < total_elements - 1; i++) // one pass
        {
            //swap
            if (sortArray[i]->getKey() > sortArray[i+1]->getKey())
            {
                swap_made = true;
                tempThing = sortArray[i];
                sortArray[i] = sortArray[i+1];
                sortArray[i+1] = tempThing;
            }
        }
        // show array after pass has been made
        cout << "\nPass # " << count;
        for (int i = 0; i < total_elements; i++)
            cout << "\n  ID: " << sortArray[i]->getID() <<
            "  Name: " << sortArray[i]->getName();
    }
}
```

Listing 9-1 *The bubble sort*

the overall performance will be $O(n * (n - 1))$. When the array is large, this value comes close to $O(n^2)$. For a large array that is significantly out of order, the bubble sort will therefore be quite slow and not a good choice.

You can improve the performance of a bubble sort by modifying it to take advantage of the fact that the each pass through the array moves the largest unsorted element into place at the bottom of the array. All you need to do is keep track of the last element that was swapped and examine only those elements above it in the array, as in Listing 9-2.

```
void ArrayMgr::bubble ()
{
    Thing * sortArray [MAX_ELEMENTS], * tempThing;
    for (int i = 0; i < total_elements; i++) // sort a copy
        sortArray[i] = theArray[i];
    bool swap_made = true;
    int count = 0; // count number of passes through array

    int unsortedIndex = total_elements - 1;
    int tmpIndex = 0;

    while (swap_made)
    {
        swap_made = false;
        count++;
        for (int i = 0; i < unsortedIndex; i++) // one pass
        {
            //swap
            if (sortArray[i]->getKey() > sortArray[i+1]->getKey())
            {
                swap_made = true;
                tempThing = sortArray[i];
                sortArray[i] = sortArray[i+1];
                sortArray[i+1] = tempThing;
                tmpIndex = i;
            }
        }
        unsortedIndex = tmpIndex;
        // show array after pass has been made
        cout << "\nPass # " << count;
        for (int i = 0; i < total_elements; i++)
            cout << "\n ID: " << sortArray[i]->getID() <<
                " Name: " << sortArray[i]->getName();
    }
}
```

Listing 9-2   A more efficient bubble sort

This modified version of the bubble sort produces performance of $O(n * (n-1)/2)$ because, on average, a pass through the array will require half the elements of the array.

> **Note:** When an array contains 16 or fewer elements, a bubble sort is as efficient as any other sort.

9.6   Selection Sort

The selection sort finds the unsorted element with the largest key and swaps it into its correct position in the array. As you can see in Figure 9-5, the selection sort makes the same number of passes through the array as a bubble sort and arranges the values in the same way (from the bottom up). Like the improved bubble sort in Listing 9-2, the selection sort also recognizes that once an element has been moved into its correct position at the bottom of the array, there is no need to deal with it again. However, the selection sort makes only one swap in each pass through the array.

The major difference between a selection sort and the improved bubble sort is the number of swaps made. The selected sort makes an average of n swaps and the improved bubble sort makes $n^2/2$. A selection sort provides an improvement over a bubble sort when the data set to be sorted is large and/or when the elements are in relatively random order.

Code for the implementation of a selection sort can be found in Listing 9-3. As you can see, the outer `for` loop begins at the last position in the array, providing the location into which the element with the largest key will be moved. Within each iteration of the loop, the code performs a sequential search of the array to find the element with the largest key. However, the search stops prior to the last element in the correct order. After finding the element with the largest key, the selection sort swaps it with whatever element is in the position the element with the largest unsorted key should occupy. The sort then decrements the index variable of the outer loop, ensuring that the next pass through the array will ignore the sorted elements.

```
Pass # 1
   ID: 20   Name: one
   ID: 5    Name: two
   ID: 18   Name: three
   ID: 29   Name: six
   ID: 4    Name: five
   ID: 85   Name: four
Pass # 2
   ID: 20   Name: one
   ID: 5    Name: two
   ID: 18   Name: three
   ID: 4    Name: five
   ID: 29   Name: six
   ID: 85   Name: four
Pass # 3
   ID: 4    Name: five
   ID: 5    Name: two
   ID: 18   Name: three
   ID: 20   Name: one
   ID: 29   Name: six
   ID: 85   Name: four
Pass # 4
   ID: 4    Name: five
   ID: 18   Name: three
   ID: 5    Name: two
   ID: 20   Name: one
   ID: 29   Name: six
   ID: 85   Name: four
Pass # 5
   ID: 4    Name: five
   ID: 18   Name: three
   ID: 5    Name: two
   ID: 20   Name: one
   ID: 29   Name: six
   ID: 85   Name: four
```

Figure 9-5 Progress of a selection sort

```
void ArrayMgr::selection ()
{
    Thing * sortArray [MAX_ELEMENTS], * tempThing;
    int maxIndex, maxKey; // index of maximum element

    for (int i = 0; i < total_elements; i++) // sort a copy
        sortArray[i] = theArray[i];

    int passcount = 1;
    // if all items are in place except the last one,
    // then last one must be too.
    // therefore can stop loop at 1 rather than 0.
    for (int i = total_elements - 1; i >= 1; i--)
    {
        // find element with max key value
        // that isn't in the right place yet
        maxKey = sortArray[0]->getKey();
        maxIndex = 0;
        for (int j = 1; j <= i; j++)
        {
            if (sortArray[j]->getKey() > maxKey)
            {
                maxKey = sortArray[j]->getKey();
                maxIndex = j;
                break;
            }
        }

        // move it to the bottom; i represents bottom of array
        tempThing = sortArray[maxIndex];
        sortArray[maxIndex] = sortArray[i];
        sortArray[i] = tempThing;

        // show array after swap has been made
        cout << "\nPass # " << passcount++;
        for (int k = 0; k < total_elements; k++)
            cout << "\n  ID: " << sortArray[k]->getID() <<
            "  Name: " << sortArray[k]->getName();
    }
}
```

Listing 9-3 Selection sort

9.7   The Insertion Sort

An insertion sort works by examining an element and then inserting it in the correct position in the array, moving other elements to make room for the inserted element. There are two ways to perform an insertion sort: Insert elements into the array as they are created, keeping the array always in order, and use the insertion process on an existing array.

> **Note:** When you insert an element into an ordered linked list, you are actually performing an insertion sort. You can therefore insert into an ordered linked list as well as to an array, as demonstrated in this section.

In either case, the performance can be expressed as $O(n^2)$. This Big Oh function, however, can be misleading. If an array is already in order, then inserting a new element means, in the worst case, making $n - 1$ comparisons. On average, the sort routine will make $(n - 1) / 2$ comparisons. An insertion sort therefore is probably the most efficient sort you can use when you are adding elements to an array or list that is already in order.

Also keep in mind that when you are inserting new elements into an array or list, rather than sorting an array in place, n starts at 1 and increases as elements are added. Performance will therefore be better when inserting into a new data structure rather than sorting one in place.

9.7.1 Insertion Sort into a New Array

Figure 9-6 demonstrates the progress of an insertion sort where elements are sorted as they are added to a new array. As you can see, each element is placed in its correct position as it is added, ensuring that the array is always in order. This type of sorting is most useful when you want to be able to perform a fast search that requires an ordered data set (for example, a binary search) at any time. It also uses less processing time than sorting the complete array once all elements are present.

> **Note:** Sorting to a new data structure does require additional main memory, but given the hardware configurations of today's computers, this is usually less of a constraint than the amount of processing time.

```
Insertion # 1
   ID: 5   Name: two
   ID: 20   Name: one
Insertion # 2
   ID: 5   Name: two
   ID: 18   Name: three
   ID: 20   Name: one
Insertion # 3
   ID: 5   Name: two
   ID: 18   Name: three
   ID: 20   Name: one
   ID: 85   Name: four
Insertion # 4
   ID: 4   Name: five
   ID: 5   Name: two
   ID: 18   Name: three
   ID: 20   Name: one
   ID: 85   Name: four
Insertion # 5
   ID: 4   Name: five
   ID: 5   Name: two
   ID: 18   Name: three
   ID: 20   Name: one
   ID: 29   Name: six
   ID: 85   Name: four
```

Figure 9-6 Progress of an insertion sort into a new array

You can find the code for an insertion sort into a new array in Listing 9-4. The outer `for` loop makes one iteration through the input data set. Inside this loop, the sort routine uses another `for` loop to perform a sequential search to find the location where the new element should be placed. (A binary search would be faster, but since we haven't discussed that technique yet, we'll stick to the sequential search.) Once the insertion spot has been found, the sort routine must move existing elements down to make room for the new element. It can then insert the new element into the hole that has been left for it.

```cpp
void ArrayMgr::insertion1 ()
{
    Thing * sortArray [MAX_ELEMENTS]; // target of sort
    sortArray[0] = theArray[0];
    int sortCount = 0; // last element used in sort array
    //loop through original array
    for (int i = 1; i < total_elements; i++)
    {
        int insert_spot = -1;
        for (int j = sortCount; j >= 0; j--)
        {
            // find insert spot
            if (theArray[i]->getKey() > sortArray[j]->getKey())
                insert_spot = j + 1;
            if (insert_spot > -1)
                break;
        }
        if (insert_spot == -1)
            insert_spot = 0;

        for (int k = sortCount; k >= insert_spot; k--)
            sortArray[k+1] = sortArray[k]; //move down
        sortArray[insert_spot] = theArray[i]; // insert
        sortCount++; // used to limit display to valid elements

        // show array after insertion has been made
        cout << "\nInsertion # " << i;
        for (int k = 0; k <= sortCount; k++)
            cout << "\n  ID: " << sortArray[k]->getID() <<
                "  Name: " << sortArray[k]->getName();
    }
}
```

Listing 9-4 Insertion sort into a new array

9.7.2 Insertion Sort on a Source Array

An insertion sort can also be performed on an existing array. Because the array contains all elements to be sorted before the sort begins, the progress of the sort looks somewhat different than that when sorting into a new array (see Figure 9-7).

The code for the insertion sort into an existing array can be found in Listing 9-5. As with the previous version, the sort routine makes one pass through the data set, which in this case consists of all the elements in the array. During each iteration, the routine does the following:

1. Determine whether the current element is out of order. If it is not, return to the top of the loop to consider the next element.

2. Save the element to be moved in a temporary variable.

3. Save the index of the element to be moved.

4. Enter a loop that continues until the correct place is found to insert the element being moved.

5. Move the element below up into the current array position. (The first time the sort routine does this, it overwrites the element being moved. This is why it has to be saved in another variable.

6. Determine whether the place to insert the element being moved has been found. If so, insert the element from the temporary variable. If not, return to step 5.

The sort is complete when all elements in the source array have been examined and moved as needed.

9.8 Shell Sort

A computer scientist named Donald Shell introduced yet another improvement to the bubble sort. His purpose was to cut down the number of comparisons by starting with increments of more than 1 between the compared elements. The idea is to move elements "closer" to their correct position in each pass. Each time the sort routine makes a pass through the array, it

```
Insertion # 1
  ID: 5   Name: two
  ID: 20  Name: one
  ID: 18  Name: three
  ID: 85  Name: four
  ID: 4   Name: five
  ID: 29  Name: six
Insertion # 2
  ID: 5   Name: two
  ID: 18  Name: three
  ID: 20  Name: one
  ID: 85  Name: four
  ID: 4   Name: five
  ID: 29  Name: six
Insertion # 3
  ID: 5   Name: two
  ID: 18  Name: three
  ID: 20  Name: one
  ID: 85  Name: four
  ID: 4   Name: five
  ID: 29  Name: six
Insertion # 4
  ID: 4   Name: five
  ID: 5   Name: two
  ID: 18  Name: three
  ID: 20  Name: one
  ID: 85  Name: four
  ID: 29  Name: six
Insertion # 5
  ID: 4   Name: five
  ID: 5   Name: two
  ID: 18  Name: three
  ID: 20  Name: one
  ID: 29  Name: six
  ID: 85  Name: four
```

Figure 9-7 Progress of an insertion sort into the same array

```
void ArrayMgr::insertion2 ()
{
    Thing * sortArray[MAX_ELEMENTS], * tempThing;
    for (int i = 0; i < total_elements; i++) // sort a copy
        sortArray[i] = theArray[i];

    for (int i = 1; i < total_elements; i++)
    {
        // if out of order
        if (sortArray[i]->getKey() < sortArray[i-1]->getKey())
        {
            tempThing = sortArray[i]; // save element to be moved
            // index into sorted portion of array
            int sortedIndex = i;
            bool found = false;
            while (!found) // look for place to insert element
            {
                // move an element up
                sortArray [sortedIndex] = sortArray[sortedIndex - 1];
                sortedIndex--;
                if (sortedIndex == 0)
                    found = true;
                else
                    found = sortArray[sortedIndex - 1]->getKey()
                        <= tempThing->getKey();
            }
            sortArray[sortedIndex] = tempThing;
        }

        // show array after insertion has been made
        cout << "\nInsertion # " << i;
        for (int k = 0; k < total_elements; k++)
            cout << "\n  ID: " << sortArray[k]->getID() <<
                " Name: " << sortArray[k]->getName();
    }
}
```

Listing 9-5 An insertion sort on a source array

decreases the increment, with the last increment being 1. As you can see in Figure 9-8, sorting the sample array using a Shell sort takes only two passes, rather than the five passes required by the bubble and insertion sorts.

```
Increment: 3
Pass # 1
   ID: 20   Name: one
   ID: 4    Name: five
   ID: 18   Name: three
   ID: 85   Name: four
   ID: 5    Name: two
   ID: 29   Name: six
Increment: 1
Pass # 2
   ID: 4    Name: five
   ID: 5    Name: two
   ID: 18   Name: three
   ID: 20   Name: one
   ID: 29   Name: six
   ID: 85   Name: four
```

Figure 9-8 Progress of a Shell sort

There is no specific formula for choosing the increments that determine the distance between elements being compared (and possibly swapped). However, increments that are *not* powers of 2 are usually most effective. The sample implementation you will see uses an initial increment equal to half the total elements. From that point on, the increment is the current increment divided by 2.2. The code could just as easily have divided the total elements by 3 or used a mod 3 operation or any other computation that generated reasonable intervals relative to the size of the array.

Because the way in which the increment is determined is left up to the programmer, it is not possible to specify a Big Oh formula for the performance of a Shell sort. However, anecdotal evidence shows that the Shell sort is a relatively good performing sort algorithm.

An implementation of a Shell sort can be found in Listing 9-6. Notice that the first step in the algorithm is to compute an initial increment. The function then enters a `while` loop that continues as long as the increment is greater than or equal to 1. (Dividing an increment of 1 by 2.2 produces an integer result of 0, stopping the loop.)

```
void ArrayMgr::shell ()
{
    Thing * sortArray[MAX_ELEMENTS], * tempThing;
    for (int i = 0; i < total_elements; i++) // sort a copy
        sortArray[i] = theArray[i];

    int passcount = 1; // used for display only
    int increment = total_elements /2;
    int sortIndex;

    while (increment >= 1)
    {
        for (int i = increment; i < total_elements; i++)
        {
            tempThing = sortArray[i];
            for (sortIndex = i - increment; sortIndex >= 0 &&
                tempThing->getKey() < sortArray[sortIndex]->getKey();
                sortIndex -= increment)
                    sortArray[sortIndex + increment] =
                        sortArray[sortIndex];
            sortArray[sortIndex + increment] = tempThing;
        }
        // show array after one pass
        cout << "\nIncrement: " << increment;
        cout << "\nPass # " << passcount++;
        for (int k = 0; k < total_elements; k++)
            cout << "\n  ID: " << sortArray[k]->getID() <<
            "  Name: " << sortArray[k]->getName();
        // compute new increment
        if (increment == 2)  // last increment must be 1
            increment = 1;
        else
            increment = increment / 2.2;
    }
}
```

Listing 9-6 Shell sort

The `for` loop inside the `while` makes a single pass through the array being sorted. Beginning with the element that is *increment* elements from the top of the array, it compares each element with the element that is *increment* elements above it. For example, if the increment is three, the first comparison is between elements 3 and 0; the second comparison is between elements 4 and 1. If the elements are in the wrong order, they are swapped.

Once all comparisons have been completed, the Shell sort computes a new increment and then begins a new pass through the array. Notice that if the new increment ends up as 2, it is set explicitly to 1. (The division by 2.2 prevents the increment from reaching 1 when the previous increment is 2.)

9.9   Quicksort

The sort methods that you have seen to this point have been similar in that each makes a comparison between the keys of two elements and, if the keys are out of order, swaps the elements. The next set of sort routines we will examine take a different approach, often known as *divide and conquer*. The main idea is to break the array into small pieces, sort those pieces, and then somehow combine them into a completely sorted array.

There are two techniques that can be used to write divide and conquer sorts: with recursion and without recursion. In some cases, a recursive solution can be less complex and actually require less memory than a nonrecursive solution.

Quicksort (developed by C. A. R. Hoare) is a very efficient sort and can be used to sort large data sets. On average, its performance is measured as $O(n \log n)$, although in the worst-case scenario (when the elements are already in the correct order), its performance degrades to $O(n^2)$.

The basic procedure behind a quicksort is to pick the median key value (the key for which half the other keys will be higher and half lower). The index of this element is known as the *pivot point*. Then the sort partitions the data set into two subsets, one containing higher keys and one containing lower keys. Then you sort each partition by dividing it again, repeating the process until the size of a partition is 1. Eventually, you put all the parts back together in sorted order.

A quicksort doesn't actually search the array for the median key value. Instead, it picks an element arbitrarily—often the first element in the array—under the assumption that the chance of the first element having the median key is as good as that of any other element.

9.9.1 Recursive Quicksort

In Figure 9-9 you can see the progress of a recursive quicksort. The output appears before each recursive call and also displays the array index of the pivot point each time it changes. To help you understand how the sort works, first take a look at the code in Listing 9-7. Notice that there are three functions. The first—`quick1`—jump starts the sort by placing the initial call to `quicksort`, which partitions the array by calling `partition` and then calls itself to sort the top half of the array and calls itself to sort the bottom half of the array. The initial pivot point is set in `partition` to the lowest index in the subset of the array being handled. The pivot point used within the first call to `partition` is therefore 0, but since it never leaves the `partition` function, it does not appear in Figure 9-9.

The second pivot is 3. It is set at the end of `partition` and returned to the calling function and therefore appears in Figure 9-9. The output you see from the second call through the seventh call is sorting just the first four elements. The eighth and ninth calls, using a pivot of 5, are working on the last two elements.

The actual sorting occurs in the `partition` function, which works in the following way:

1. Accept the indexes of the lowest and highest elements in the portion of the array being partitioned.
2. Set the initial pivot point to the lowest element in the part of the array being handled.
3. Save the key of the pivot point's element.

```
Call # 1                          Call # 5
  ID: 20   Name: one                ID: 4    Name: five
  ID: 5    Name: two                ID: 5    Name: two
  ID: 18   Name: three             ID: 18   Name: three
  ID: 85   Name: four              ID: 20   Name: one
  ID: 4    Name: five              ID: 85   Name: four
  ID: 29   Name: six               ID: 29   Name: six
Pivot point: 3                    Call # 6
                                    ID: 4    Name: five
Call # 2                            ID: 5    Name: two
  ID: 4    Name: five              ID: 18   Name: three
  ID: 5    Name: two               ID: 20   Name: one
  ID: 18   Name: three             ID: 85   Name: four
  ID: 20   Name: one               ID: 29   Name: six
  ID: 85   Name: four             Call # 7
  ID: 29   Name: six               ID: 4    Name: five
Pivot point: 0                      ID: 5    Name: two
                                    ID: 18   Name: three
Call # 3                            ID: 20   Name: one
  ID: 4    Name: five              ID: 85   Name: four
  ID: 5    Name: two               ID: 29   Name: six
  ID: 18   Name: three            Pivot point: 5
  ID: 20   Name: one
  ID: 85   Name: four
  ID: 29   Name: six              Call # 8
Call # 4                            ID: 4    Name: five
  ID: 4    Name: five              ID: 5    Name: two
  ID: 5    Name: two               ID: 18   Name: three
  ID: 18   Name: three             ID: 20   Name: one
  ID: 20   Name: one               ID: 29   Name: six
  ID: 85   Name: four              ID: 85   Name: four
  ID: 29   Name: six              Call # 9
Pivot point: 1                      ID: 4    Name: five
                                    ID: 5    Name: two
                                    ID: 18   Name: three
                                    ID: 20   Name: one
                                    ID: 29   Name: six
                                    ID: 85   Name: four
```

Figure 9-9 Progress of a recursive quicksort

```
void ArrayMgr::quick1 ()
{
    Thing * sortArray[MAX_ELEMENTS];
    for (int i = 0; i < total_elements; i++) // sort a copy
        sortArray[i] = theArray[i];

    // initiate the sort
    quicksort (sortArray, 0, total_elements - 1);
}

void ArrayMgr::quicksort (Thing * theArray[], int low, int high)
{
    int pivotPoint;
    // show array at beginning of each recursive call
    static int passcount = 1;
    cout << "\nCall # " << passcount++;

    for (int k = 0; k < total_elements; k++)
        cout << "\n  ID: " << theArray[k]->getID() <<
            "  Name: " << theArray[k]->getName();

    if (low < high)
    {
        // partition the array
        partition (theArray, low, high, pivotPoint);
        cout << "\nPivot point: " << pivotPoint << endl;
        // sort the top half
        quicksort (theArray, low, pivotPoint - 1);
        // sort the bottom half
        quicksort (theArray, pivotPoint + 1, high);
    }
}

void ArrayMgr::partition (Thing * theArray[], int low,
        int high, int & pivotPoint)
{
    Thing * tempThing;
    pivotPoint = low;
    int pivotKey = theArray[pivotPoint]->getKey();
```

Listing 9-7 Recursive quicksort

```
while (low <= high)
{
    if (theArray[low]->getKey() <= pivotKey)
        low++;
    else if (theArray[high]->getKey() >= pivotKey)
        high--;
    else
    {
        tempThing = theArray[high]; //swap
        theArray[high] = theArray[low];
        theArray[low] = tempThing;
        low++;
        high--;
    }
}
tempThing = theArray[high];
theArray[high] = theArray[pivotPoint];
theArray[pivotPoint] = tempThing;
// this is the spot between the two partitions
pivotPoint = high;
}
```

Listing 9-7 (Continued) Recursive quicksort

4. Enter a `while` loop that continues as long as the index of the lowest element is less than or equal to that of the highest element. When the low index becomes greater than the high index, skip to step 8.

5. If the key of the element with the lowest index is less than or equal to the key of the element at the pivot point, raise the lowest index by 1 and return to Step 4.

6. If the key of the element with the highest index is greater than or equal to the key of the element at the pivot point, lower the highest index by 1 and return to Step 4.

7. Otherwise, swap the elements at the high and low indexes of the partition. Return to Step 4.

8. Swap the element at the high index with the element at the pivot point.

9. Set the pivot point to the high index.

The result of a call to `partition` is to move elements to the correct side of the pivot point and then to move the pivot point to the middle of the high end of the array subset. Therefore, the general process for a recursive quicksort is:

1. Partition the array.
2. Call the quicksort function again on the top half of the array.
3. Call the quicksort function again on the bottom half of the array.

Keep in mind that when the sort routine performs Step 2, it actually partitions the top half, and then calls itself twice again, once to sort each half of the top half. This continues until the size of the partitions in the top half is 1. Then the sort routine calls itself to handle the bottom half.

9.9.2 Nonrecursive Quicksort

If you would prefer to avoid recursion, you can code a quicksort without it by using two stacks, one to hold array indexes above the pivot point and one to hold array indexes below the pivot point. The stacks keep track of which elements have been sorted.

You can find the progress of a nonrecursive quicksort in Figure 9-10. When you compare it to Figure 9-9, you can see that although the nonrecursive version makes fewer passes through the array, the two implementations order the array in much the same manner: The top four elements are sorted first, followed by the last two.

The code for the nonrecursive version can be found in Listing 9-8. In addition to the `quick2` function, the nonrecursive quicksort uses the same `partition` function as the recursive version.

Notice first in Listing 9-8 that there is only a single stack pointer. This means that the low and high stacks are always in sync. The sort routine also maintains high and low pointers for the array indexes at the top and bottom of a partition.

The nonrecursive quicksort works in the following way:

1. Enter a `do while` loop that continues until the stacks are empty (`stackPtr = -1`).

```
Pass # 1
   ID: 4   Name: five
   ID: 5   Name: two
   ID: 18  Name: three
   ID: 20  Name: one
   ID: 85  Name: four
   ID: 29  Name: six
Pass # 2
   ID: 4   Name: five
   ID: 5   Name: two
   ID: 18  Name: three
   ID: 20  Name: one
   ID: 29  Name: six
   ID: 85  Name: four
Pass # 3
   ID: 4   Name: five
   ID: 5   Name: two
   ID: 18  Name: three
   ID: 20  Name: one
   ID: 29  Name: six
   ID: 85  Name: four
Pass # 4
   ID: 4   Name: five
   ID: 5   Name: two
   ID: 18  Name: three
   ID: 20  Name: one
   ID: 29  Name: six
   ID: 85  Name: four
```

Figure 9-10 Progress of a nonrecursive quicksort

```
void ArrayMgr::quick2 ()
{
    Thing * sortArray[MAX_ELEMENTS];
    for (int i = 0; i < total_elements; i++) // sort a copy
        sortArray[i] = theArray[i];

    int low = 0;
    int high = total_elements - 1;
```

Listing 9-8   Nonrecursive quicksort

```
int pivotPoint;
int stackPtr = -1;
int lowStack [STACK_SIZE], highStack [STACK_SIZE];
int passcount = 1;

do
{
    if (stackPtr > -1)
    {
        low = lowStack [stackPtr];
        high = highStack [stackPtr];
        stackPtr--;
    }

    while (low < high)
    {
        partition (sortArray, low, high, pivotPoint);
        if (pivotPoint - low < high - pivotPoint)
        {
            if (stackPtr >= STACK_SIZE)
            {
                cout << "\nStack overflow. Cannot complete sort.";
                return;
            }
            stackPtr++;
            lowStack[stackPtr] = pivotPoint + 1;
            highStack[stackPtr] = high;
            high = pivotPoint - 1;
        }
        else
        {
            if (stackPtr >= STACK_SIZE)
            {
                cout << "\nStack overflow. Cannot complete sort.";
                return;
            }
            stackPtr++;
            lowStack[stackPtr] = low;
            highStack[stackPtr] = pivotPoint - 1;
            low = pivotPoint - 1;
```

Listing 9-8 (Continued)   Nonrecursive quicksort

```
        }

        cout << "\nPass # " << passcount++;
        for (int k = 0; k < total_elements; k++)
            cout << "\n   ID: " << sortArray[k]->getID()
                << "   Name: " << sortArray[k]->getName();
    }
} while (stackPtr > -1);
}
```

Listing 9-8 (Continued)   Nonrecursive quicksort

2. If the stack is not empty, set the low and high indexes to the top of the appropriate stacks and decrement the stack pointer, effectively popping the top values off both stacks.

3. Enter a `while` loop that continues until the low index becomes greater than or equal to the high index. When the low index is greater than or equal to the high index, go to step 7.

4. Partition the array by calling `partition`.

5. If the pivot point returned by `partition` minus the low pointer is less than the high pointer minus the pivot point:

    a. Increment the stack pointer.

    b. Push the pivot point plus 1 onto the low stack.

    c. Push the high index onto the high stack.

    d. Reset the high index to the pivot point minus 1.

    e. Go to step 3.

6. Otherwise:

    a. Increment the stack pointer.

    b. Push the low index onto the low stack.

    c. Push the pivot point minus 1 onto the high stack.

    d. Reset the low index to the pivot point plus 1.

    e. Go to step 3.

7. If the stack is not empty, go to step 2.

As you can see, the stacks keep track of sets of low and high pointers, simulating the effect of recursion. The recursive version of the quicksort requires less code than the nonrecursive version and also uses less main memory. (It doesn't have to maintain the stacks.) However, some programmers prefer to avoid recursion because they find it more conceptually complex than nonrecursive code.

9.10 Merge Sort

Like the quicksort, a merge sort most commonly is implemented using recursion and has a performance of $O(n \log n)$. However, because a merge sort requires a copy of the array into which elements can be merged, it takes more main memory than a quicksort.

Merge sort is based on the idea of splitting the data set into equal halves that are sorted and then merged back together. The recursive implementation continues to split the halves in half again until the smallest part contains only one element. It is then merged with a second part that contains one element, creating a part of two elements. Merging two parts of two elements generates a part of four elements, and so on, until the data set is reassembled into the correct order.

The progress of the sort on our sample data set can be found in Figure 9-11. The output appears after each recursive call to the `mergesort` function and again after each call to `domerge`.

The code for the merge sort appears in Listing 9-9. Its organization is very similar to the quicksort: The `merge` function initiates the sort with a call to `mergesort`, which then computes the middle index of the portion of the array being sorted, calls itself to sort the top half, calls itself to sort the bottom half, and then calls `domerge` to put the two halves back together.

The recursive calls move three indexes: low (lowest index in the portion of the array being sorted), high (highest index), and mid (the middle index).

```
Call # 1                 Call # 6                  After merge
   ID: 20   Name: one       ID: 5    Name: two        ID: 5    Name: two
   ID: 5    Name: two       ID: 20   Name: one        ID: 18   Name: three
   ID: 18   Name: three     ID: 18   Name: three      ID: 20   Name: one
   ID: 85   Name: four      ID: 85   Name: four       ID: 4    Name: five
   ID: 4    Name: five      ID: 4    Name: five       ID: 85   Name: four
   ID: 29   Name: six       ID: 29   Name: six        ID: 29   Name: six
Call # 2                 After merge               Call # 11
   ID: 20   Name: one       ID: 5    Name: two        ID: 5    Name: two
   ID: 5    Name: two       ID: 18   Name: three      ID: 18   Name: three
   ID: 18   Name: three     ID: 20   Name: one        ID: 20   Name: one
   ID: 85   Name: four      ID: 85   Name: four       ID: 4    Name: five
   ID: 4    Name: five      ID: 4    Name: five       ID: 85   Name: four
   ID: 29   Name: six       ID: 29   Name: six        ID: 29   Name: six
Call # 3                 Call # 7                  After merge
   ID: 20   Name: one       ID: 5    Name: two        ID: 5    Name: two
   ID: 5    Name: two       ID: 18   Name: three      ID: 18   Name: three
   ID: 18   Name: three     ID: 20   Name: one        ID: 20   Name: one
   ID: 85   Name: four      ID: 85   Name: four       ID: 4    Name: five
   ID: 4    Name: five      ID: 4    Name: five       ID: 29   Name: six
   ID: 29   Name: six       ID: 29   Name: six        ID: 85   Name: four
Call # 4                 Call # 8                  After merge
   ID: 20   Name: one       ID: 5    Name: two        ID: 4    Name: five
   ID: 5    Name: two       ID: 18   Name: three      ID: 5    Name: two
   ID: 18   Name: three     ID: 20   Name: one        ID: 18   Name: three
   ID: 85   Name: four      ID: 85   Name: four       ID: 20   Name: one
   ID: 4    Name: five      ID: 4    Name: five       ID: 29   Name: six
   ID: 29   Name: six       ID: 29   Name: six        ID: 85   Name: four
Call # 5                 Call # 9
   ID: 20   Name: one       ID: 5    Name: two
   ID: 5    Name: two       ID: 18   Name: three
   ID: 18   Name: three     ID: 20   Name: one
   ID: 85   Name: four      ID: 85   Name: four
   ID: 4    Name: five      ID: 4    Name: five
   ID: 29   Name: six       ID: 29   Name: six
After merge              Call # 10
   ID: 5    Name: two       ID: 5    Name: two
   ID: 20   Name: one       ID: 18   Name: three
   ID: 18   Name: three     ID: 20   Name: one
   ID: 85   Name: four      ID: 85   Name: four
   ID: 4    Name: five      ID: 4    Name: five
   ID: 29   Name: six       ID: 29   Name: six
```

Figure 9-11 Progress of a merge sort

Subarrays are put back together by `domerge`, which works in the following way:

1. Initialize a top pointer to the lowest index in the portion of the array
   being merged.

```
void ArrayMgr::merge ()
{
    Thing * sortArray[MAX_ELEMENTS];
    for (int i = 0; i < total_elements; i++) // sort a copy
        sortArray[i] = theArray[i];

    // initiate the sort
    mergesort (sortArray, 0, total_elements - 1);
}

void ArrayMgr::mergesort (Thing * theArray[], const int & low,
    const int & high)
{
    // show array at the beginning of each recursive call
    static int passcount = 1;
    cout << "\nCall # " << passcount++;
    for (int k = 0; k < total_elements; k++)
        cout << "\n  ID: " << theArray[k]->getID() <<
        "  Name: " << theArray[k]->getName();

    if (low < high)
    {
        int mid = (low + high) / 2; // find the middle element

        mergesort (theArray, low, mid); // sort top half
        mergesort (theArray, mid + 1, high); // sort bottom half
        // merge the halves back together
        domerge (theArray, low, mid, high);

        cout << "\nAfter merge ";
        for (int k = 0; k < total_elements; k++)
            cout << "\n  ID: " << theArray[k]->getID() <<
            "  Name: " << theArray[k]->getName();
    }
}

void ArrayMgr::domerge (Thing * theArray[], const int  & low,
    const int & mid, const int & high)
{
    int topPtr = low; // pointer to top half of array
```

Listing 9-9 Merge sort

```
int midPtr = mid + 1; // pointer to middle; start of bottom half
int resultPtr = 0;   // pointer to merged array
Thing * tempArray [MAX_ELEMENTS];

// copy into temporary array from two sorted halves in
// correct order
while (topPtr <= mid && midPtr <= high)
{
    if (theArray[topPtr]->getKey() <
        theArray[midPtr]->getKey())
    {
        tempArray[resultPtr] = theArray[topPtr];
        topPtr++;
    }
    else
    {
        tempArray[resultPtr] = theArray[midPtr];
        midPtr++;
    }
    resultPtr++;
}

// copy remaining elements;
// at most one of these two loops will execute
while (topPtr <= mid)
{
    tempArray[resultPtr] = theArray[topPtr];
    topPtr++;
    resultPtr++;
}
while (midPtr <= high)
{
    tempArray[resultPtr] = theArray[midPtr];
    midPtr++;
    resultPtr++;
}

// now copy back to original array
topPtr = low;
resultPtr = 0;
```

Listing 9-9 (Continued) Merge sort

```
while (topPtr <= high)
{
    theArray[topPtr] = tempArray[resultPtr];
    topPtr++;
    resultPtr++;
}
}
```

Listing 9-9 (Continued) Merge sort

2. Initialize a middle pointer to one above the mid index of the array sub-set. This marks the start of the bottom half of the array subset.

3. Initialize a pointer to the merged array to 0.

4. Allocate storage for the merged array.

5. Enter a `while` loop. When either the top pointer becomes less than or equal to the original mid index or the middle pointer becomes less than or equal the original high index, skip to step 8.

6. Compare the keys of the elements at the top of the portions of the array that are being merged.

7. Copy the element with the larger key to the result array and increment the appropriate pointers. Go to step 5.

8. Copy the remaining elements from whichever array hasn't been transferred completely to the result array.

9. Copy all elements back to the original array.

9.11 Radix Sort

The radix sort is conceptually quite different from anything encountered earlier in this chapter. In fact, if you look at the sort progress in Figure 9-12, you may not be able to see any logic to it at all.

To decipher the mystery, first assume that all key values are the same length: 20, 05, 18, 85, 04, 29. Now, sort the elements in order based on the rightmost digit; that's what you see at the end of Pass #2. Then, sort the array of the leftmost digit, producing the sorted array. A radix sort works

```
Pass #:1
    ID: 20   Name: one
    ID: 5    Name: two
    ID: 18   Name: three
    ID: 85   Name: four
    ID: 4    Name: five
    ID: 29   Name: six
Pass #:2
    ID: 20   Name: one
    ID: 4    Name: five
    ID: 5    Name: two
    ID: 85   Name: four
    ID: 18   Name: three
    ID: 29   Name: six
Pass #:3
    ID: 4    Name: five
    ID: 5    Name: two
    ID: 18   Name: three
    ID: 20   Name: one
    ID: 29   Name: six
    ID: 85   Name: four
Pass #:4
    ID: 4    Name: five
    ID: 5    Name: two
    ID: 18   Name: three
    ID: 20   Name: one
    ID: 29   Name: six
    ID: 85   Name: four
```

Figure 9-12 Progress of a radix sort

by sorting on the least significant digit or character first, moving to the next character or digit to the left, and so on, until all elements are sorted. The performance of such a sort is measured as $O(n)$.

Because a radix sort works on digits or characters, there are several ways to implement one. If the key on which the sort is based is a string, then comparisons will be made on individual characters in the string. If the key is an integer, then you can either work at the digit level, as you will see in this example, or you can work at the byte level, using shift operations to isolate the bytes in the value.

The code for a digit-based radix sort appears in Listing 9-10. Like a merge sort, it requires a copy of the array. As you will see, the elements are copied from the source array, to the copy, and back as the sort progresses. In addition, it requires a second copy of the array to provide an index to where sorted elements should be copied.

```
void ArrayMgr::radix ()
{
    Thing * destArray [MAX_ELEMENTS];
    Thing * sortArray[MAX_ELEMENTS];
    for (int i = 0; i < total_elements; i++) // sort a copy
        sortArray[i] = theArray[i];

    int maxKey = theArray[0]->getKey(); // first find largest key
    for (int i = 1; i < total_elements; i++)
        if (sortArray[i]->getKey() > maxKey)
        {
            maxKey = theArray[i]->getKey();
            break;
        }

    int passcount = 1;
    int numb_digits = log10 (maxKey) + 1;

    // This loop contains what at first looks to be redundant code.
    // However, it actually copies data between two arrays.
    for (int i = 0; i <= numb_digits; i+=2)
    {
        radixsort (i, destArray, sortArray);
        cout << "\nPass #:" << i + 1;
        for (int k = 0; k < total_elements; k++)
            cout << "\n  ID: " << destArray[k]->getID() << "  Name: "
            << destArray[k]->getName();
        radixsort (i+1, sortArray, destArray);
        cout << "\nPass #:" << i + 2;
        for (int k = 0; k < total_elements; k++)
```

Listing 9-10 Radix sort

```
            cout << "\n  ID: " << sortArray[k]->getID() << "  Name: "
                << sortArray[k]->getName();
    }
}

void ArrayMgr::radixsort (int theDigit, Thing * destArray [],
        Thing * sortArray [])
// Note that this function must also have access to the total
// number of items being sorted and the array containing the
// original items.
{
    int frequency [10];
    // initialize frequency counting array
    for (int i = 0; i < 10; i++)
        frequency[i] = 0;

    int digit;
    float value;
    // count occurrences of each value
    for (int i = 0; i < total_elements; i++)
    {
        value = ((float) sortArray[i]->getKey() /
            (pow (10, theDigit)));
        digit = (int) ((float) sortArray[i]->getKey() /
            (pow (10, theDigit)));
        digit = (int) ((value - (float) digit) * 10);
        frequency [digit]++;
    }

    int index [MAX_ELEMENTS];
    index[0] = 0;
    for (int i = 1; i < MAX_ELEMENTS; i++)
        index[i] = index[i-1]+frequency[i-1];

    for (int i = 0; i < total_elements; i++)
    {
        value = ((float) sortArray[i]->getKey() /
            (pow (10, theDigit)));
        digit = (int) ((float) sortArray[i]->getKey() /
            (pow (10, theDigit)));
```

Listing 9-10 (Continued) Radix sort

```
        digit = (int) ((value - (float) digit) * 10);
        destArray[index[digit]++] = sortArray[i];
    }
}
```

Listing 9-10 (Continued) Radix sort

This implementation of a radix sort uses two functions: `radix`, which controls the progress of the sort, and `radixsort`, which actually does the sorting. Much of what appears in `radix` involves preparing to handle the individual digits in the number:

1. Find the largest key value in the array.
2. Find the maximum number of digits in any key value by taking the log of the maximum key value and adding 1.
3. Enter a `for` loop that processes each digit in the keys. The loop increments by two until it reaches the total digits in the key. If the maximum key has an odd number of digits, then there will be one extra pass through the array. This is unavoidable.
4. Call `radixsort`, moving data from the source array to the copy.
5. Call `radixsort`, moving data from the copy to the source array.
6. Return to step 3.

The actual sorting of the elements by one digit takes place in `radixsort`. The method used takes advantage of the fact that there are only 10 possible values for a digit. It counts the frequency of occurrence of each digit, storing the frequencies in a 10-element array. It can then create an index to where elements should be moved because it knows how many of each value to leave space for in the destination array.

> **Note:** To sort by characters, you would need a frequency array with one position for each possible character; to sort by bytes, you would need a 256 position frequency array.

The `radixsort` function works in the following way:

1. Initialize the frequency counting array.

2. Perform a `for` loop that counts the occurrences of each value in the digit position being sorted.

Isolating a digit requires the following math:

```
value = ((float) sortArray[i]->getKey() /
   (pow (10, theDigit)));
digit = (int) ((float) sortArray[i]->getKey() /
   (pow (10, theDigit)));
digit = (int) ((value - (float) digit) * 10);
```

3. Perform a `for` loop that loads the index array based on the frequencies of each value.

4. Perform a `for` loop that copies elements from the source array to the destination array based on the index array.

Because of the work needed to isolate the individual digits for a radix sort by digit, a radix sort isn't the best choice for an integer sort. However, it can be very efficient when sorting strings, especially if you have pointers to the strings in the array so that you are moving just pointers rather than the strings themselves in main memory.

9.12 The Binary Search

One of the most important reasons for sorting a data structure is to order it so that it can be searched by a binary search. A binary search uses a divide and conquer strategy. It looks first at the middle element in an array. If the middle element is not the target element, then the search can at least determine whether the target element is above or below the middle element. In this way, the search can immediately eliminate half the elements in the array from consideration. The search continues in this fashion—eliminating half the elements with each comparison of the search key to an element's key—until either the correct element is found or the search determines that the target element is not in the data set.

Just how fast is a binary search? To get a feeling for its performance, let's first consider a sequential search in which you begin at the first element in an array and check each successive element, in order, until you either find the desired element or reach the bottom of the array, at which point you can determine that the element you want isn't in the array. If the array contains 1000 elements, then, on average, you will need to make 500 comparisons to find an element that is in the array. In the "worst-case scenario"—the desired element is not in the array—then you will need to make 1000 comparisons.

If you perform a binary search on the same 1000 element array, the comparisons shrink the array being searched in the following way:

1. First comparison: 500 elements
2. Second comparison: 125 elements
3. Third comparison: 62 elements
4. Fourth comparison: 31 elements
5. Fifth comparison: 15 elements
6. Sixth comparison: 7 elements
7. Seventh comparison: 3 elements
8. Eighth comparison: 1 element

When the portion of the array being searched contains only one element and that element is not the desired element, then the search has failed. This means that it takes a maximum of eight comparisons in the worst-case scenario for a binary search, making it more than 100 times as efficient as a failed sequential search on an array of size 1000. When the element being sought is in the array, it takes an average of six or less comparisons to find that element.

The benefits of a binary search increase exponentially with the size of the array. For example, if we increase the size of the array to 10,000 elements, then the sequential search needs 10,000 comparisons to determine that a search has failed. But the binary search needs only 13, nearly 770 times less than the sequential search.

An implementation of a binary search can be found in Listing 9-11. Although there is more than one way to code the search, this particular method is relatively efficient, in that it stops as soon as the desired element is found, rather than continuing until the entire array has been searched.

```
Thing * ArrayMgr::search (int ID)
{
    int top, bottom, middle;
    top = 0;
    bottom = total_elements - 1;

    bool found = false;
    Thing * result = 0;

    while (top <= bottom && !found)
    {
        middle = (top + bottom) / 2; // find a new middle element
        if (theArray[middle]->getID() == ID)
        {
            result = theArray[middle]; // found it!
            found = true;
        }
        else if (theArray[middle]->getID() < ID)
            top = middle + 1; // in bottom half; move top down
        else
            // must be in top half; move bottom up
            bottom = middle - 1;

    }
    return result; // desired element wasn't found
}
```

Listing 9-11 Implementation of a binary search

The search function works in the following way:

1. Declare three pointers, one to the top of the array (element 0), one to the bottom of the array (last valid array element used), and one to point to the middle element.

2. Declare a boolean that flags when the desired element has been found.

3. Declare a local variable to hold a pointer to the found element. Initialize it to 0. Returning a 0 will indicate that the search failed.

4. Enter a while loop that continues while the top pointer is less than or equal to the bottom pointer and the desired element hasn't been found. (In other words, a failed search is detected when the top and bottom pointers cross). When the loop stops, go to step 9.

5. Compute the middle element by adding the top and bottom element indexes and dividing by 2.

6. If the middle element is the desired element (its key matches the key of the desired element), store the contents of the middle element in the result variable and set the `found` boolean to `true`. Go to step 4.

7. If the key of the middle element is less than the key of the element being sought, move the top down to one element below the middle. Go to step 4.

8. Otherwise, the desired element must be in the top half of the array. Move the bottom pointer up to one element above the middle. Go to step 4.

9. Return the result.

9.13 Summary

In this chapter you have been introduced to a variety of methods for sorting data:

- Bubble sort
- Selection sort
- Insertion sort
- Shell sort
- Quicksort (recursive and nonrecursive)
- Merge sort
- Radix sort

You can also sort items by inserting them into an ordered linked list or binary inserting them into a binary tree.

Once a direct access data structure has been sorted, you can use it for a binary search, a very fast search technique that uses a divide and conquer approach.

CHAPTER 10

Hash Tables

A binary tree and a binary search provide fast access to a single element based on a key value. On average, however, both a search of a binary tree and a binary search on a sorted array will require multiple comparisons to locate a desired element. To cut down on the number of comparisons, it would be useful to have a data structure that allowed more direct access to elements.

One solution is to use *hashing*, a technique in which a mathematical transformation of a key value produces the location in an array or file where an element can be found. The term itself comes from the idea that a program chops up the key (makes "hash" of it) to generate a storage location.

In CODASYL database management systems—database systems that used a simple network data model in which all relationships (one-to-one or one-to-many only) were hard-coded into the data set—hashing was used to provide a fast access path to data stored in database files. In that case, the result of the key transformation produced an identifier that referred to a location in a direct access file. For example, the hash key would include the file page (or bucket) number and the page directory entry for the data. The DBMS would consult the page or bucket directory for the byte offset from the start of the page or bucket that indicated the start of the required data. The hashing therefore determined the physical placement of data in the file.

Hashing can also be used to keep an index to data stored elsewhere. The collection of references to data locations, known as a *hash table*, can be kept either in main memory or in a disk file. When a hash table is kept in main memory, the underlying data structure is an array and the array elements are pointers. However, when a hash table is kept in a disk file, the hashed elements must be data identifiers, such as the disk page numbers and page directory entry numbers as described in the preceding paragraph.

10.1 Hash Table Concepts

The easiest way to conceptualize a hash table is to think of it as an array. (In this case, a vector won't work because it doesn't necessarily have a fixed size throughout its life.) When a program stores an element in the array, the element's key is transformed by a *hash function* that produces an array index within the range of valid indexes for that array. The intent is that over the life of the hash table, elements will be relatively randomly and uniformly distributed.

To find an element in the table, a program rehashes the key, producing the array index at which the element is stored. The program can then go directly to the desired element.

Unfortunately, it isn't quite that clean and simple. As the array begins to fill, keys will unavoidably produce the same array index when transformed by the hash function. (If you find this hard to believe, consider that you need only 24 people in a room to have a 50/50 chance that two people have the same birthday.) When more than one element tries to occupy the same array position, you have a *collision*.

Note: In some cases it is possible to generate a hash function that never produces a collision. This is known as a *pure hash function*. Finding a pure hash function that works for a given data set can be extremely time consuing, and perhaps even impossible. We therefore must live with collisions.

10.1.1 Collision Resolution Techniques

In most cases, collisions are inevitable. They can't be avoided, so they must be handled. There are two general techniques for doing so: using adjacent locations in the array and using linked lists. You will see examples of both techniques in this chapter. Which is a better technique depends on the size of your data set, the size of the hash table, whether you need to delete elements, and the randomness of locations generated by the hash function.

10.1.1.1 Collision Resolution Using Adjacent Elements

If you are using adjacent elements for collision resolution, your program stores the first element that generates a specific array index at that index. For example, if the key generates 55, then you use array index 55. When a second element generates 55, the program begins a sequential search starting at location 55, looking for the first open location. The second element whose key generates 55 will be stored at 56, the third at 57, and so on. Of course, if 56 and 57 are already occupied by elements that have collided with an earlier index value, then colliding a value will be stored farther away from the location generated by the hash function.

When it comes time to retrieve a value, the program recomputes the hash index and checks the key of the element stored at that location. If the desired key value isn't at that location, then the search function begins a sequential search of the array that continues until either the desired element is found or the search encounters an unused position in the array, indicating that the element is not present.

There are three disadvantages to this approach. First, as the number of collisions increases, the distance from the array index computed by the hash function and the actual location of an element increases, increasing search time. Second, elements tend to cluster around elements that produce collisions. As the array fills, there will be gaps of unused locations. Finally, the hash table has a fixed size. At some point all the elements in the array will be filled. The only alternative at that point is to expand the table, which also means modifying the hash function to accommodate the increased address space.

On the other hand, all of the elements (or pointers to the elements) are placed in contiguous storage. This will speed up the sequential searches when collisions do occur.

There are slight variations to the preceding scheme that attempt to space out the elements, avoiding the clustering of elements that occurs with adjacent placement. For example, collided elements can be placed some fixed number of locations away from the location generated by the hash function. For example, suppose we decided to place the elements four locations apart. If the first element is stored at location 55, the second element whose hashed key generated 55 would be stored at 59, the third at 63, and so on. If a location is occupied, the program adds four and checks again, until it finds an unused location.

10.1.1.2 Collision Resolution Using Linked Lists

The major alternative to using adjacent storage is to use linked lists. In this case, the elements in the hash table are list managers. Each element that generates a given location is added to the end of the list at that location.

There is one major advantage to this approach: The hash table's size is limited only by available storage space. Unless performance becomes unacceptable, you do not need to expand the table and recreate the hash function.

However, as the lists of collided elements (*collision chains*) become long, searching them for a desired element begins to take longer and longer.

10.1.2 Creating Hash Functions

There is no magic formula for the creation of a hash function. It can be any mathematical transformation that produces a relatively random and uniform distribution of values within the address space of the storage into which elements are being hashed. Although some of the development of a hash function is trial and error, here are some hints that may make the process easier:

- Set the size of the storage space to a prime number. This will help generate a more uniform distribution of addresses. For example, the demonstration program in this chapter uses an array of 203 elements.

- Use modulo arithmetic. In other words, transform the key in such a way that you can perform a % ARRAY_SIZE to generate the address.

- To transform a numeric key, try something like adding the digits together or picking every other digit.

- To transform a string key, take advantage of C++'s automatic typecasting and treat each character as an integer. Then either add the values together or pick every other character or some other combination that works. The sample program in this chapter adds the ASCII codes of the characters in a string key and then performs modulo division.

10.1.3 Hash Table Iteration

The data structures that you have seen to this point—with the exception of the stack and queue—have been accompanied by iterators that produce the elements in key order. Given the random nature of storage in a hash table, however, it isn't possible to iterate in key order. Two keys that generate the same value from the hash function are not necessarily next to each other in numeric or alphabetic order!

The only iteration that is feasible for a hash table is to produce the elements based on their physical placement in the hash table. If you are using adjacent elements for collision resolution, then this will simply be a listing of the entire storage space. If you are using linked lists, then iteration means using each stored array manager to iterate its own list. Given that we have working linked list code to handle this, iterating a hash table that uses linked lists isn't as difficult as might first appear.

10.2 Using Adjacent Elements to Handle Collisions

The first demonstration program we will consider implements a hash table using adjacent elements for collision resolution. You can find the program's main menu in Figure 10-1.

```
1. Add an element
2. Find one Thing
3. View contents of table
9. Exit

Choice: |
```

Figure 10-1 Menu for the hash table demonstration program

The data set used for this demonstration (as well as the linked list version of the hash table) consists of thirty `Thing` objects. The ID numbers are 1 through 30; the names are the values written out (*one* through *thirty*). The values were entered in order so that you could track how the hash function actually placed the elements. After pointers to all 30 objects have been added, the table looks like Figure 10-2.

The first collision appears as the ninth element is added! However, some of the elements that are in adjacent locations do not represent collisions, but merely adjacent locations generated directly by the hash function. In fact, only indexes 55 (one collisions) and 139 (two collisions) actually generated collisions.

A declaration for a hash table class that uses adjacent elements for collision resolution can be found in Listing 10-1. Notice that the hash table stores pointers to `Thing` objects. The `computeIndex` function—the actual has function—takes the string key and returns an index within the range of the array (0 through 202).

One of the things you may have noticed from looking at both Figure 10-1 and Listing 10-1 is that there is no function to remove elements from the hash table. This is not a trivial omission: Removing elements from this type of hash table and leaving the table in such a state that it will still function is

```
Index 20:  ID = 5   Name = five
Index 21:  ID = 9   Name = nine
Index 29:  ID = 18  Name = eighteen
Index 30:  ID = 11  Name = eleven
Index 35:  ID = 21  Name = twenty-one
Index 38:  ID = 4   Name = four
Index 39:  ID = 28  Name = twenty-eight
Index 46:  ID = 23  Name = twenty-three
Index 53:  ID = 26  Name = twenty-six
Index 54:  ID = 12  Name = twelve
Index 55:  ID = 13  Name = thirteen
Index 56:  ID = 27  Name = twenty-seven
Index 59:  ID = 22  Name = twenty-two
Index 60:  ID = 14  Name = fourteen
Index 67:  ID = 30  Name = thirty
Index 74:  ID = 20  Name = twenty
Index 119:  ID = 1   Name = one
Index 123:  ID = 8   Name = eight
Index 124:  ID = 10  Name = ten
Index 128:  ID = 15  Name = fifteen
Index 130:  ID = 3   Name = three
Index 137:  ID = 6   Name = six
Index 139:  ID = 7   Name = seven
Index 140:  ID = 25  Name = twenty-five
Index 141:  ID = 29  Name = twenty-nine
Index 143:  ID = 2   Name = two
Index 157:  ID = 24  Name = twenty-four
Index 159:  ID = 16  Name = sixteen
Index 161:  ID = 17  Name = seventeen
Index 162:  ID = 19  Name = ninetween
```

Figure 10-2 The distribution of elements in a hash table that uses adjacent elements for collision resolution

extremely difficult, well beyond the scope of this book. Compilers, for example, use hash tables with adjacent elements for collision resolution to build symbol tables. In such an application, the strategy works well because elements never have to be removed from the table.

```
#ifndef HASHTABLE
#define HASHTABLE

#include "stringclass.h"
#include "thing.h"

#define TABLE_SIZE 203

class Hashtable
{
    private:
        Thing * table [TABLE_SIZE];
        int computeIndex (String key);
    public:
        Hashtable();
        bool insert (Thing *);
        Thing * find (String);
        Thing * getThing (int);
};

#endif
```

Listing 10-1 Declaration of a hash table class that uses adjacent elements for collision resolution

10.2.1 Adding Elements

You can find the code for adding an element to the hash table in Listing 10-2. Notice first that the `hashtable` class's constructor fills the array with 0s, making it easy to detect unused elements.

```
Hashtable::Hashtable ()
{
    for (int i = 0; i < TABLE_SIZE; i++)
        table[i] = 0;
}

bool Hashtable::insert (Thing * newThing)
{
    String key;
```

Listing 10-2   Adding an element to a hash table that places collisions in adjacent locations

```
newThing->getKey (key);
int index = computeIndex (key);
bool result = true;

if (table[index] == 0) // first entry at that hash value
    table[index] = newThing;
else
{
    while (table[++index] != 0 && index < TABLE_SIZE)
        ; // find next open spot
    if (index == TABLE_SIZE)
    {
        int index = -1;
        // start again at top
        while (table[++index] != 0 && index < computedindex -1)
            ;
        if (index == computedindex)
            result = false; //  table is full
        else
            table[index] = newThing;
    }
    else
        table[index] = newThing;
}
return result;
}

int Hashtable::computeIndex (String key)
{
    long sum = 0;
    for (int i = 0; i < key.len(); i++)
        sum += key[i];
    return sum % TABLE_SIZE;
}
```

Listing 10-2 (Continued) Adding an element to a hash table that places collisions in adjacent

To add an element, the `insert` function can then do the following:

1. Retrieve the key of the object being stored in the hash table.

2. Compute the hash table index for the new object by calling `com-puteIndex`.

3. If the index position in the array is empty, insert the pointer to the new object. Return `true` indicating a successful insertion.

4. Otherwise, search forward in the array to find the next empty element. If you reach the end of the array without finding an empty spot, go back to the beginning and search from the beginning to one above the original computed index position. If there is no empty element, return `false`, indicating that the hash table is full.

5. Otherwise, insert the new object into the hash table at the location of the found index. Return `true` indicating a successful insertion.

10.2.2 Finding Elements

As you can see in Listing 10-3, finding an element is very much the same as storing it. The `find` function computes the hash index and then checks to see if the desired element is stored at that index. If not, it searches forward in the array until it either finds the element, encounters a 0 (in which case the element is not in the array), or reaches the end of the array. If it reaches the end of the array, it starts at the beginning and searches sequentially until one before the computed index location. If it still hasn't found the desired element, then it isn't in the hash table.

```
Thing * Hashtable::find (String key)
{
    int index = computeIndex (key);
    int computedIndex = index;
    Thing * theThing = 0;
    String theKey;
    table[index]->getKey (theKey);

    if (theKey != key)
    {
        while (theKey != key && table[index] !=0
            && index < TABLE_SIZE)
            table[++index]->getKey (theKey);

        if (theKey == key)
            theThing = table[index];
```

Listing 10-3   Finding an element in a hash table that places collisions in adjacent locations

```
        else if (index == TABLE_SIZE)
        {
            index = -1; // start at beginning again
            while (theKey != key && table[++index] != 0 &&
                index < computedIndex)
                table[index]->getKey (theKey);
            if (theKey == key)
                theThing = table[index];
        }
    }
    else
        theThing = table[index];
    return theThing;
}
```

Listing 10-3 (Continued)   Finding an element in a hash table that places collisions in adjacent

10.2.3 Listing the Elements

An iterator class to list the elements in a hash table that places collisions in adjacent locations is relatively simple. As you can see in Listing 10-4, it needs only a constructor to initialize an iterator object with the table being iterated and a getNext function.

```
#ifndef HASHTABLEITR
#define HASHTABLEITR

#include "hashtable.h"

class HashtableItr
{
    private:
        Hashtable * theTable;
        int index;
    public:
        HashtableItr (Hashtable *);
        bool getNext(Thing * &, int &);
};
```

Listing 10-4   Declaration of an iterator class for a hash table that places collisions in adjacent locations

```
#endif
```

Listing 10-4 (Continued) Declaration of an iterator class for a hash table that places collisions in adjacent locations

The `getNext` function (Listing 10-5) begins by locating the first nonzero location in the array. It then assigns the index of that location to a reference parameter and returns a boolean that indicates whether the traversal is complete.

```
#include "hashtableitr.h"

HashtableItr::HashtableItr (Hashtable * whichTable)
{
    theTable = whichTable;
    index = -1;
}

bool HashtableItr::getNext(Thing * & theThing, int & position)
{
    bool done = false;

    // find next used position in table
    while (theTable->getThing(++index) == 0 && index < TABLE_SIZE)
         ;

        if (index == TABLE_SIZE)
        {
            done = true;
            theThing = 0;
            position = -1;
        }
        else
        {
            theThing = theTable->getThing(index);
            position = index; //  for demonstration purposes only
        }
    return done;
}
```

Listing 10-5 Implementation of an iterator class for a hash table (collisions in adjacent locations)

This function also provides the index of the element provided in another reference parameter. This is particularly useful for the demonstration program because it means that you can see which indexes in the array have actually been filled.

10.3 Using Linked Lists to Handle Collisions

Using a linked list to handle collisions is actually simpler than using adjacent elements if you have working list manager and list iterator classes. To insert, you either create a new list manager or insert a node into an existing list. To search, you use the list manager's search function. Iteration means finding each list and letting the list manager iterate through its own members.

In addition, it is also possible to support removing elements from the hash table: You use the list manager's removal function to do so. This is a major advantage over using adjacent elements, where deletion of an element is extremely difficult to implement.

Using the same data set as that for the previous version of the hash table, the table loads as in Figure 10-3. Notice that this illustration makes it clear where the collisions have occurred: Those elements with identical indexes represent the collisions. They are chained together into a linked list whose manager resides at the specified index.

The declaration for the class can be found in Listing 10-6. In this case, the contents of the hash table are list manager objects. The class therefore must include a function (getList) that returns the location of the list manager in a given array position to be used by the array iterator.

```
Index 20:  ID = 5   Name = five
Index 20:  ID = 9   Name = nine
Index 29:  ID = 18  Name = eighteen
Index 30:  ID = 11  Name = eleven
Index 35:  ID = 21  Name = twenty-one
Index 38:  ID = 4   Name = four
Index 39:  ID = 28  Name = twenty-eight
Index 42:  ID = 19  Name = nineteen
Index 46:  ID = 23  Name = twenty-three
Index 53:  ID = 26  Name = twenty-six
Index 54:  ID = 12  Name = twelve
Index 55:  ID = 13  Name = thirteen
Index 55:  ID = 27  Name = twenty-seven
Index 59:  ID = 22  Name = twenty-two
Index 60:  ID = 14  Name = fourteen
Index 67:  ID = 30  Name = thirty
Index 74:  ID = 20  Name = twenty
Index 119: ID = 1   Name = one
Index 123: ID = 8   Name = eight
Index 124: ID = 10  Name = ten
Index 128: ID = 15  Name = fifteen
Index 130: ID = 3   Name = three
Index 137: ID = 6   Name = six
Index 139: ID = 7   Name = seven
Index 139: ID = 25  Name = twenty-five
Index 139: ID = 29  Name = twenty-nine
Index 143: ID = 2   Name = two
Index 157: ID = 24  Name = twenty-four
Index 159: ID = 16  Name = sixteen
Index 161: ID = 17  Name = seventeen
```

Figure 10-3 The distribution of elements in a hash table that uses linked lists for collision resolution

10.3.1 Adding Elements

Adding an element to a hash table that is using linked lists for collision resolution is simpler than adding to a table using adjacent placement. As you can see from Listing 10-7, the insertion works in the following way:

1. Retrieve the key from the object being hashed into the table.

2. Compute the hash key.

3. If the computed location is empty (i.e., it contains a 0), create a new list manager object and store a pointer to it in the computed location. Then ask the list manager to insert the object being hashed into the table.

4. If a list manager already occupies the location, then a collision has occurred and the new element must be added to the list at that location. Ask the list manager to insert the object being hashed into the table.

The list manager `insert` routine being used by the hash table (Listing 10-8) is different from the `insert` function used to maintain an ordered linked list. Elements are always added to the end of the list. Therefore, the list manager needs to maintain a pointer to the last element its list and inserting requires only setting the last element to point to the new element and resetting the last variable to point to the new .node.

```
#ifndef HASHTABLE
#define HASHTABLE

#include "listmgr.h"
#include "stringclass.h"

#define TABLE_SIZE 203

class Hashtable
{
    private:
        ListMgr * table [TABLE_SIZE];
        int computeIndex (String key);
    public:
        Hashtable();
        void insert (Thing *);
        bool remove (String);
        Thing * find (String);
        ListMgr * getList (int);
};

#endif
```

Listing 10-6 Declaration of a hash table class that uses linked lists for collision resolution

```
Hashtable::Hashtable ()
{
    for (int i = 0; i < TABLE_SIZE; i++)
        table[i] = 0;
}

void Hashtable::insert (Thing * newThing)
{
    String key;
    newThing->getKey (key);
    int index = computeIndex (key);

    if (table[index] == 0) // first entry at that hash value
        table[index] = new ListMgr ();
    table[index]->insert (newThing);
}

int Hashtable::computeIndex (String key)
{
    long sum = 0;
    for (int i = 0; i < key.len(); i++)
        sum += key[i];
    return sum % TABLE_SIZE;
}
```

Listing 10-7 Adding an element to a hash table that uses linked lists for collision resolution

```
void ListMgr::insert (Thing * theThing)
{
    Node * newNode;

    newNode = new Node (theThing); // create a node object

    if (first == 0) // list is empty
    {
        first = newNode;
        last = newNode;
    }
    else  // insert last in collision chain
    {
```

Listing 10-8   A list manager function to insert a new element at the end of a list

```
        last->setNext (newNode);
        last = newNode;
    }
}
```

Listing 10-8 (Continued) A list manager function to insert a new element at the end of a list

> **Note:** Using ordered linked lists will not produce an in-order iteration. As you can see from Figure 10-3, a collision does not mean that there is any logical ordering between the collided elements. Since it is faster to use a linked list that always puts new elements first or last, there is no reason not to do so.

10.3.2 Finding Elements

To find an element, the hash table that uses linked lists for collision resolution does the following in Listing 10-9:

```
Thing * Hashtable::find (String key)
{
    int index = computeIndex (key);
    Thing * theThing = 0;
    if (table[index] != 0)
        theThing = table[index]->find (key);
    return theThing;
}
```

Listing 10-9 Finding an element in a hash table that uses linked lists for collision resolution

1. Compute the hash key for the desired key value.
2. If the element at the computed index value is a 0, then there is no object in the table with the desired key. Return 0.
3. Otherwise, ask the list manager to search its elements to find the object.

The original list manager class you saw earlier in this book used an integer key. However, the hash table is using a string key. Therefore, the list manager now contains an overloaded find function that searches with a string key (see Listing 10-10).

```
Thing * ListMgr::find (String key)
{
    Thing * currentThing, * theThing = 0;
    Node * current;
    current = first; // start at head of list
    String currentKey;
    bool found = false;

    while (current != 0 && !found)
    {
        currentThing = current->getThing();
        currentThing->getKey(currentKey);
        if (key == currentKey)
        {
            theThing = currentThing;
            found = true;
        }
        else
            current = current->getNext ();
    }
    return theThing; // not found
}
```

Listing 10-10 A list manager function to find an element using a string key

10.3.3 Removing an Element

To remove an element from a hash table using linked lists for collision resolution, you can once again take advantage of existing list manager functionality (Listing 10-11):

```
bool Hashtable::remove (String key)
{
    Thing * theThing;
    bool result = false;
    int ID;

    int index = computeIndex (key);
    if (table[index] != 0)
```

Listing 10-11   Removing an element from a hash table that uses linked lists for collision resolution

```
      theThing = table[index]->find (key);
   if (theThing != 0)
   {
      theThing->getKey (ID);
      result = table[index]->remove (ID);
   }
   return result;
}
```

Listing 10-11 (Continued) Removing an element from a hash table that uses linked lists for collision

1. Compute the hash table index of the element to be removed.
2. If the value at the computed index location is 0, then the desired element is not in the table. Return `false`.
3. Otherwise, call `find` for the list manager stored at the computed index.
4. If find returns 0, the desired element was not in the table. Return `false`.
5. Otherwise, ask the list manager to remove the found element.
6. Return `true`.

10.3.4 Listing the Elements

Conceptually, iterating a hash table that uses linked lists is more difficult than iterating one that uses adjacent elements for collision resolution. Not only does the iterator need to keep track of the current array element, but it must keep track of where it is in the list being iterated. If you already happen to have a list iterator class, then you can allow the list iterator to keep track of its own position.

The declaration of the iterator class appears in Listing 10-12. It keeps track of the index currently being processed as well as a pointer to the current list iterator. It also uses a boolean to determine when it is time to move on to the next element in the hash table's array.

```
#ifndef HASHTABLEITR
#define HASHTABLEITR
```

Listing 10-12 Declaration of an iterator class for a hash table (linked lists for collision resolution)

```
#include "hashtable.h"
#include "listitr.h"

class HashtableItr
{
    private:
        Hashtable * theTable;
        int index;
        bool newList;
        ListItr * theItr;
    public:
        HashtableItr (Hashtable *);
        bool getNext(Thing * &, int &);
};
#endif
```

Listing 10-12 (Continued) Declaration of an iterator class for a hash table (linked lists for collision

The implementation of the iterator class can be found in Listing 10-13. The constructor initializes the iterator with a pointer to the hash table. It also sets the newList boolean to true and initializes a variable to hold the current array index.

```
#include "hashtableitr.h"

HashtableItr::HashtableItr (Hashtable * whichTable)
{
    theTable = whichTable;
    index = -1;
    newList = true;
}

bool HashtableItr::getNext(Thing * & theThing, int & position)
{
    bool done = false;

    if (newList)
    {
```

Listing 10-13 Implementation of an iterator class for a hash table (linked lists for collision resolution)

```
        // find next used position in table
        while (theTable->getList(++index) == 0 &&
            index < TABLE_SIZE)
            ;

        if (index == TABLE_SIZE)
            done = true;
        else
        {
            theItr = new ListItr (theTable->getList(index));
            newList = false;
        }
    }

    if (!done)
    {
        theThing = theItr->getNext();
        position = index; // for demonstration purposes only
        if (theItr->getNextNode() == 0) // if last in list
            newList = true; // need new list next time
    }
    return done;
}
```

Listing 10-13 (Continued) Implementation of an iterator class for a hash table (linked lists for collision

The getNext function, which returns a pointer to a Thing object in a reference parameter, works in the following way:

1. Set the done boolean to false, indicating that the iteration has not finished.

2. If the previous call to the function resulted in the end of a list (or this is the first call), search through the table for the next occupied location.

3. If the end of the hash table is encountered without finding another list manager, set the done boolean to true and go to step 8.

4. Once a valid list manager has been found, retrieve a pointer to the list and set the newList boolean to false.

5. Create a new list iterator object, initializing it with the list pointer returned by
   3. Set the newList boolean to false.

6. Request the next `Thing` object from the list iterator.

7. If the `Thing` object is 0, then the end of the list has been reached. Set `newList` to `true`.

8. Return `done`.

This function also returns the index of the array manager being iterated using a reference parameter.

10.4 Summary

A hash table is a storage area in which storage locations are directly addressable. Elements are placed in the structure by performing a mathematical transformation on a key, generating a value randomly distributed within the storage area's address range. To retrieve an element, a program performs the key transformation again to regenerate the storage location.

In most cases, the mathematical key transformation (a hash function) does not generate a unique value for every key. Duplicate hash values are called a collision. Given the collisions are generally unavoidable, a hash table must have some way to handle them.

One strategy is to place colliding data in physically adjacent storage locations. This makes it easy to iterate through the hash table, but tends to cluster elements, leaving the hash table with blocks of unused storage locations. This strategy also tends to complicate the logic of storing and finding elements. It also means that the number of elements that can be stored is limited by the size of the hash table.

The second alternative is to chain colliding elements together into linked lists. Although this makes it more difficult to iterate through the hash table, it avoids the clustering problem and removes the limitation that the number of stored elements can be no more than the size of the hash table.

There is no efficient way to iterate the values of a hash table in key order.

CHAPTER 11　*Dictionaries*

Dictionaries are a conceptual data structure that are typically used to provide indexes to stored data. They provide access to its elements using a single immutable key. Associated with the key is a value that can be modified as needed. To use a dictionary to index a data set in an object-oriented environment, the value is typically a pointer to an object in main memory or a disk file location.

A dictionary must be able to do the following:

- Add an element.
- Remove an element.
- Find an element and return its value.
- If the element isn't present, create a new element with the specified key.
- Set an element's value.

Notice that the preceding says nothing about the implementation structure of a dictionary. In fact, a dictionary can be implemented as a linked list (poor for quick search access but no size limitations), an array (good for quick access but subject to size limitations), or a binary search tree (good for quick access and dynamic in size). Because a binary search tree provides both quick access to elements and dynamic sizing, the example you will see in this chapter uses that data structure. The example also presents templates for the binary search tree and its adjunct classes.

Note: You could also use a vector to implement a dictionary and avoid the size limitation of an array. Research has shown that there is often little difference in search performance between using a vector and a binary tree, but the time necessary to expand the vector when it is full can slow overall application performance.

11.1 Associations

The type of element managed by a dictionary is known as an *association*. As you can see in Listing 11-1, an association has only two variables: its key and its value. It has member functions to return the key and the value and a member function to set the value. In this particular example, the value is an object of the String class, but it could just as easily be a pointer to an object in main memory or a disk file location The implementation of an association (Listing 11-2) is similarly straightforward.

```
#ifndef ASSOCIATION
#define ASSOCIATION

#include "stringclass.h"

class Association
{
    private:
        int key; // key cannot be modified
        String value;
    public:
        Association (int, String);
        void getKey (int &);
```

Listing 11-1   Declaration of an association class

```
        String getValue ();
        void setValue (String);
        // no setKey function because key cannot be modified
};

#endif
```

Listing 11-1 (Continued) Declaration of an association class

```
#include "association.h"

Association::Association (int iKey, String iValue)
{
    key = iKey;
    value = iValue;
}

void Association::getKey (int & oKey)
    { oKey = key; }

String Association::getValue ()
    { return value; }

void Association::setValue (String iValue)
    { value = iValue; }
```

Listing 11-2 Implementation of an association class

Note: Yes, an association does look a great deal like the Thing objects that have been used in the demonstration programs throughout this book. However, keep in mind that there is one major difference: An association's key cannot be modified. (This is an essential restriction for database processing, for example, if the key happens to be a physical location in a disk file.) The Thing class has no such restriction.

11.2 The Dictionary Class

You can find the declaration of the dictionary class in Listing 11-3. A dictionary object stores a default value to assign to associations that are created automatically with just a key, as well as the binary tree that stores the associations.

```
#ifndef DICTIONARY
#define DICTIONARY

#include "association.h"
// template for binary search tree; includes node.h
#include "tree.h"
#include "stringclass.h"

class Dictionary
{
    private:
        String defaultValue;
        Tree <Association, int> * theTree;
    public:
        Dictionary ();
        Dictionary (String); // sets default value
        String operator [] (int);
        Association * getAssociation (int);
        void insert (Association *);
        void deleteAllValues ();
        bool includesKey (int);
        bool isEmpty ();
        bool removeKey (int);
        // set a default value for new associations
        void setDefault (String);
        Tree<Association, int> * getTree ();
};

#endif
```

Listing 11-3 Declaration of a dictionary class

The binary tree is created from two templates: *node.h* (Listing 11-4) and *tree.h* (Listing 11-5). These are essentially the same as the header files and class implementations that manipulate `Thing` objects, with only some minor changes to make them generic. For example, the word "Thing" in function names has be changed to "Element."

```
#ifndef NODE
#define NODE

template <class E, class K> class Node
{
    private:
        K key;
        Node * right_child, * left_child;
        E * theElement;
    public:
        Node (E *);
        void getKey (K &);
        E * getElement ();
        Node * getRight();
        Node * getLeft();
        void setRight (Node *);
        void setLeft (Node *);
};

template <class E, class K>
Node<E, K>::Node (E * iElement)
{
    theElement = iElement;
    theElement->getKey(key);
    right_child = 0;
    left_child = 0;
}

template <class E, class K>
void Node<E, K>::getKey(K & oKey)
    { oKey = key; }

template <class E, class K>
E * Node<E, K>::getElement ()
    { return theElement; }
```

Listing 11-4   The binary tree node template class

```
template <class E, class K>
Node<E, K> * Node<E, K>::getRight ()
    { return right_child; }

template <class E, class K>
Node<E, K> * Node<E, K>::getLeft ()
    { return left_child; }

template <class E, class K>
void Node<E, K>::setRight (Node * iNode)
    { right_child = iNode; }

template <class E, class K>
void Node<E, K>::setLeft (Node * iNode)
    { left_child = iNode; }

#endif
```

Listing 11-4 (Continued) The binary tree node template class

```
#ifndef TREE
#define TREE

#include "node.h"

template <class E, class K>
class Tree
{
    private:
        Node<E, K> * root;
        // used by deleteNode function only
        Node<E, K> * find (int, Node<E, K> * &, char &);
    public:
        Tree ();
        void insert (E *);
        bool deleteNode (K);
        E * find (K);
        Node<E, K> * find (K, Node<E, K> * &, char &);
        Node<E, K> * getRoot();
        bool isEmpty();
};
```

Listing 11-5 The binary tree template class

```
template <class E, class K>
Tree<E, K>::Tree()
{
    root = 0;
}

template <class E, class K>
void Tree<E, K>::insert (E * theElement)
{
    Node<E, K> * current, * child, * newNode;
    K key;
    theElement->getKey(key);

    if (root) // if root node exists
    {
        current = root;
        while (current) // keep going while there's a pointer
        {
            K currentKey;
            current->getKey (currentKey);
            if (currentKey < key)
            {
                // go down right side
                child = current->getRight();
                if (!child) // if no right child, insert
                {
                    newNode =
                        new Node<Association, int> (theElement);
                    current->setRight (newNode);
                    return;
                }
            }
            else
            {
                // go down left side
                child = current->getLeft();
                if (!child) // if no left child, insert
                {
                    newNode =
                        new Node<Association, int> (theElement);
                    current->setLeft (newNode);
```

Listing 11-5 (Continued) The binary tree template class

```
                    return;
               }
          }
          current = child;
       }
   }
   else
       root = new Node<Association, int> (theElement);
}

template <class E, class K>
bool Tree<E, K>::deleteNode (K key)
{
   Node<E, K> * previous = 0;   // use to save parent of found node
   char direction;
   Node<E, K> * theNode = find (key, previous, direction);

   if (theNode == 0)
       return false; // key not found in tree
   // needed to delete the object pointed to
   E * theElement = theNode->getElement ();

   // if no children, just disconnect; set parent pointer to 0
   if (theNode->getRight() == 0 && theNode->getLeft() == 0)
   {
       if (theNode == root)
           root = 0; // empty tree
       else
           if (direction == 'r')
               previous->setRight (0);
           else
               previous->setLeft (0);
   }
   // right subtree but no left subtree
   else if (theNode->getRight() != 0 && theNode->getLeft() == 0)
   {
       Node<E, K> * subtree = theNode->getRight();
       if (theNode == root)
           root = subtree;
       else
       {
```

Listing 11-5 (Continued) The binary tree template class

```
            if (direction == 'r')
                previous->setRight (subtree);
            else
                previous->setLeft (subtree);
        }
    }
    // left subtree but no right subtree
    else if (theNode->getRight() == O && theNode->getLeft() != 0)
    {
        Node<E, K> * subtree = theNode->getLeft();
        if (theNode == root)
            root = subtree;
        else
        {
            if (direction == 'r')
                previous->setRight (subtree);
            else
                previous->setLeft (subtree);
        }
    }
    else // must have both left and right subtrees
    {
        Node<E, K> * next;
        Node<E, K> * current = theNode->getLeft();
        // if there is a right subtree of left child...
        if (current->getRight() != 0)
        {
            next = current->getRight();
            while (next->getRight() != 0) // find last right child
            {
                current = next;
                next = current->getRight();
            }

            // replace deleted node with node found
            current->setRight (next->getLeft());
            next->setLeft (theNode->getLeft());
            next->setRight (theNode->getRight());
            // set parent pointers
            if (theNode != root)
                if (direction == 'l')
```

Listing 11-5 (Continued) The binary tree template class

```
                    previous->setLeft (next);
                else
                    previous->setRight (next);
            else root = next;
        }
        // since no right subtree, replace with left child
        else
        {
            next = current;
            next->setRight (theNode->getRight());
            if (theNode != root)
                if (direction == 'l')
                    previous->setLeft (next);
                else
                    previous->setRight (next);
            else root = next;
        }
    }

    // remove the node from memory
    delete theNode;
    return true;
}

template <class E, class K>
Node<E, K> * Tree<E, K>::find (K key, Node<E, K> * & previous,
        char & direction) // for deletion only
{
    Node<E, K> * current;

    if (root) // make sure there is at least one node
    {
        current = root;
        previous = current;
        while (current) // as long as there's a pointer
        {
            int currentKey;
            current->getKey (currentKey);
            if (currentKey == key)
                return current; // send back pointer to Node object
            // if less, go down right side
```

Listing 11-5 (Continued) The binary tree template class

```
            if (currentKey < key)
            {
                previous = current;
                direction = 'r';
                current = current->getRight();
            }
            // if greater, go down left side
            else
            {
                previous = current;
                direction = 'l';
                current = current->getLeft();
            }
        }
    }
    return 0;
}

template <class E, class K>
E * Tree<E, K>::find (K key)   // search by key
{
    Node<E, K> * current;

    if (root) // make sure there is at least one node
    {
        current = root;
        K currentKey;
        current->getKey (currentKey);
        while (current) // as long as there's a pointer
        {
            if (currentKey == key)
                // send back pointer to Thing object
                return current->getElement();
            // if less, go down right side
            if (currentKey < key)
                current = current->getRight();
            // if greater, go down left side
            else
                current = current->getLeft();
            if (current)
                current->getKey (currentKey);
```

Listing 11-5 (Continued) The binary tree template class

```
        }
    }
    return 0; // Element not found
}

template <class E, class K>
Node<E, K> * Tree<E, K>::getRoot ()
    { return root; }

template <class E, class K>
bool Tree<E, K>::isEmpty()
    { return (root == 0); }

#endif
```

Listing 11-5 (Continued) The binary tree template class

Working with the templates, the dictionary class can then include declarations such as

```
Tree <Association, int> * theTree;
```

to declare a binary tree object that uses an integer key and stores an association as its data value.

The implementation of the dictionary can then use the functions defined for the binary tree to perform most of its actions. As you can see in Listing 11-6, to insert an association into the dictionary, the dictionary class simply calls the binary tree's insert function. Deletion occurs in the same way.

```
#include "dictionary.h"
#include "preorderitr.h"

Dictionary::Dictionary ()
{
    theTree = new Tree<Association, int> ();
    defaultValue = "Default";
}
```

Listing 11-6 Implementation of a dictionary class

```
Dictionary::Dictionary (String iDefault)
{
    theTree = new Tree<Association, int> ();
    defaultValue = iDefault;
}

void Dictionary::insert (Association * newAssociation)
    { theTree->insert (newAssociation); }

String Dictionary::operator[] (int key)
{
    Association * theAssociation = getAssociation (key);
    // if not already in tree, create an association for this key
    if (!theAssociation)
    {
        theAssociation = new Association (key, defaultValue);
        theTree->insert (theAssociation);
    }
    return theAssociation->getValue();
}

void Dictionary::deleteAllValues()
{
    PreOrderItr<Association, int> theItr;
    // traverse the tree
    Association * theAssociation;
    for (theItr.init (theTree); !theItr; ++theItr)
    {
        theAssociation = theItr();
        if (theAssociation)
            theAssociation->setValue ("/0");
    }
}

bool Dictionary::includesKey (int key)
    { return (getAssociation (key) != 0); }

bool Dictionary::isEmpty ()
    { return theTree->isEmpty(); }
```

Listing 11-6 (Continued) Implementation of a dictionary class

```
bool Dictionary::removeKey (int key)
   { return (theTree->deleteNode (key)); }

void Dictionary::setDefault (String iValue)
   { defaultValue = iValue; }

Association * Dictionary::getAssociation (int key)
   { return (theTree->find (key)); }

Tree <Association, int> * Dictionary::getTree ()
   { return theTree; }
```

Listing 11-6 (Continued) Implementation of a dictionary class

The dictionary has three functions that locate associations:

- The overloaded [] operator takes the key supplied in the brackets and searches the dictionary for the key. If the key is not found, the function creates an association with that key and uses the stored default for its value. In either case, the function returns the association's value. An application can then determine whether a new association was created by checking for the default value.

- The getAssociation function takes a key as input and returns the association's value. If the key is not in the dictionary, the function returns the 0 provided by the binary tree's find function.

- The includesKey function determines whether an association with a specified key is in the dictionary and returns the appropriate boolean.

A dictionary typically also includes a function to delete all values (deleteAllValues), leaving the associations (and their keys) intact. To do this, the dictionary needs to traverse the tree, visiting each association, although the order in which this occurs is not important. The simplest way is to use an existing binary tree iterator, in this case, the preorder iterator (Listing 11-7).

This iterator uses the same node template as the binary tree (Listing 11-4) and a template for the stack class (Listing 11-8).

```
#ifndef PREORDER
#define PREORDER

#include "tree.h"
#include "stack.h"

template <class E, class K>
class PreOrderItr
{
    private:
        Node<E, K> * root;
        Stack<E, K> * theStack;
    public:
        PreOrderItr ();
        bool init (Tree<E, K> *);
        bool operator++ (); // find node
        bool operator! (); // check for end of traversal
        // return pointer to element pointed to by current node
        E * operator() ();
};

template <class E, class K>
PreOrderItr<E, K>::PreOrderItr()
{
    theStack = new Stack<E, K>();
    root = 0;
}

template <class E, class K>
bool PreOrderItr<E, K>::init (Tree<E, K> * tree)
{
    root = tree->getRoot(); // initialize current node to root
    if (root)
        theStack->push (root); // push root onto stack
    return theStack->is_empty(); // is stack empty?
}

template <class E, class K>
bool PreOrderItr<E, K>::operator++ ()
{
    Node<E, K> * current = theStack->getTop();
```

Listing 11-7   *A template class for a binary tree preorder traversal*

```
    Node<E, K> * next = current->getLeft();

    bool found = false;

    if (next)
    {
        theStack->push (next);
        found = true;
    }
    else
    {
        // while stack still has elements
        while (theStack->is_empty())
        {
            current = theStack->pop();
            next = current->getRight();
            if (next)
            {
                theStack->push (next);
                found = true;;
            }
        }
    }
    return found;
}

template <class E, class K>
E * PreOrderItr<E, K>::operator() ()
{
    Node<E, K> * theNode = theStack->getTop();
    // current node is top of stack
    return theNode->getElement ();
}

template <class E, class K>
bool PreOrderItr<E, K>::operator! ()
    { return theStack->is_empty(); } // check for end of traversal

#endif
```

Listing 11-7 (Continued)   A template class for a binary tree preorder traversal

```
#ifndef STACK
#define STACK

#include "node.h"

#define STACK_SIZE 25

template <class E, class K>
class Stack
{
   private:
      int stackPtr;
      Node<E, K> * stack [STACK_SIZE];
   public:
      Stack ();
      bool is_empty ();
      bool push (Node<E, K> *);
      Node<E, K> * pop ();
      Node<E, K> * getTop ();
      Node<E, K> * getElement (int);
      int getStackPtr ();
};

template <class E, class K>
Stack<E, K>::Stack ()
   { stackPtr = -1; }

// Returns false if the stack is empty
template <class E, class K>
bool Stack<E, K>::is_empty()
   { return stackPtr >= 0; }

template <class E, class K>
bool Stack<E, K>::push (Node<E, K> * theNode)
{
   if (stackPtr + 1 == STACK_SIZE)
      return false;
   stack[++stackPtr] = theNode;
   return true;
}
```

Listing 11-8   A stack template class

```
template <class E, class K>
Node<E, K> * Stack<E, K>::pop ()
    { return stack[stackPtr--]; }

template <class E, class K>
Node<E, K> * Stack<E, K>::getTop ()
    { return stack[stackPtr]; }

template <class E, class K>
Node<E, K> * Stack<E, K>::getElement (int pos)
{
    if (pos < 0 || pos > stackPtr)
        return 0;
    return stack [pos];
}

template <class E, class K>
int Stack<E, K>::getStackPtr ()
    { return stackPtr; }

#endif
```

Listing 11-8 (Continued) A stack template class

11.3 Listing the Dictionary's Contents

As mentioned at the beginning of this chapter, dictionaries do not necessarily have iterators designed to provide a listing in key order. However, since the underlying data structures typically do have iterators, it is relatively straightforward to provide one (see Listing 11-9 and Listing 11-10).

```
#ifndef DICT_ITR
#define DICT_ITR

#include "inorderitr.h"
#include "dictionary.h"
```

Listing 11-9 Declaration of a dictionary iterator class

```
class DictionaryItr
{
    private:
        Dictionary * theDictionary;
        InOrderItr<Association, int> theItr;
    public:
        DictionaryItr(Dictionary *);
        Association * getNext();
};

#endif
```

Listing 11-9 (Continued) Declaration of a dictionary iterator class

```
#include "dictionaryitr.h"

DictionaryItr::DictionaryItr (Dictionary * iDictionary)
{
    theDictionary = iDictionary;
    theItr.init (theDictionary->getTree());
}

Association * DictionaryItr::getNext()
{
    Association * theAssociation = 0;
    if (!theItr)
    {
        theAssociation = theItr ();
        ++theItr;
    }
    return theAssociation;
}
```

Listing 11-10 Implementation of a dictionary iterator class

The dictionary iterator makes use of the template version of the binary tree class's in-order iterator (Listing 11-11), which in turn uses the template version of the stack class (Listing 11-8) and the same node template as the binary tree template (Listing 11-4).

```
#ifndef INORDER
#define INORDER

#include "tree.h"
#include "stack.h"

template <class E, class K>
class InOrderItr
{
    private:
        Node<E, K> * root;
        void goLeft (Node<E, K> *);
        Stack<E, K> * theStack;
    public:
        InOrderItr ();
        bool init (Tree<E, K> *);
        bool operator++ (); // find node
        bool operator! (); // check for end of traversal
        // return pointer to thing pointed to by current node
        E * operator() ();
};

template <class E, class K>
InOrderItr<E, K>::InOrderItr()
{
    root = 0;
    theStack = new Stack<E, K> ();
}

template <class E, class K>
bool InOrderItr<E, K>::init (Tree<E, K> * tree)
{
    root = tree->getRoot(); // initialize current node to root
    goLeft (root); // go down left side of tree
    return theStack->is_empty(); // is stack empty?
}

template <class E, class K>
bool InOrderItr<E, K>::operator++ ()
{
    Node<E, K> * parent, * child;
```

Listing 11-11   A template class for an in-order binary tree iterator

```
    if (theStack->is_empty())
    {
        parent = theStack->pop();
        child = parent->getRight();
        if (child)
            goLeft (child);
    }
    return theStack->is_empty();
}

template <class E, class K>
// current node is top of stack
E * InOrderItr<E, K>::operator() ()
{
    Node<E, K> * theNode = theStack->getTop();
    return theNode->getElement ();
}

template <class E, class K>
void InOrderItr<E, K>::goLeft (Node<E, K> * node)
{
    while (node)
    {
        theStack->push (node);
        node = node->getLeft();
    }
}

template <class E, class K>
bool InOrderItr<E, K>::operator! ()
    { return theStack->is_empty(); } // check for end of traversal

#endif
```

Listing 11-11 (Continued) A template class for an in-order binary tree iterator

11.4 *Summary*

A dictionary is a conceptual data structure that provides access to data values or objects using a single, immutable key. A dictionary can be implemented using an array, linked list, or binary search tree that stores an object known as an association. Dictionaries typically are used as indexes to stored data.

Part IV: Sample Implementations

To this point, we have been looking at the technical aspects of data structures: how they are built, how they operate. But there is more to using data structures than simply being able to program them. You need to be able to make reasonable choices as to which data structures you should use in a given situation. Although we have talked about appropriate uses of data structures in general, you haven't seen them in action in a specific program.

Most of the time, there isn't any single right data structure for a particular task: There are almost always tradeoffs. Therefore, the purpose of this part of the book is to show you how some of those decisions were made for two specific applications. You may disagree with the choices. You may believe that if you were writing the code, you would have chosen something else. That's OK. What's important is that you see the reasoning behind the choices and that you have good, logical reasons for what you do.

There is a lot of code in Chapters 12 and 13. Nonetheless, the applications aren't complete. Both use a simplistic text-based menu system to keep them platform-neutral. Both are missing a great deal of functionality. Why? Because they are the basic underpinnings of very large programs that often take years to develop.

What you will see, however, is the underlying data manipulation code, including file and keyboard I/O. You will see how the data structures are built and how they integrate into the overall structure of the program. You will also see template classes for many of the data structures.

CHAPTER 12

The Video Store

It seems as though no programming book today is complete without a sample program that models the operation of a video store, and this book is no exception. Actually, a video store supports an excellent demonstration of how data structures can be used to provide organization and access to a variety of data. The store must manage its inventory (copies of videos and games that are rented), its customers, and rental and return activity.

As mentioned in the introduction to this part of this book, the example programs presented here aren't complete. For this example, a video store application should at a minimum provide a listing of overdue rentals and should allow searches by genre and star. It should also support modification of its entity classes. However, adding those functions is really more of what is already in the program. If you can handle the file I/O and data entry from the keyboard, correctly building the data structures as needed, then most of what is necessary for the remainder of the program is already in place.

The discussion in this chapter begins with a look at the entity classes and their inheritance hierarchy. You will then read about the way in which data structures were chosen to handle objects created from those entity classes.

The discussion will then turn to the application class and how it manipulates the data structures to perform its work.

12.1 *The Entity Classes*

The video store program is based on three groups of entity classes: the customers, the titles of videos and games, and the copies of videos and games. Keep in mind that it is *copies* of videos and games that are being rented. The store's inventory therefore consists of multiple copies of many titles.

12.1.1 The Customer Class

The declaration of the Customer class can be found in Listing 12-1. The only somewhat unusual feature of the class is that one of its variables is an object of the class DoubleListMgr. This list hold pointers to the copies of items that the customer has rented.

```
#ifndef CUSTOMER
#define CUSTOMER

#include "stringclass.h"
#include "doublelistmgr.h"
#include "treeable.h"
#include "itemcopy.h"
#include <fstream.h>

class Customer : public Treeable
{
    private:
        int custID;
        String fname, lname, street, CSZ, phone;
        String creditCardNumb;
        DoubleListMgr<ItemCopy, int> * itemsRented;
    public:
        Customer ();
```

Listing 12-1   Declaration of the Customer class

```
      Customer (int, String, String, String, String,
          String, String);
      Customer (ifstream &);
      int getCustID();
      DoubleListMgr<ItemCopy, int> * getList();
      void write (ofstream &);
      void getKey (int &);
      void getKey (String &);
      void addRental (ItemCopy *);
      void removeRental (int);
};

#endif
```

Listing 12-1 (Continued) Declaration of the Customer class

Note: The `Treeable` class from which `Customer` inherits is the same mix-in class to which you were introduced in Chapter 5.

The `Customer` class has implemented two of the `getKey` functions from the `Treeable` mix-in class, one for an integer key (the customer ID number) and one for a string key (last name followed immediately by first name). These will be used in different data structures, the reasons for which will become clear in Section 12.3.

The implementation of the `Customer` class appears in Listing 12-2. Notice that manipulation of the list of rented items is quite straightforward: just call the appropriate list manager function.

```
#include "customer.h"

Customer::Customer ()
    { }

Customer::Customer (int inumb, String ifname, String ilname,
        String istreet, String iCSZ, String iphone, String iccn)
```

Listing 12-2 Implementation of the Customer class

```
{
    custID = inumb;
    strcpy (fname, ifname);
    strcpy (lname, ilname);
    strcpy (street, istreet);
    strcpy (CSZ, iCSZ);
    strcpy (phone, iphone);
    strcpy (creditCardNumb, iccn);
    itemsRented = new DoubleListMgr<ItemCopy, int> ();
}

Customer::Customer (ifstream & fin)
{

    fin >> custID;
    fin.get (); // "eat" blank following integer
    fin.getline (fname, 80, '\0');
    fin.getline (lname, 80, '\0');
    fin.getline (street, 80, '\0');
    fin.getline (CSZ, 80, '\0');
    fin.getline (creditCardNumb, 80, '\0');
}

int Customer::getCustID()
    { return custID; }

DoubleListMgr<ItemCopy, int> * Customer::getList ()
    { return itemsRented; }

void Customer::write (ofstream & fout)
{
    fout << custID << ' ';
    fout << fname.getcString() << '\0';
    fout << lname.getcString() << '\0';
    fout << street.getcString() << '\0';
    fout << CSZ.getcString() << '\0';
    fout << creditCardNumb.getcString() << '\0';
}


void Customer::getKey (int & theKey)
```

Listing 12-2 (Continued) Implementation of the Customer class

```
       { theKey = custID; }

void Customer::getKey (String & theKey)
{
    theKey = lname;
    theKey += fname;
}

void Customer::addRental (ItemCopy * theItem)
    { itemsRented->insert (theItem); }

void Customer::removeRental (int key)
    { itemsRented->remove (key); }
```

Listing 12-2 (Continued) Implementation of the Customer class

The template for the double linked list manager can be found in Listing 12-3 and its node in Listing 12-4. The major change to this code from what you saw in Chapter 3 is the name of the class and its node, which was done to distinguish between the various types of list and node classes.

```
#ifndef DOUBLE_LISTMGR
#define DOUBLE_LISTMGR

#include "doublenode.h"

template <class E, class K>
class DoubleListMgr
{
    private:
        DoubleNode<E> * first, * last;
    public:
        DoubleListMgr ();
        void insert (E *);
        E * find (K); // traverse list to locate by key
        bool remove (K); // use key number to locate for removal
        DoubleNode<E> * getFirst();
        DoubleNode<E> * getLast ();
};
```

Listing 12-3   Template class for the double linked list manager

```
template <class E, class K>
DoubleListMgr<E, K>::DoubleListMgr()
{
    first = 0;
    last = 0;
}

template <class E, class K>
void DoubleListMgr<E, K>::insert (E * theElement)
{
    DoubleNode<E> * newNode, * current, * previous;
    E * currentElement;

    // create a node object
    newNode = new DoubleNode<E> (theElement);
    K newKey;
    theElement->getKey(newKey);

    if (first == 0) // list is empty
    {
        first = newNode;
        last = newNode;
    }
    else
    {
        bool firstNode = true;
        K currentKey;
        current = first; // start at head of list
        while (current != 0)
        {
            currentElement = current->getElement();
            currentElement->getKey(currentKey);
            if (newKey < currentKey)
        // spot found (between current and current's previous node)
                break;
            current = current->getNext ();
            firstNode = false; // not the first node
        }

        if (current == 0) // insert as new last node
```

Listing 12-3 (Continued) Template class for the double linked list manager

```
        {
            newNode->setPrior (last);
            last->setNext (newNode);
            last = newNode;
        }
        else if (!firstNode)  // insert in the middle of the list
        {
            previous = current->getPrior ();
            previous->setNext (newNode);
            newNode->setNext (current);
            newNode->setPrior (previous);
            current->setPrior (newNode);
        }
        else // have new first in list
        {
            first->setPrior (newNode);
            newNode->setNext (first);
            first = newNode;
        }
    }
}

template <class E, class K>
E * DoubleListMgr<E, K>::find (K searchKey)
{
    E * currentElement;
    DoubleNode * current;
    K currentKey;
    current = first; // start at head of list

    while (current != 0)
    {
        currentElement = current->getElement();
        currentElement->getKey(currentkey);
        if (searchKey == currentKey)
            return currentElement;
        current = current->getNext ();
    }
    return 0; // not found
}
```

Listing 12-3 (Continued) Template class for the double linked list manager

```
template <class E, class K>
bool DoubleListMgr<E, K>::remove (K searchKey)
{
    E * currentElement;
    DoubleNode<E> * current, * previous, * next;

    if (first == 0)
        return false; // list is empty

    bool firstNode = true;
    K currentKey;
    current = first;

    while (current != 0)
    {
        currentElement = current->getElement();
        currentElement->getKey(currentKey);
        if (searchKey == currentKey)
            break; // jump out of loop
        current = current->getNext ();
        firstNode = false; // not the first node
    }

    if (current == 0)
        return false; // node not found

    if (current->getNext () == 0) // if last node
    {
        previous = current->getPrior ();
        previous->setNext (0);
        last = previous;
    }
    else if (!firstNode) // if in the middle of the list
    {
        // get node after node being removed
        next = current->getNext ();
        // get node preceding node being removed
        previous = current->getPrior ();
        previous->setNext (next);
        next->setPrior (previous);
```

Listing 12-3 (Continued) Template class for the double linked list manager

```
        }
    else // must be first in list
        // sets first to node after node being removed
        first = current->getNext ();

    delete current; // remove node object from memory

    return true; // remove was successful
}

template <class E, class K>
DoubleNode<E> * DoubleListMgr<E, K>::getFirst()
    { return first; }

template <class E, class K>
DoubleNode<E> * DoubleListMgr<E, K>::getLast ()
    { return last; }

#endif
```

Listing 12-3 (Continued) Template class for the double linked list manager

```
#ifndef DOUBLE_NODE
#define DOUBLE_NODE

template <class E>
class DoubleNode
{
    private:
        E * theElement; // pointer to object being linked
        DoubleNode * next; // pointer to next node in list
        DoubleNode * prior; // pointer to prior node in list
    public:
        DoubleNode (E *);
        DoubleNode * getNext ();
        DoubleNode * getPrior ();
        E * getElement ();
        void setNext (DoubleNode *);
        void setPrior (DoubleNode *);
};
```

Listing 12-4   Template class for the double linked list node

```
template <class E>
DoubleNode<E>::DoubleNode (E * theObject)
{
    theElement = theObject;
    next = 0;
    prior = 0;
}

template <class E>
DoubleNode<E> * DoubleNode<E>::getNext ()
    { return next; }

template <class E>
DoubleNode<E> * DoubleNode<E>::getPrior ()
    { return prior; }

template <class E>
E * DoubleNode<E>::getElement ()
    { return theElement; }

template <class E>
void DoubleNode<E>::setNext (DoubleNode * nextNode)
    { next = nextNode; }

template <class E>
void DoubleNode<E>::setPrior (DoubleNode * priorNode)
    { prior = priorNode; }

#endif
```

Listing 12-4 (Continued) Template class for the double linked list node

Why use a linked list to hold rented items? Why not use something like a tree or hash table that provides faster access? Because a linked list is a simple, dynamic data structure that uses memory efficiently. None of the lists are likely to grow very long. (Twenty elements would be a lot, assuming the store allowed a single customer to have that many items rented at one time!) Therefore, traversing a list won't take much more time than searching any other data structure.

The linked list used in the current implementation has an integer key (the item number). Another alternative would be to use the date a rented item is due as the key. The list manager would then keep the items in chronological order. The double linked list could be used to provide access in either chronological or reverse-chronological order, depending on whether the program used an ascending or descending iterator. Note that doing this also requires that a function with a prototype of

```
void getKey (Date &);
```

be added to the `Customer` class.

12.1.2 The Merchandise Item Hierarchy

The merchandise item inheritance hierarchy represents the titles carried by the video store. As you can see in Figure 12-1, there are five classes. The concrete classes are persistent; they can write themselves to a file and read themselves back in.

`MerchandiseItem` (Listing 12-5 and Listing 12-6) is an abstract base class for all titles. It contains the variables that are common to all types of items along with a list manager for the copies of each item currently in the inventory.

The `Video` class (Listing 12-7 and Listing 12-8) is another abstract base class. The concrete classes `Movies` (Listing 12-9 and Listing 12-10) and `Other` videos (Listing 12-11 and Listing 12-12) inherit from it.

The `Game` class (Listing 12-13 and Listing 12-14) inherits directly from `MerchandiseItem`. Like the other two concrete classes in this hierarchy it must iterate through its list of copies when writing itself to a file. The video store program therefore also includes a template for an iterator of the double linked list (Listing 12-15).

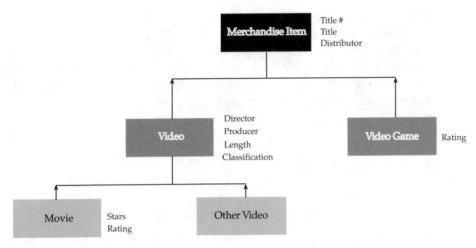

Figure 12-1   The merchandise item inheritance hierarchy

```
#ifndef MERCHANDISE_ITEM
#define MERCHANDISE_ITEM

#include "stringclass.h"
#include "doublelistmgr.h"
#include "itemcopy.h"
#include <fstream.h>

class MerchandiseItem : public Treeable
{
    protected:
        int titleNumb, copyCount, itemType;
        String title;
        String distributor;
        DoubleListMgr<ItemCopy, int> * itemList;
    public:
        MerchandiseItem ();
        MerchandiseItem (int, String, String);
        MerchandiseItem (ifstream &);
        // true = keyboard; false = file
        void addCopy (ItemCopy *, bool);
        void removeCopy (int);
```

Listing 12-5   Declaration of the MerchandiseItem class

```
        char * getTitle( );
        int getCopyCount( ); // return number of copies
        int getItemType ( );
        int getTitleNumb( );
        // check to see if any copies are available
        ItemCopy * available ( );
        virtual void write (ofstream &) = 0;
        void getKey (int &);
        void getKey (String &);
};

#endif
```

Listing 12-5 (Continued)   Declaration of the MerchandiseItem class

```
#include "merchandiseitem.h"
#include "doublelistitrasc.h"

MerchandiseItem::MerchandiseItem ()
    { }

MerchandiseItem::MerchandiseItem (int iTnumb, String iTitle,
        String iDistributor)
{
    titleNumb = iTnumb;
    copyCount = 0;
    title = iTitle;
    distributor = iDistributor;
    itemList = new DoubleListMgr<ItemCopy, int> ();
}

MerchandiseItem::MerchandiseItem (ifstream & fin)
{
    itemList = new DoubleListMgr<ItemCopy, int> ();
    fin >> titleNumb;
    fin >> copyCount;
    fin.get ();
    fin.getline (title, 80, '\0');
    fin.getline (distributor, 80, '\0');
}
```

Listing 12-6   Implementation of the MerchandiseItem class

```
void MerchandiseItem::addCopy (ItemCopy * newCopy,
     bool incrementCount)
{
   itemList->insert (newCopy);
   if (incrementCount)
      copyCount++;
}

void MerchandiseItem::removeCopy (int inventoryNumb)
{
   itemList->remove (inventoryNumb);
   copyCount--;
}

char * MerchandiseItem::getTitle()
   { return title; }

int MerchandiseItem::getCopyCount ()
   { return copyCount; }

ItemCopy * MerchandiseItem::available()
{
   DoubleListItrAsc<ItemCopy, int> * theItr =
      new DoubleListItrAsc<ItemCopy, int> (itemList);

   ItemCopy * current = theItr->getNext();
   bool status = true;
   if (current)
      status = current->getStatus();
   while (current && !status)
   {
      current = theItr->getNext();
      if (current)
         status = current->getStatus();
   }
   if (!current)
      return 0; // no copies available
   else
      return current; // first available copy
```

Listing 12-6 (Continued) Implementation of the MerchandiseItem class

```
}

int MerchandiseItem::getItemType()
    { return itemType; }

int MerchandiseItem::getTitleNumb()
    { return titleNumb; }

void MerchandiseItem::getKey (int & theKey)
    { theKey = titleNumb; }

void MerchandiseItem::getKey (String & theKey)
    { theKey = title; }
```

Listing 12-6 (Continued) Implementation of the MerchandiseItem class

```
#ifndef VIDEO
#define VIDEO

#include "stringclass.h"
#include "merchandiseitem.h"

#define MAX_STARS 20

class Video : public MerchandiseItem
{
    protected:
        String director;
        String producer;
        String classification;
        int runningTime;
    public:
        Video (int, String, String, String, String, String, int);
        Video (ifstream &);
        virtual void write (ofstream &) = 0;
};

#endif
```

Listing 12-7 Declaration of the Video class

355

```
#include "video.h"
#include <fstream.h>

Video::Video (int iTnumb, String iTitle, String iDistributor,
        String iDirector, String iProducer, String iClass,
        int iLength)
    : MerchandiseItem (iTnumb, iTitle, iDistributor)
{
    director = iDirector;
    producer = iProducer;
    classification = iClass;
    runningTime = iLength;
}

Video::Video (ifstream & fin)
    : MerchandiseItem (fin)
{
    fin.getline (director, 80, '\0');
    fin.getline (producer, 80, '\0');
    fin.getline (classification, 80, '\0');
    fin >> runningTime;
    fin.get ();
}
```

Listing 12-8 Implementation of the Video class

```
#ifndef MOVIE
#define MOVIE

#include "video.h"
#include <fstream.h>
#include "stringclass.h"

#define MOVIE_VIDEO 0

class Movie : public Video
{
    private:
        String stars[MAX_STARS]; // array of strings for stars
        int numbStars;
```

Listing 12-9 Declaration of the Movie class

```
      String rating;
   public:
      Movie (int, String, String, String, String, String, int,
         int, String [], String);
      Movie (ifstream &);
      void write (ofstream &);
};

#endif
```

Listing 12-9 (Continued) Declaration of the Movie class

```
#include "movie.h"
#include "doublelistitrasc.h"
#include "videocopy.h"

Movie::Movie (int iTnumb, String iTitle, String iDistributor,
      String iDirector, String iProducer, String iClass,
      int iLength, int inumbStars, String iStars[],
      String iRating)
   : Video (iTnumb, iTitle, iDistributor, iDirector, iProducer,
      iClass, iLength)
{
   numbStars = inumbStars;
   for (int i = 0; i < numbStars; i++)
      stars[i] = iStars[i];
   rating = iRating;
   itemType = MOVIE_VIDEO;
}

Movie::Movie (ifstream & fin)
   : Video (fin)
{
   fin >> numbStars;
   fin.get ();
   for (int i = 0; i < numbStars; i++)
      fin.getline (stars[i], 80, '\0');
   fin.getline (rating, 10, '\0');
   itemType = MOVIE_VIDEO;
}
```

Listing 12-10   Implementation of the Movie class

```
void Movie::write (ofstream & fout)
{
    fout << titleNumb << ' ';
    fout << copyCount << ' ';
    fout << title.getcString() << '\0';
    fout << distributor.getcString() << '\0';
    fout << director.getcString() << '\0';
    fout << producer.getcString() << '\0';
    fout << classification.getcString() << '\0';
    fout << runningTime << ' ';
    fout << numbStars << ' ';
    for (int i = 0; i < numbStars; i++)
        fout << stars[i].getcString() << '\0';
    fout << rating.getcString() << '\0';
    DoubleListItrAsc<ItemCopy, int> * theItr =
        new DoubleListItrAsc<ItemCopy, int> (itemList);
    ItemCopy * theCopy = theItr->getNext ();
    while (theCopy)
    {
        theCopy->write (fout);
        theCopy = theItr->getNext ();
    }
}
```

Listing 12-10 (Continued) Implementation of the Movie class

```
#ifndef OTHER
#define OTHER

#include "stringclass.h"
#include "video.h"
#include <fstream.h>

#define OTHER_VIDEO 1

class Other : public Video
{
    public:
```

Listing 12-11 Declaration of the Other class

```
        Other (int, String, String, String, String, String, int);
        Other (ifstream &);
        void write (ofstream &);
};

#endif
```

Listing 12-11 (Continued) Declaration of the Other class

```
#include "other.h"
#include "doublelistitrasc.h"
#include "videocopy.h"

Other::Other (int iTnumb, String iTitle, String iDistributor,
        String iDirector, String iProducer, String iClass,
        int iLength)
    : Video (iTnumb, iTitle, iDistributor, iDirector, iProducer,
        iClass, iLength)
        { itemType = OTHER_VIDEO; }

Other::Other (ifstream & fin)
    : Video (fin)
{
    // note: base class's constructor reads all data
    itemType = OTHER_VIDEO;
}


void Other::write (ofstream & fout)
{
    fout << titleNumb << ' ';
    fout << copyCount << ' ';
    fout << title.getcString() << '\0';
    fout << distributor.getcString() << '\0';
    fout << director.getcString() << '\0';
    fout << producer.getcString() << '\0';
    fout << classification.getcString() << '\0';
    fout << runningTime << ' ';
    DoubleListItrAsc<ItemCopy, int> * theItr =
        new DoubleListItrAsc<ItemCopy, int> (itemList);
```

Listing 12-12 Implementation of the Other class

```
    ItemCopy * theCopy = theItr->getNext ();
    while (theCopy)
    {
        theCopy->write (fout);
        theCopy = theItr->getNext ();
    }
}
```

Listing 12-12 (Continued) Implementation of the Other class

```
#ifndef GAME
#define GAME

#include "string.h"
#include "merchandiseitem.h"
#include <fstream.h>

#define VIDEO_GAME 2

class Game : public MerchandiseItem
{
    private:
        String rating;
    public:
        Game (int, String, String, String);
        Game (ifstream &);
        void write (ofstream &);
};

#endif
```

Listing 12-13 Declaration of the Game class

```
#include "game.h"
#include "doublelistitrasc.h"
#include "gamecopy.h"

Game::Game (int iTnumb, String iTitle, String iDistributor,
        String iRating)
    : MerchandiseItem (iTnumb, iTitle, iDistributor)
```

Listing 12-14 Implementation of the Game class

```
{
    rating = iRating;
    itemType = VIDEO_GAME;
}

Game::Game (ifstream & fin)
    : MerchandiseItem (fin)
{
    fin.getline (rating, 80, '\0');
    itemType = VIDEO_GAME;
}

void Game::write (ofstream & fout)
{
    fout << titleNumb << ' ';
    fout << copyCount << ' ';
    fout << title.getcString() << '\0';
    fout << distributor.getcString() << '\0';
    fout << rating.getcString() << '\0';
    DoubleListItrAsc<ItemCopy, int> * theItr =
        new DoubleListItrAsc<ItemCopy, int> (itemList);
    ItemCopy * theCopy = theItr->getNext ();
    while (theCopy)
    {
        theCopy->write (fout);
        theCopy = theItr->getNext ();
    }
}
```

Listing 12-14 (Continued) Implementation of the Game class

```
#ifndef LISTITR_ASC
#define LISTITR_ASC

#include "doublenode.h"
#include "doublelistmgr.h"

template <class E, class K>
class DoubleListItrAsc
{
```

Listing 12-15 The template class for an ascending order iterator for a double linked list

```
    private:
        DoubleNode<E> * current;
        DoubleListMgr<E, K> * theList;
    public:
        DoubleListItrAsc (DoubleListMgr<E, K> *);
        E * getNext ();
};

template <class E, class K>
DoubleListItrAsc<E, K>::DoubleListItrAsc
        (DoubleListMgr<E, K> * whichList)
{
    current = 0;
    theList = whichList;
}

template <class E, class K>
E * DoubleListItrAsc<E, K>::getNext ()
{
    if (current == 0)
        current = theList->getFirst ();
    else
        current = current->getNext ();

    if (current != 0)
        return current->getElement();
    else
        return 0;
}

#endif
```

Listing 12-15 (Continued) The template class for an ascending order iterator for a double linked list

12.1.3 The Item Copy Hierarchy

The item copy hierarchy (Figure 12-2) contains three classes: the abstract base class `ItemCopy`, `VideoCopy` for movies and other videos, and `GameCopy` for games. Although there is a logical relationship between a merchandise item and a copy of an item, it isn't an inheritance ("is a") relationship, but a one-to-many relationship (one item to many copies) in a database relationship sense. Therefore, this hierarchy must remain independent of the merchandise item hierarchy.

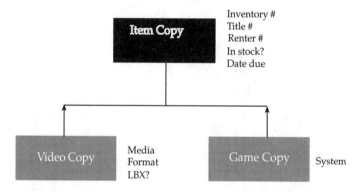

Figure 12-2 The item copy inheritance hierarchy

`ItemCopy` (Listing 12-16 and Listing 12-17) takes care of most of the basic copy functionality, including setting the variables that indicate whether a copy is rented (`status`), who rented it (`custID`), and when it is due back (`dateDue`).

```
#ifndef ITEMCOPY
#define ITEMCOPY

#include "stringclass.h"
#include "date.h"
#include "treeable.h"
#include <fstream.h>
```

Listing 12-16   Declaration of the ItemCopy class

```
class ItemCopy : public Treeable
{
    protected:
        int inventoryNumb, titleNumb, custID;
        bool status;
        Date * dateDue;
    public:
        ItemCopy ();
        ItemCopy (int, int);
        ItemCopy (ifstream &);
        void rentCopy (int, String);
        void returnCopy ();
        int getStatus();
        int getInventoryNumb();
        virtual void write (ofstream &) = 0;
        void getKey (int &);
        int getCustID ();
};

#endif
```

Listing 12-16 (Continued) Declaration of the ItemCopy class

```
#include "itemcopy.h"

ItemCopy::ItemCopy ()
    { }

ItemCopy::ItemCopy (int iNumb, int iTnumb)
{
    inventoryNumb = iNumb;
    titleNumb = iTnumb;
    custID = 0;
    status = true;
    dateDue = 0;
}

ItemCopy::ItemCopy (ifstream & fin)
{
    fin >> inventoryNumb;
```

Listing 12-17 Implementation of the ItemCopy class

```
      fin >> titleNumb;
      fin >> custID;
      fin >> status;
      fin.get ();
      String whenDue;
      fin.getline (whenDue, 80, '\0');
      if (whenDue.len() > 1)
          dateDue = new Date (whenDue);
      else
          dateDue = 0;
}

void ItemCopy::rentCopy (int renter, String whenDue)
{
   custID = renter;
   dateDue = new Date (whenDue);
   status = false;
}

void ItemCopy::returnCopy()
{
   custID = 0;
   dateDue = 0;
   status = true;
}

int ItemCopy::getStatus()
   { return status; }

int ItemCopy::getInventoryNumb()
   { return inventoryNumb; }

void ItemCopy::getKey (int & theKey)
   { theKey = inventoryNumb; }

int ItemCopy::getCustID ()
   { return custID; }
```

Listing 12-17 (Continued) Implementation of the ItemCopy class

In fact, the only reason for having VideoCopy (Listing 12-18 and Listing 12-19) and GameCopy (Listing 12-20 and Listing 12-21) is to store additional information about the specific types of copies. If the application were to be extended, it could provide for searches by, for example, game system or whether a video is letterboxed.

```cpp
#ifndef VIDEOCOPY
#define VIDEOCOPY

#include "itemcopy.h"
#include "stringclass.h"
#include <fstream.h>

class VideoCopy : public ItemCopy
{
    private:
        String media, format;
        bool LBX;
    public:
        VideoCopy (int, int, String, String, bool);
        VideoCopy (ifstream &);
        void write (ofstream &);
};

#endif
```

Listing 12-18 Declaration of the VideoCopy class

```cpp
#include "videocopy.h"

VideoCopy::VideoCopy (int iNumb, int iTnumb, String iMedia, String
iFormat, bool iLBX)
    : ItemCopy (iNumb, iTnumb)
{
    media = iMedia;
    format = iFormat;
    LBX = iLBX;
}
```

Listing 12-19 Implementation of the VideoCopy class

```
VideoCopy::VideoCopy (ifstream & fin)
   : ItemCopy (fin)
{
   fin.getline (media, 80, '\0');
   fin.getline (format, 80, '\0');
   fin >> LBX;
   fin.get ();
}

void VideoCopy::write (ofstream & fout)
{
   fout << inventoryNumb << ' ';
   fout << titleNumb << ' ';
   fout << custID << ' ';
   fout << status << ' ';
   if (dateDue != 0)
   {
       String theDate;
       fout << dateDue->showDate(theDate) << '\0';
   }
   else
       fout << '\0';
   fout << media.getcString() << '\0';
   fout << format.getcString() << '\0';
   fout << LBX << ' ';
}
```

Listing 12-19 (Continued) Implementation of the VideoCopy class

```
#ifndef GAMECOPY
#define GAMECOPY

#include "itemcopy.h"
#include "stringclass.h"
#include "date.h"
#include <fstream.h>

class GameCopy : public ItemCopy
{
   private:
```

Listing 12-20 Declaration of the GameCopy class

```
        String system;
    public:
        GameCopy (int, int, String);
        GameCopy (ifstream &);
        void write (ofstream &);
};

#endif
```

Listing 12-20 (Continued) Declaration of the GameCopy class

```
#include "gamecopy.h"

GameCopy::GameCopy (int iNumb, int iTnumb, String iSystem)
    : ItemCopy (iNumb, iTnumb)
{
    system = iSystem;
}

GameCopy::GameCopy (ifstream & fin)
    : ItemCopy (fin)
{
    fin.getline (system, 80, '\0');
}

void GameCopy::write (ofstream & fout)
{
    fout << inventoryNumb << ' ';
    fout << titleNumb << ' ';
    fout << custID << ' ';
    fout << status << ' ';
    if (dateDue != 0)
    {
        String dateString;
        fout << dateDue->showDate (dateString) << '\0';
    }
    else
        fout << '\0';
    fout << system.getcString() << '\0';
}
```

Listing 12-21 Implementation of the GameCopy class

12.2 The Utility Classes

There are three utility classes used by this program (and the pharmacy program in Chapter 13). They are included here so you can get a feeling for what they do.

12.2.1 String

Although a string class is part of the recent C++ libraries, not all compilers support that class. The sample programs therefore use the `String` class in Listing 12-22 and Listing 12-23 to make the programs more compiler-independent.

```
#ifndef STRING
#define STRING

class String
{
    // operators overloaded as friend functions

    // equal to
    friend int operator== (String, char *);
    friend int operator== (char *, String);

    // not equal to
    friend int operator!= (String, char *);
    friend int operator!= (char *, String);

    // greater than
    friend int operator> (String, char *);
    friend int operator> (char *, String);

    // greater than or equal to
    friend int operator>= (String, char *);
    friend int operator>= (char *, String);

    // less than
    friend int operator< (String, char *);
```

Listing 12-22   Declaration of the String class

```
    friend int operator< (char *, String);

    // less than or equal to
    friend int operator<= (String, char *);
    friend int operator<= (char *, String);

private:
    char cString[256]; // 255 character C string
public:
    String (); // create and initialize to null
    String (String &);
    String (char *);
    char * getcString (); // return pointer to the string itself
    int len (); // get length of string

    // overloaded operators

    // assignment
    // assignment between two String objects
    void operator= (String *);
    void operator= (char *); // assignment from a literal

    // relationship
    int operator== (String);
    int operator> (String);
    int operator>= (String);
    int operator< (String);
    int operator<= (String);
    int operator!= (String);

    // concatenation
    void operator+= (String);
    void operator+= (char *);

    // character access
    // program sends in array index; use on right side of =
    char operator[] (int);

    // type conversion (lets you use String in place of char *)
    operator char*();
```

Listing 12-22 (Continued) Declaration of the String class

```
};

#endif
```

Listing 12-22 (Continued) Declaration of the String class

```
#include <string.h>
#include "stringClass.h"

// *************************************************************
// · The String class
// *************************************************************

String::String ()  // default constructor
    { strcpy (cString,""); } // set string to null

String::String (String & inObject) // copy constructor
    { *this = inObject; }

String::String (char * inString)
    { strcpy (cString, inString); }

char * String::getcString ()
    { return cString; }

int String::len()
    { return strlen (cString); }

void String::operator= (String * inObject)
    { strcpy (cString, inObject->cString); }

void String::operator= (char * inString)
    { strcpy (cString, inString); }

int String::operator== (String inObject)
    { return (strcmp (cString, inObject.cString) == 0); }

int String::operator> (String inObject)
    { return (strcmp (cString, inObject.cString) > 0); }
```

Listing 12-23 Implementation of the String class

```
int String::operator>= (String inObject)
    { return (strcmp (cString, inObject.cString) >= 0); }

int String::operator< (String inObject)
    { return (strcmp (cString, inObject.cString) < 0); }

int String::operator<= (String inObject)
    { return (strcmp (cString, inObject.cString) >= 0); }

int String::operator!= (String inObject)
    { return (strcmp (cString, inObject.cString) != 0); }

void String::operator+= (String inObject)
    { strcat (cString, inObject.cString); }

void String::operator+= (char * inString)
    { strcat (cString, inString); }

char String::operator[] (int Index)
    { return cString[Index]; }

String::operator char*()
    { return cString; }

// operators overloaded as friend functions

int operator== (String inObject, char * inString)
    { return (strcmp (inObject.cString, inString) == 0); }

int operator== (char * inString, String inObject)
    { return (strcmp (inObject.cString, inString) == 0); }

int operator != (String inObject, char * inString)
    { return (strcmp (inObject.cString, inString) != 0); }

int operator!= (char * inString, String inObject)
    { return (strcmp (inObject.cString, inString) != 0); }

int operator> (String inObject, char * inString)
    { return (strcmp (inObject.cString, inString) > 0); }
```

Listing 12-23 (Continued) Implementation of the String class

```
int operator> (char * inString, String inObject)
   { return (strcmp (inObject.cString, inString) > 0); }

int operator>= (String inObject, char * inString)
   { return (strcmp (inObject.cString, inString) >= 0); }

int operator>= (char * inString, String inObject)
   { return (strcmp (inObject.cString, inString) >= 0); }

int operator< (String inObject, char * inString)
   { return (strcmp (inObject.cString, inString) < 0); }

int operator< (char * inString, String inObject)
   { return (strcmp (inObject.cString, inString) < 0); }

int operator<= (String inObject, char * inString)
   { return (strcmp (inObject.cString, inString) <= 0); }

int operator<= (char * inString, String inObject)
   { return (strcmp (inObject.cString, inString) <= 0); }
```

Listing 12-23 (Continued) Implementation of the String class

12.2.2 Date

The Date class used by the sample programs (Listing 12-24 and Listing 12-25) provides basic date manipulations. It stores dates internally as three integers, allowing it to handle two- and four-digit years. A program can choose to write the three individual parts of the date to a file or to write a formatted string using the showDate function. Because the class can convert a formatted string to its internal format, the video store program uses showDate when writing to a file.

```
#ifndef DATECLASS
#define DATECLASS

class Date
{
    friend Date operator+ (int, Date);
    friend Date operator+ (Date, int);

    private:
        int month, day, year;
        // convert two-digit integer back to ASCII; not part of
        // standard C libraries, although some compilers have
        // their own.
        void itoa (int, char *);
    public:
        Date (char *);
        int getMonth ();
        int getDay ();
        int getYear ();
        char * showDate (char *);
        // overloaded operators
        int operator== (Date);
        int operator!= (Date);
        int operator> (Date);
        int operator>= (Date);
        int operator< (Date);
        int operator<= (Date);
        // assignment--lets you copy one date to another
        void operator= (Date&);
};

#endif
```

Listing 12-24 Declaration of the Date class

```
#include <string.h>
#include <stdlib.h>
#include <iostream.h>
#include <math.h>
#include "date.h"
```

Listing 12-25   Implementation of the Date class

```
Date::Date (char * stringDate)
{
    char Tstring[5];
    int i = 0, j = 0;

    while (stringDate[i] != '/' && stringDate[i] != '-')
        Tstring[i++] = stringDate[i]; // copy month
    Tstring[i] = '\0';
    month = atoi (Tstring); // convert to integer
    i++; // skip over delimiter
    while (stringDate[i] != '/' && stringDate[i] != '-')
        // get day; need to start over at 0 with Tstring
        Tstring[j++] = stringDate[i++];
    Tstring[j] = '\0';
    day = atoi (Tstring); // convert to integer
    i++; // skip over delimiter
    // get rest of string for year
    strcpy (Tstring, &stringDate[i]);
    year = atoi (Tstring); // convert to integer
}

void Date::itoa (int integer, char * string)
{
    // characters, not a string
    char numbers[] = {'0','1','2','3','4','5','6','7','8','9'};
    int digit, power = 0, divisor, temp;

    temp = integer;
    while (temp > 0) // find highest power of 10
    {
        power++;
        temp /= 10;
    }

    // Note: The following decrement is necessary to avoid having a
    // leading zero in
    // front of each number. However, if you want a leading zero in
    // front of single
    // digit values (i.e., for a date), then replace the decrement
    // statement with:
    //          if (power > 1) power--;
```

Listing 12-25 (Continued) Implementation of the Date class

```
        power--;
        divisor = pow (10,power);

        for (int i = 0; i <= power; i++)
        {
            digit = integer / divisor;
            string[i] = numbers[digit];
            integer = integer % divisor;
            divisor = divisor / 10;
        }
        string[i] = '\0';
}

int Date::getMonth()
    { return month;}

int Date::getDay()
    { return day; }

int Date::getYear()
    { return year; }

char * Date::showDate (char * stringDate)
{
    char Tstring[5];

    itoa (month, Tstring);
    strcpy (stringDate, Tstring);
    strcat (stringDate, "/");
    itoa (day,Tstring);
    strcat (stringDate,Tstring);
    strcat (stringDate,"/");
    itoa (year,Tstring);
    strcat (stringDate,Tstring);
    return stringDate;
}

int Date::operator== (Date inDate)
{
    if (month == inDate.getMonth() && day == inDate.getDay() &&
            year == inDate.getYear())
```

Listing 12-25 (Continued) Implementation of the Date class

```
        return true;
    return false;
}

int Date::operator!= (Date inDate)
{
    if (month == inDate.getMonth() && day == inDate.getDay() &&
            year == inDate.getYear())
        return false;
    return true;
}

int Date::operator> (Date inDate)
{
    if (year > inDate.getYear())
        return true;
    if (year == inDate.getYear())
    {
        if (month > inDate.getMonth())
            return false;
        if (month == inDate.getMonth() && day > inDate.getDay())
            return true;
    }
    return false;
}

int Date::operator>= (Date inDate)
{
    if (*this > inDate)
        return true;
    if (*this == inDate)
        return true;
    return false;
}

int Date::operator< (Date inDate)
{
    if (year < inDate.getYear())
        return true;
    if (year == inDate.getYear())
    {
```

Listing 12-25 (Continued) Implementation of the Date class

377

```
        if (month < inDate.getMonth())
            return true;
        if (month == inDate.getMonth() && day < inDate.getDay())
            return true;
    }
    return false;
}

int Date::operator<= (Date inDate)
{
    if (*this < inDate)
        return true;
    if (*this == inDate)
        return true;
    return false;
}

void Date::operator= (Date& inDate) // copy
{
    month = inDate.getMonth();
    day = inDate.getDay();
    year = inDate.getYear();
}

Date operator+ (int days2add, Date inDate)
{
    inDate.day += days2add;
    if (inDate.month == 2 && inDate.day > 28)
    {
        inDate.day -= 28;
        inDate.month++;
    }
    else if ((inDate.month == 4 || inDate.month == 6 ||
        inDate.month == 9 || inDate.month == 11) && inDate.day > 30)
    {
        inDate.day -= 30;
        inDate.month++;
    }
    else if (inDate.day > 31)
    {
        inDate.day -= 31;
```

Listing 12-25 (Continued) Implementation of the Date class

```
        inDate.month++;
    }
    if (inDate.month > 12)
    {
        inDate.month--;
        inDate.year++;
    }
    return inDate;
}

// same as preceding but parameters are reversed
Date operator+ (Date inDate, int days2add)
{
    inDate.day += days2add;
    if (inDate.month == 2 && inDate.day > 28)
    {
        inDate.day -= 28;
        inDate.month++;
    }
    else if ((inDate.month == 4 || inDate.month == 6 ||
        inDate.month == 9 || inDate.month == 11) && inDate.day > 30)
    {
        inDate.day -= 30;
        inDate.month++;
    }
    else if (inDate.day > 31)
    {
        inDate.day -= 31;
        inDate.month++;
    }
    if (inDate.month > 12)
    {
        inDate.month--;
        inDate.year++;
    }
    return inDate;
}
```

Listing 12-25 (Continued) Implementation of the Date class

12.2.3 Menu

It's certainly not possible to provide a generic GUI for a C++ program. However, to help make the interface a bit more consistent, the sample programs use the Menu class in Listing 12-26 and Listing 12-27. The main menu (Figure 12-3) is supported by a pseudo-resource file (Listing 12-28) that is simply included in the application class implementation file.

```
#ifndef MENUCLASS
#define MENUCLASS

#include "stringclass.h"

#define MAX_ITEMS 20

class Menu      // class for a menu of up to MAX_ITEMS
{
    private:
        String menutitle;
        String menuitems [MAX_ITEMS];  // array to hold the items
        int count; // # of options in the menu

    public:
        Menu (String, String [], int); // constructor
        void displaymenu (void);
        int chooseoption (void);
};

#endif
```

Listing 12-26 Declaration of the Menu class

```
#include <iostream.h>
#include "menu.h"

Menu::Menu (String title, String menutext[], int numbItems)
{
    menutitle = title;
    count = numbItems;
```

Listing 12-27 Implementation of the Menu class

```
   for (int i = 0; i <= count; i++)
      menuitems[i] = menutext[i];
}

void Menu::displaymenu ()
{
   cout << endl;
   cout << "---------- " << menutitle << " ----------"
      << endl << endl;
   for (int i = 0; i < count; i++)
      cout << menuitems[i] << endl;
   cout << endl;
}

int Menu::chooseoption ()
{
   int choice;

   cout << "Enter an option: ";
   cin >> choice;
   cin.get();
   return choice;
}
```

Listing 12-27 (Continued) Implementation of the Menu class

12.3 *Choosing the Data Structures*

It is up to the application manipulating entity objects to declare the data structures that will organize those objects. If the entity classes have been properly designed, then they will be completely independent of any data structures in which they are used. The data structures should be able to be changed at any time without requiring modifications of the entity objects.

You can see the choices made for the video store program in the declaration of its application class (Listing 12-29). There are three vectors and two binary search trees. As you will see shortly, these structures provide fast access by a key and also rebuild properly when read back in from a data file.

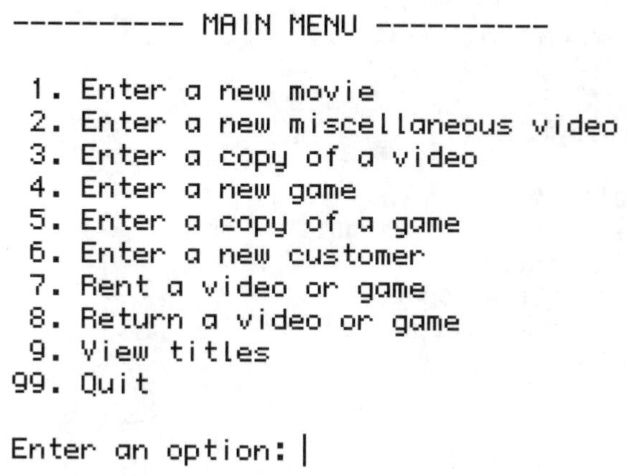

```
---------- MAIN MENU ----------

     1. Enter a new movie
     2. Enter a new miscellaneous video
     3. Enter a copy of a video
     4. Enter a new game
     5. Enter a copy of a game
     6. Enter a new customer
     7. Rent a video or game
     8. Return a video or game
     9. View titles
    99. Quit

Enter an option: |
```

Figure 12-3 The video store program's menu

```
#include "menu.h"

String maintitle = "MAIN MENU";
String mainmenu [] = {" 1. Enter a new movie",
                      " 2. Enter a new miscellaneous video",
                      " 3. Enter a copy of a video",
                    " 4. Enter a new game",
                    " 5. Enter a copy of a game",
                    " 6. Enter a new customer",
                    " 7. Rent a video or game",
                    " 8. Return a video or game",
                     " 9. View titles",
                    "99. Quit"};

int mainmenucount = 10;

const NEW_MOV = 1;
const NEW_OTH = 2;
const VID_COPY = 3;
const NEW_GAM = 4;
const GAM_COPY = 5;
const NEW_CUST = 6;
```

Listing 12-28   The resource file for the video store program's menu

```
const RENT = 7;
const RETURN = 8;
const VIEW = 9;
const MAIN_QUIT = 99;
```

Listing 12-28 (Continued) The resource file for the video store program's menu

```
#include "tree.h"
#include "vectormgr.h"
#include "customer.h"
#include "merchandiseitem.h"
#include "stringclass.h"
#include "itemcopy.h"

#define ITEMS_VECTOR_SIZE 20
#define COPIES_VECTOR_SIZE 50
#define CUST_VECTOR_SIZE 20

class AppClass
{
    private:
        VectorMgr<MerchandiseItem, int> * items;
        Tree<MerchandiseItem, String> * titles;
        VectorMgr<ItemCopy, int> * copies;
        VectorMgr<Customer, int> * customers;
        Tree<Customer, String> * names;
        int lastTitleNumb, lastCopyNumb; // kept in master file
        int movieCount, otherCount, gameCount, custCount;
        bool load ();
        bool write ();
        void enterMovie ();
        void enterOther ();
        void enterVideoCopy ();
        void enterGame ();
        void enterGameCopy ();
        void enterCustomer ();
        void rentItem ();
        void returnItem ();
        void view ();
    public:
```

Listing 12-29 Declaration of the application class for the video store program

```
        AppClass ();
        bool run ();
};
```

Listing 12-29 (Continued) Declaration of the application class for the video store program

But why use vectors instead of all trees? A vector has to be explicitly enlarged, and all its elements copied, whenever it fills. A tree never has to be copied; it doesn't even need contiguous storage, as does a vector. To answer this question, we need to look at the types of access the program requires as well as the way in which the keys are assigned.

The video store program needs the following basic types of access to its data:

- Customers by name and customer ID number.
- Merchandise items by title and title number.
- Item copies by inventory number.

Customer ID numbers, title numbers, and inventory numbers are assigned automatically by the application program. They are generated sequentially by incrementing a variable that stores the last used number of each type. What this means is that those data structures that use the numeric keys will receive the keys in numeric order. Now, consider what that does to a binary tree: You end up with the equivalent of a linked list, with every new element becoming a right child on a new level of the tree. This means that a standard binary search tree isn't a good choice in this case.

What about an AVL tree? That would rotate the elements so the tree would remain balanced. However, because the elements are entering in key order, rotations would be frequent, increasing execution time. Given that the keys arrive in order, the elements that are inserted into a vector will be in key order, already sorted. This means that you can use a binary search on the vector for quick access without having to sort the vector. In most cases, then, the vector will provide better performance than the AVL tree, with slowdowns occurring only when the vector has to be expanded. The frequency with which the vector expands can be adjusted by changing the size of the increase. (The larger the increase, the more wasted memory space but the less frequently expansion needs to occur.)

The names of customers and the titles of items arrive randomly. Therefore, a binary search tree can be used to access objects by those keys.

As mentioned earlier, the application program needs to be able to reconstruct the data structures it uses when loading data from a text file. (You don't store data structures because they use pointers; you store only the data. Each time a program runs it may be located in different areas of main memory and the pointers will be different.) The choice of an iterator for a vector is no problem: You write the data in key order and read in back in the same order.

However, you must be careful when writing binary search trees. If you use an in-order iterator, the elements will be written to a file in key order. When you read the items back, rebuilding the tree as you go, the items will arrive in order, producing a linked list. To avoid this problem, use a preorder iterator so that the tree will be rebuilt in exactly the same order as it was before it was written to the file.

12.3.1 Vector Class Enhancements

The template for the Vector class used by the video store (Listing 12-30) is slightly enhanced from that used in Chapter 8. First notice that it has been modified to handle pointers to objects rather than the objects themselves. In addition, it contains a binary search function.

```
#ifndef VECTOR_MGR
#define VECTOR_MGR

template <class E, class K>
class VectorMgr
{
    private:
        int total_elements, current_size;
        E ** theVector;
```

Listing 12-30   The Vector template class, modified to manage pointers rather than objects

```
    public:
        VectorMgr (int); // pass in initial size
        VectorMgr (VectorMgr *); // copy constructor
        ~VectorMgr ();
        bool addElement (E *); // pass in a single element
        bool addElement (E *, int); // pass in a element and index
        bool setElement (E *, int);// pass in element and index
        E * getElement (int); // pass in ordinal position of element
        // pass in ordinal position of element to delete
        bool deleteElement (int);
        // pass in key value; return ordinal value
        bool findElement (K, int & pos);
        int getNumbElements (); // return total elements in vector
        void decrementNumbElements ();
        int getSize (); // return current size
        bool isEmpty (); // true if vector is empty
        void resize (int); // pass in new size
        E * find (K);
};

template <class E, class K>
VectorMgr<E, K>::VectorMgr (int size)
{
    theVector = new E * [size];
    // holds next array index as well as total elements
    total_elements = 0;
    current_size = size;
}

template <class E, class K>
VectorMgr<E, K>::VectorMgr (VectorMgr * iVector)
{
    current_size = iVector->getSize();
    theVector = new E * [current_size];
    total_elements = iVector->getNumbElements();
    for (int i = 0; i < total_elements; i++)
        iVector->getElement (i, theVector[i]);
}

template <class E, class K>
```

Listing 12-30 (Continued) The Vector template class, modified to manage pointers rather than objects

```
VectorMgr<E, K>::~VectorMgr ()
    { delete [] theVector; }

template <class E, class K>
bool VectorMgr<E, K>::addElement (E * theElement)
{
    bool result = true;
    if (total_elements == current_size)
        result = false; // vector is full
    else
    {
        theVector [total_elements] = theElement;
        total_elements++;
    }
    return result;
}

template <class E, class K>
bool VectorMgr<E, K>::addElement (E * theElement, int index)
{
    bool result = true;
    if (index <= total_elements)
    {
        theVector [index] = theElement;
        total_elements++;
    }
    else
        result = false;
    return result;
}

template <class E, class K>
bool VectorMgr<E, K>::setElement (E * theElement, int index)
{
    bool result = true;
    if (index <= total_elements)
        theVector [index] = theElement;
    else
        result = false;
    return result;
```

Listing 12-30 (Continued)   The Vector template class, modified to manage pointers rather than objects

```
}

template <class E, class K>
E * VectorMgr<E, K>::getElement (int index)
{
    E * theElement;
    if (index >= total_elements)
        theElement = false;
    else
        theElement = theVector [index];
    return theElement;
}

template <class E, class K>
bool VectorMgr<E, K>::deleteElement (int element)
{
    bool result = true;
    if (element >= total_elements)
        result = false;
    else
    {
        for (int i = element; i < total_elements - 1; i++)
            theVector[i] = theVector[i+1];
        total_elements--;
    }
    return result;
}

template <class E, class K>
bool VectorMgr<E, K>::findElement (K searchValue, int & element)
{
    int result = true;
    int i = 0;
    while (i < total_elements)
    {
        if (theVector[i].getKey() == searchValue)
            element = i;
        i++;
    }
    if (i > total_elements)
```

Listing 12-30 (Continued)   The Vector template class, modified to manage pointers rather than objects

```
        result = false;
    return result;
}

template <class E, class K>
int VectorMgr<E, K>::getNumbElements ()
    { return total_elements; }

template <class E, class K>
void VectorMgr<E, K>::decrementNumbElements ()
    { total_elements--; }

template <class E, class K>
int VectorMgr<E, K>::getSize ()
    { return current_size; }

template <class E, class K>
bool VectorMgr<E, K>::isEmpty ()
{
    if (total_elements == 0)
        return true;
    return false;
}

template <class E, class K>
void VectorMgr<E, K>::resize (int newSize)
{
    E * newVector = new E * [newSize];
    for (int i = 0; i < total_elements; i++)
        newVector[i] = theVector[i];
    theVector = newVector;
    delete [] theVector;
    current_size = newSize;
}

template <class E, class K>
E * VectorMgr<E, K>::find (K key)
{
    int top, bottom, middle;
    top = 0;
```

Listing 12-30 (Continued)   The Vector template class, modified to manage pointers rather than objects

```
    bottom = total_elements - 1;

    bool found = false;
    E * result = 0;

    while (top <= bottom && !found)
    {
        middle = (top + bottom) / 2; // find a new middle element
        K middleKey;
        theVector[middle]->getKey(middleKey);
        if (middleKey == key)
        {
            result = theVector[middle]; // found it!
            found = true;
        }
        else if (middleKey < key)
            top = middle + 1; // in bottom half; move top down
        else
        // must be in top half; move bottom up
            bottom = middle - 1;

    }
    return result; // desired element wasn't found
}
#endif
```

Listing 12-30 (Continued)   The Vector template class, modified to manage pointers rather than objects

To create a dynamic array of pointers, you must first declare the vector itself to be a handle (a pointer to a pointer):

```
E ** theVector;
```

Then the constructor can allocate space for the array of pointers:

```
theVector = new E * [size];
```

All of the other functions in the Vector class have been modified to use the pointers. The binary search function is unchanged from what you read about in Chapter 9.

Similar modifications have been made to the vector iterator template to reflect the changes made to the vector manager (see Listing 12-31).

```
#ifndef VECTOR_ITR
#define VECTOR_ITR

#include "VectorMgr.h"

template <class E, class K>
class VectorItr
{
    private:
        VectorMgr<E, K> * theVector;
        int numb_elements;
        int current_index;

    public:
        VectorItr (VectorMgr<E, K> *, int); // pass in the vector
manager and total elements
        bool getNext (E * &);
};

template <class E, class K>
VectorItr<E, K>::VectorItr (VectorMgr<E, K> * inVector, int
iElements)
{
    theVector = inVector;
    numb_elements = iElements;
    current_index = 0;
}

template <class E, class K>
bool VectorItr<E, K>::getNext (E * & nextObject)
{
    bool result = false;
    if (current_index < numb_elements)
    {
        nextObject = theVector->getElement (current_index);
        result = true;
        current_index++;
    }
    return result;
}
```

Listing 12-31   Modified vector iterator template class

```
#endif
```

Listing 12-31 (Continued) Modified vector iterator template class

12.3.2 Tree Class Enhancements

The binary tree class template used in the video store program is the same as that in Listing 11-5 on page 322, with one exception: The node class (Listing 11-4 on page 321) has been renamed TreeNode to distinguish it from other types of nodes.

12.4 Manipulating the Data Structures within the Application Class

As well as managing the user interface, the application class is responsible for creating and manipulating the data structures used by the program. The video store's application class constructor (Listing 12-32) takes care of allocating memory for the data structures as well as initializing internal counters used by the application. All the counters are written to the data files so they can be restored during the next program run.

```
AppClass::AppClass ()
{
    items =
        new VectorMgr<MerchandiseItem, int> (ITEMS_VECTOR_SIZE);
    titles = new Tree <MerchandiseItem, String> ();
    copies = new VectorMgr<ItemCopy, int> (COPIES_VECTOR_SIZE);
    customers = new VectorMgr<Customer, int> (CUST_VECTOR_SIZE);
    names = new Tree<Customer, String> ();
    lastTitleNumb = 0;
    lastCopyNumb = 0;
    movieCount = 0;
    otherCount = 0;
    gameCount = 0;
```

Listing 12-32 Application class constructor

```
    custCount = 0;
}
```

Listing 12-32 (Continued) Application class constructor

Notice that the data structures for the items and item copies use the base classes rather than the concrete classes from which objects are actually created. This allows all items, for example, to be stored together.

12.4.1 Managing the User Interface

Given its simple user interface, the application class's run function (Listing 12-33) has only a few tasks:

```
bool AppClass::run ()
{
    bool result = load();
    if (!result)  // failure in load; user asked to cancel
        return false;

    // parameters come from menu.rsc file
    Menu * mainMenu =
        new Menu (maintitle, mainmenu, mainmenucount);
    int choice = 0;

    while (choice != MAIN_QUIT)
    {
        mainMenu->displaymenu();
        choice = mainMenu->chooseoption();
        switch (choice)
        {
            case NEW_MOV:
                enterMovie ();
                break;
            case NEW_OTH:
                enterOther ();
                break;
            case VID_COPY:
                enterVideoCopy ();
```

Listing 12-33   Application class run function

```
                    break;
            case NEW_GAM:
                enterGame ();
                break;
            case GAM_COPY:
                enterGameCopy ();
                break;
            case NEW_CUST:
                enterCustomer ();
                break;
            case RENT:
                rentItem ();
                break;
            case RETURN:
                returnItem ();
                break;
            case VIEW:
                view ();
                break;
            case MAIN_QUIT:
                result = write ();
                if (!result)
                    cout <<
                "\nWrite error. Data not saved. Exit anyway? (y/n) ";
                char yes_no;
                cin >> yes_no;
                if (yes_no == 'n')
                    choice = 0;
                break;
            default:
                cout << "\nYou've entered an unavailable option."
                    << endl;
        }
    }
    if (result)
        return true;
    else
        return false;
}
```

Listing 12-33 (Continued)   Application class run function

- Create a main menu object at the beginning of the program run.
- Call the private function that loads data into data files at the beginning of the program run.
- Display the main menu and accept a menu choice from the user.
- Analyze the menu choice and dispatch the program to the correct private function.
- When the user decides to exit the application, save the all data back to the data files.

12.4.2 File I/O

The program we are examining is RAM-based; all data reside in main memory while the program is running. (The sample program in Chapter 13 is disk-based, with data brought into RAM from disk only as needed.) The `load` and `write` functions (Listing 12-34) manage the reading and writing, respectively.

```
bool AppClass::load ()
{
    char yes_no;
    ifstream masterIn ("Master"); // master file
    if (!masterIn.is_open())
    {
        cout << "\nMaster file not found. Continue? (y/n) ";
        cin >> yes_no;
        if (yes_no == 'n')
            return false;
    }
    masterIn >> lastTitleNumb >> lastCopyNumb;
    masterIn.close();

    // Have to get customers in first so program can insert
    // copies when encountered during load
    ifstream custIn ("Customers"); // customers file
    if (!custIn.is_open())
    {
        cout << "Customers file not found. Continue? (y/n) ";
```

Listing 12-34   The application class file I/O functions

```
        cin >> yes_no;
        if (yes_no == 'n')
            return false;
        else
            return true;
    }
    custIn >> custCount;
    custIn.get ();
    Customer * newCust;
    for (int i = 1; i <= custCount; i++)
    {
        newCust = new Customer (custIn);
        customers->addElement (newCust);
        names->insert (newCust);
    }
    custIn.close();

    // read in movies
    ifstream movieIn ("Movies"); // movie file
    if (!movieIn.is_open())
    {
        cout << "Movie file not found. Continue? (y/n) ";
        cin >> yes_no;
        if (yes_no == 'n')
            return false;
    }
    movieIn >> movieCount;
    movieIn.get ();
    Movie * newMovie;
    VideoCopy * newVideo;
    for (int i = 1; i <= movieCount; i++)
    {
        newMovie = new Movie (movieIn);
        items->addElement (newMovie);
        titles->insert (newMovie);
        for (int j = 1; j <= newMovie->getCopyCount(); j++)
        {
            newVideo = new VideoCopy (movieIn);
            copies->addElement (newVideo);
            newMovie->addCopy (newVideo, false);
```

Listing 12-34   (Continued) The application class file I/O functions

```
        int custNumb = newVideo->getCustID();
        if (custNumb != 0)
        {
            Customer * theCustomer = customers->find (custNumb);
            theCustomer->addRental (newVideo);
        }
    }
}
movieIn.close();

ifstream otherIn ("Others"); // other videos file
if (!otherIn.is_open())
{
    cout << "Other video file not found. Continue? (y/n) ";
    cin >> yes_no;
    if (yes_no == 'n')
        return false;
}
otherIn >> otherCount;
otherIn.get ();
Other * newOther;
for (int i = 1; i <= otherCount; i++)
{
    newOther = new Other (otherIn);
    items->addElement (newOther);
    titles->insert (newOther);
    for (int j = 1; j <= newOther->getCopyCount(); j++)
    {
        newVideo = new VideoCopy (otherIn);
        copies->addElement (newVideo);
        newOther->addCopy (newVideo, false);
        int custNumb = newVideo->getCustID();
        if (custNumb != 0)
        {
            Customer * theCustomer = customers->find (custNumb);
            theCustomer->addRental (newVideo);
        }
    }
}
otherIn.close();
```

Listing 12-34   (Continued)The application class file I/O functions

```
ifstream gamesIn ("Games"); // games file
if (!gamesIn.is_open())
{
    cout << "Games file not found. Continue? (y/n) ";
    cin >> yes_no;
    if (yes_no == 'n')
        return false;
}
gamesIn >> gameCount;
gamesIn.get ();
Game * newGame;
GameCopy * newGC;
for (int i = 1; i <= gameCount; i++)
{
    newGame = new Game (gamesIn);
    items->addElement (newGame);
    titles->insert (newGame);
    for (int j = 1; j <= newGame->getCopyCount(); j++)
    {
        newGC = new GameCopy (gamesIn);
        copies->addElement (newGC);
        newGame->addCopy (newGC, false);
        int custNumb = newGC->getCustID();
        if (custNumb != 0)
        {
            Customer * theCustomer = customers->find (custNumb);
            theCustomer->addRental (newGC);
        }
    }
}
gamesIn.close();

    return true;
}

bool AppClass::write ()
{
    bool result = true;
    ofstream masterOut ("Master");
```

Listing 12-34 (Continued)The application class file I/O functions

```
if (!masterOut.is_open())
    { result = false;}
else
{
    masterOut << lastTitleNumb << ' ' << lastCopyNumb;

    ofstream custOut ("Customers");
    if (!custOut.is_open())
        { result = false; }
    else
    {
        custOut << custCount << ' ';
        VectorItr<Customer, int> * writer =
            new VectorItr<Customer, int> (customers, custCount);
        Customer * currentCust;
        bool validObject = writer->getNext (currentCust);
        while (validObject)
        {
            currentCust->write (custOut);
            validObject = writer->getNext (currentCust);
        }
        delete writer;

        ofstream movieOut ("Movies");
        ofstream otherOut ("Others");
        ofstream gameOut ("Games");
        if (!movieOut.is_open() || !otherOut.is_open() ||
                !gameOut.is_open())
            result = false;
        else
        {
            movieOut << movieCount << ' ';
            otherOut << otherCount << ' ';
            gameOut << gameCount << ' ';
            VectorItr<MerchandiseItem, int> * writer =
                new VectorItr<MerchandiseItem, int>
                (items, movieCount + otherCount + gameCount);
            MerchandiseItem * currentItem;
            validObject = writer->getNext (currentItem);
            int type;
```

Listing 12-34   (Continued) The application class file I/O functions

```
            while (validObject)
            {
                type = currentItem->getItemType();
                if (type == MOVIE_VIDEO)
                    currentItem->write (movieOut);
                else if (type == OTHER_VIDEO)
                    currentItem->write (otherOut);
                else
                    currentItem->write (gameOut);
                validObject = writer->getNext (currentItem);
            }
            delete writer;
        }
    }
}
    return result;
}
```

Listing 12-34   (Continued)The application class file I/O functions

The application class is mostly isolated from the internal structure of the data files. It knows the structure of the small master file that holds the last title number and last inventory number used. It also knows that each data file has a counter as the first piece of data. Beyond that, however, the layout of the data files is determined by the entity objects; that's where the actual code for reading and writing lies.

This is an essential part of object-oriented organization. The major benefit, of course, is that you can change the structure of the entity classes without having to modify the load and write functions.

> **Note:** There are certainly many ways the files for this application could be organized. All data could be kept in one file; all items and copies could be in one file and customers in another; items, copies, and customers could be in separate files. When you have a file processing application such as this one, the trick is to make the application class's load and write functions match the high-level file structure, whatever it happens to be.

As you can see in Listing 12-34, the `load` function rebuilds the data structures, just as they are built when adding new elements. The one usual aspect of this is the `MerchandiseItem` class's `addCopy` function. It has a boolean parameter that indicates whether the copy being added to an item is a new copy or whether it is being read from a file. In the latter case, the boolean suppresses the incrementing of the copy counter because the copy count has been read in from the file.

The lists of copies—whether they be item copies or copies rented by customers—are the only instance in which entity objects manage data structures. A list of item copies is a private part of each item and customer object rather than being a structure used by the application. In fact, the application object doesn't know how the copies are organized by the items and customers. Therefore, all the application has to do is give an item or customer object an item copy object and ask the item or customer object to insert the item copy into its private list.

12.4.3 Adding Objects

The functions to add objects to the video store program (Listing 12-35) all follow basically the same pattern:

- Initialize local variables to hold object data.
- Increment the counter for the type of object being created.
- Collect data from the user. (In a commercial application, this would probably be done through a dialog box or other form of data entry window, but the overall structure of the function would remain the same.)
- Create the new object.
- Insert the new object into all data structures of which it should be a part.

```
void AppClass::enterMovie ()
{
    int titleNumb, iLen;
    String iTitle, iDistributor, iDirector, iProducer, iClass;
    int numbStars = 0;
    String iStars[MAX_STARS];
```

Listing 12-35 Application class functions to add elements to the video store

```
    String iRating;

    titleNumb = ++lastTitleNumb;
    cout << "\nTitle: ";
    gets (iTitle);
    cout << "Distributor: ";
    gets (iDistributor);
    cout << "Director: ";
    gets (iDirector);
    cout << "Producer: ";
    gets (iProducer);
    cout << "Classification: ";
    gets (iClass);
    cout << "Length in minutes: ";
    cin >> iLen;
    cin.get();
    cout << "Star: ";
    cin.getline (iStars[numbStars], 80);
    while (strlen (iStars[numbStars++]) > 0)
    {
        cout << "Star: ";
        cin.getline (iStars[numbStars],80);
    }
    numbStars--;
    cout << "Rating: ";
    cin.getline (iRating, 10);
    Movie * newMovie = new Movie (titleNumb, iTitle, iDistributor,
        iDirector, iProducer, iClass, iLen, numbStars, iStars,
        iRating);
    items->addElement (newMovie);
    titles->insert (newMovie);
    ++movieCount;
}

void AppClass::enterOther ()
{
    int TitleNumb, iLen;
    String iTitle, iDistributor, iDirector, iProducer, iClass;

    TitleNumb = ++lastTitleNumb;
```

Listing 12-35 (Continued) Application class functions to add elements to the video store

```
    cout << "\nTitle: ";
    gets (iTitle);
    cout << "Distributor: ";
    gets (iDistributor);
    cout << "Director: ";
    gets (iDirector);
    cout << "Producer: ";
    gets (iProducer);
    cout << "Classification: ";
    gets (iClass);
    cout << "Length in minutes: ";
    cin >> iLen;
    Other * newOther = new Other
        (TitleNumb, iTitle, iDistributor, iDirector, iProducer,
        iClass, iLen);
    items->addElement (newOther);
    titles->insert (newOther);
    ++otherCount;
}

void AppClass::enterVideoCopy ()
{
    String iTitle, iMedia, iFormat;
    int newCopyNumb, iTitleNumb;
    char LBX;
    bool iLBX = true;

    cout << "\nTitle: ";
    cin.getline (iTitle, 80);
    MerchandiseItem * parent = titles->find (iTitle);
    if (parent == 0)
    {
        cout << "We don't stock that title.";
        return;
    }
    iTitleNumb = parent->getTitleNumb();
    newCopyNumb = ++lastCopyNumb;
    cout << "Give this copy inventory # " << newCopyNumb << endl;
    cout << "Media: ";
    cin.getline (iMedia, 10);
```

Listing 12-35 (Continued) Application class functions to add elements to the video store

```
        cout << "Format: ";
        cin.getline (iFormat, 30);
        cout << "Letterboxed? (y/n) ";
        cin >> LBX;
        if (LBX == 'n')
            iLBX = false;
        VideoCopy * newCopy = new VideoCopy
            (newCopyNumb, iTitleNumb, iMedia, iFormat, iLBX);
        parent->addCopy (newCopy, true);
        copies->addElement (newCopy);
}

void AppClass::enterGame ()
{
        int titleNumb;
        String iTitle, iDistributor;
        String iRating;

        titleNumb = ++lastTitleNumb;
        cout << "\nTitle: ";
        cin.getline (iTitle, 80);
        cout << "Distributor: ";
        cin.getline (iDistributor, 80);
        cout << "Rating: ";
        cin.getline (iRating, 10);
        Game * newGame = new Game
            (titleNumb, iTitle, iDistributor, iRating);
        items->addElement (newGame);
        titles->insert (newGame);
        ++gameCount;
}

void AppClass::enterGameCopy ()
{
        String iTitle, iSystem;
        MerchandiseItem * parent;
        int newCopyNumb, iTitleNumb;

        cout << "\nTitle: ";
        cin.getline (iTitle,80);
```

Listing 12-35 (Continued) Application class functions to add elements to the video store

```
    parent = titles->find (iTitle);
    if (parent == 0)
    {
        cout << "We don't stock that title.";
        return;
    }
    iTitleNumb = parent->getTitleNumb();
    newCopyNumb = ++lastCopyNumb;
    cout << "\nGame system: ";
    cin.getline (iSystem, 15);
    cout << "\nGive this copy inventory # " << newCopyNumb << endl;
    GameCopy * newCopy =
        new GameCopy (newCopyNumb, iTitleNumb, iSystem);
    parent->addCopy (newCopy, true);
    copies->addElement (newCopy);
}

void AppClass::enterCustomer ()
{
    String ifname, ilname, istreet, iCSZ, iphone, iccn;

    cout << "\nFirst name: ";
    cin.getline (ifname, 20);
    cout << "Last name: ";
    cin.getline (ilname, 20);
    cout << "Street: ";
    cin.getline (istreet, 20);
    cout << "City, State Zip: ";
    cin.getline (iCSZ, 20);
    cout << "Phone: ";
    cin.getline (iphone, 20);
    cout << "Credit card number: ";
    cin.getline (iccn, 20);
    Customer * newCust = new Customer (custCount, ifname, ilname,
        istreet, iCSZ, iphone, iccn);
    customers->addElement (newCust);
    names->insert (newCust);
    ++custCount;
}
```

Listing 12-35 (Continued) Application class functions to add elements to the video store

Although the current program doesn't provide functions to delete objects, doing so is straightforward because the functionality to manipulate the data in the data structures has already been coded into the data structure classes:

- Ask the user for the key of the object to be deleted.
- Use the data structure built on the key to retrieve a pointer to the object.
- Ask each data structure of which the object is a member to remove it.
- Delete the object from main memory.

12.4.4 Renting and Returning Copies

The code for renting and returning item copies can be found in Listing 12-36. To rent an item copy, the video store program must first find an available copy of the item, modify that copy so that it contains data about the rental, and insert a pointer to the copy in the customer's list of rentals. To return a copy, the application reverses the process, removing the copy from the customer's list and setting item copy data to indicate that the copy is in the store.

```
void AppClass::rentItem ()
{
    String iTitle, ifname, ilname;
    String due;

    cout << "\nCustomer's first name: ";
    cin.getline (ifname, 80);
    cout << "Customer's last name: ";
    cin.getline (ilname, 80);
    String longName = ilname;
    longName += ifname;
    Customer * renter = names->find (longName);
    if (renter == 0)
    {
        cout << "That customer isn't on file.";
        return;
    }
```

Listing 12-36 Application class functions to rent and return items

```
    cout << "Title: ";
    cin.getline (iTitle, 80);
    MerchandiseItem * item = titles->find (iTitle);
    if (item == 0)
    {
        cout << "We don't stock that title.";
        return;
    }
    ItemCopy * firstAvailable = item->available();
    if (firstAvailable == 0)
    {
        cout << "No copies of " << iTitle << " are available.";
        return;
    }
    cout << "\nThe first available copy has inventory # "
        << firstAvailable->getInventoryNumb() << ".";
    cout << "\nDate due: ";
    cin.getline (due, 20);
    firstAvailable->rentCopy (renter->getCustID(), due);
    renter->addRental (firstAvailable);
}

void AppClass::returnItem ()
{
    int copyNumb;

    cout << "\nInventory #: ";
    cin >> copyNumb;
    ItemCopy * item = copies->find (copyNumb);
    if (item == 0)
    {
        cout << "That inventory number isn't in use.";
        return;
    }
    int custID = item->getCustID ();
    Customer * renter = customers->find (custID);
    item->returnCopy();
    renter->removeRental (copyNumb);
}
```

Listing 12-36 (Continued) Application class functions to rent and return items

The `rentItem` function assumes that the user walks up to the customer service counter with an empty box. The application program then searches to find the inventory number of the first available copy, which an employee then takes from a shelf behind the counter. However, if the item copies are on the shelf, then the `rentItem` function should be modified to accept an inventory number as input, from which the program can find the copy's object.

12.5 Additional Functionality the Program Could Provide

What you have seen in this chapter is the basic structure of a sample video store program. By adding more data structures or traversing existing structures, the program could be enhanced to:

- Provide a list of overdue rentals. The program would need to traverse the customer vector. For each customer, it would traverse the linked list of rented items, comparing the current date against the date due of each rental. Those that were overdue would be written to a file and/or the screen.

- Search by genre, stars, rating, and so on. The program would need an additional data structure for each variable for which it wanted to provide a fast search. The memory and time needed to maintain the extra data structures would be balanced by faster retrieval time. Without the added data structures, the program would be reduced to performing sequential searches of existing structures. In the beginning, when the inventory was low, sequential searches might provide acceptable performance, but retrieval speed would degrade noticeably as the volume of the inventory becomes large.

- Provide customized inventory lists. Using the data structures described in the preceding paragraph, search results can be displayed on the screen or printed to leave in strategic places throughout the store.

- Modify customer data. The `Customer` class needs set functions to modify all variables except the customer ID number, which should never change. Once those are in place, customer information can be changed by finding the customer's object and setting those variables that need to be modified.

> **Note:** A full-featured video store application would also print customer statements, totaling up rental fees, taxes, and so on. It might also be programmed to interact directly with a credit card authorization service.

12.6 Summary

When choosing data structures for handling entity data, among the important criteria you should use are the following:

- The order in which the keys will arrive. In they arrive in order, then a binary search tree isn't a good choice.
- The type of access you need. If you need random access by key values, then a tree, vector, or array is a good choice. If you need sequential, in order access only, then a list is a good choice. A list is also a good choice for a small collection of items.
- The volatility of the data. If the number of elements increases frequently, then a structure such as a tree is better than a vector, which has to be increased in chunks.
- The organization of external storage files. An inorder iterator of a tree will produce a data file that will read back in as a linked list. A preorder iterator, however, will allow the tree to rebuild its original structure.

CHAPTER 13

The Corner Pharmacy

This chapter looks at a program that provides basic management of prescriptions for a small town pharmacy. It stores data about drugs (and their interactions with other medications), customers, and prescriptions. What makes the design of a program of this type so challenging is that over time the amount of data becomes quite large; it would be rare for a pharmacy to delete data. Therefore, it must be at least partially disk based.

For the purposes of this demonstration, data for the entity objects are kept in direct-access text files with fixed field lengths. Using variable field lengths is considerably more complex and given that the purpose of the application is to demonstrate the use and maintenance of data structures, using a more complex file organization would be more of a distraction than a help!

The program is controlled by a set of text-based, drill-down menus. As you might guess from seeing the main menu in Figure 13-1, the menus are produced by the same Menu class used in the video store program (see Listing 12-26 and Listing 12-27 on page 380). The three submenus (Figure 13-2) are also generated by objects of the Menu class.

```
---------- MAIN MENU ----------

1. Manage drug information
2. Manage customer information
3. Manage prescriptions
9. Quit


Enter an option: |
```

Figure 13-1 *The pharmacy program main menu*

```
---------- DRUG MENU ----------

1. Enter a new drug
2. Find drug
9. Return to main menu



Enter an option:
```
```
---------- CUSTOMER MENU ----------

1. Enter a new customer
2. Find customer
9. Return to main menu



Enter an option:
```
```
---------- PRESCRIPTION MENU ----------

1. Enter a new prescription
2. Refill a prescription
3. Find a prescription
9. Return to main menu


Enter an option: |
```

Figure 13-2 *The pharmacy program submenus*

13.1 The Entity Classes

Like the entity classes handled by the video store program, the entity classes in the pharmacy program are persistent. However, the video store program was RAM-based, and rewrote all data from sequential files at the end of every program run. The pharmacy program writes new objects immediately to a data file and then deletes the object from main memory. Each time an object's data are needed, they are read from the disk file by a constructor.

13.1.1 The Drug Class

The Drug class handles information about a medication, including its brand name, generic name, and other medications that may have adverse interactions with it. You can find the declaration of the class in Listing 13-1 and its implementation in Listing 13-2.

```
#ifndef DRUG
#define DRUG

#include "stringclass.h"
#include <fstream.h>

#define DRUG_NUMB_LENGTH 6
#define DRUG_NUMB_OFFSET 0

#define BRAND_NAME_LENGTH 30
#define BRAND_NAME_OFFSET 6

#define GENERIC_NAME_LENGTH 30
#define GENERIC_NAME_OFFSET 36

#define NUMB_INTERACTIONS_LENGTH 3
#define NUMB_INTERACTIONS_OFFSET 66

#define INTERACTION_LENGTH 30
#define INTERACTION_START_OFFSET 69
```

Listing 13-1   The declaration of the Drug class

```
#define DRUG_DEL_LENGTH 2
#define DRUG_DEL_OFFSET 369

#define DRUG_REC_LENGTH 371

#define MAX_INTERACTIONS 10

class Drug
{
    private:
        int drugNumb;
        String brandName, genericName;
        int numbInteractions;
        String interactions [MAX_INTERACTIONS];
        bool deleted;
    public:
        // constructor that loads data from disk--
        // stream is passed in
        Drug(ifstream &, int);
        // constructor that handles interactive I/O
        Drug(int, int, String, String, String [], fstream &, int);
        void write (fstream &, int); // function that writes to disk
        // check for drug interaction
        bool checkInteraction (String);
        int getDrugNumb();
        String getBrandName();
        String getGenericName ();
        void getKey (int &);
        bool getDeleted ();
        void setDeleted ();
        void undelete ();
};

#endif
```

Listing 13-1 (Continued) The declaration of the Drug class

```cpp
#include "drug.h"

// constructor that loads from disk
Drug::Drug(ifstream & fin, int recNumb)
{
    int recStart = recNumb * DRUG_REC_LENGTH;
    fin.seekg (recStart + DRUG_NUMB_OFFSET);
    fin >> drugNumb;
    fin.get ();
    fin.seekg (recStart + BRAND_NAME_OFFSET);
    fin.getline (brandName,BRAND_NAME_LENGTH,'\0');
    fin.seekg (recStart + GENERIC_NAME_OFFSET);
    fin.getline (genericName, GENERIC_NAME_LENGTH,'\0');
    fin.seekg (recStart + NUMB_INTERACTIONS_OFFSET);
    fin >> numbInteractions;
    fin.get ();

    for (int i = 0; i < numbInteractions; i++)
    {
        fin.seekg (recStart + INTERACTION_START_OFFSET +
            (i * INTERACTION_LENGTH));
        fin.getline (interactions[i],INTERACTION_LENGTH,'\0');
    }

    fin.seekg (recStart + DRUG_DEL_OFFSET);
    fin >> deleted;
}


// constructor for interactive drug entry
Drug::Drug(int idrugNumb, int inumbConflicts, String ibrandName,
        String igenericName, String iconflicts[], fstream & fout,
        int recNumb)
{
    drugNumb = idrugNumb;
    brandName = ibrandName;
    genericName = igenericName;
    numbInteractions = inumbConflicts;
    for (int i = 0; i < numbInteractions; i++)
        interactions[i] = iconflicts[i];
```

Listing 13-2   Implementation of the Drug class

415

```
    deleted = false;
    write (fout, recNumb);
}

void Drug::write (fstream & fout, int recNumb)
{
    int recStart = recNumb * DRUG_REC_LENGTH;
    fout.seekp (recStart + DRUG_NUMB_OFFSET);
    fout << drugNumb << ' ';
    fout.seekp (recStart + BRAND_NAME_OFFSET);
    fout << brandName.getcString() << '\0';
    fout.seekp (recStart + GENERIC_NAME_OFFSET);
    fout << genericName.getcString() << '\0';
    fout.seekp (recStart + NUMB_INTERACTIONS_OFFSET);
    fout << numbInteractions << ' ';
    for (int i = 0; i < numbInteractions; i++)
    {
        fout.seekp (recStart + INTERACTION_START_OFFSET +
            (i * INTERACTION_LENGTH));
        fout << interactions[i].getcString() << '\0';
    }
    fout.seekp (recStart + DRUG_DEL_OFFSET);
    fout << deleted << ' ';
}

bool Drug::checkInteraction (String drug2Check)
{
    for (int i = 0; i < numbInteractions; i++)
    {
        if (drug2Check == interactions[i] == 0 )
            return false;   // drug not OK
    }
    return true;
}

int Drug::getDrugNumb()
    { return drugNumb; }

String Drug::getBrandName()
    { return brandName; }
```

Listing 13-2 (Continued) Implementation of the Drug class

```
String Drug::getGenericName ()
    { return genericName; }

void Drug::getKey (int & key)
    { key = drugNumb; }

bool Drug::getDeleted ()
    { return deleted; }

void Drug::setDeleted ()
    { deleted = true; }

void Drug::undelete ()
    { deleted = false; }
```

Listing 13-2 (Continued) Implementation of the Drug class

The major decision that had to be made when designing the Drug class was how to store the names of interacting drugs. There was one overriding issue: The data structure had to be of fixed size because of the fixed field length file storage. An array is therefore the only data structure that can be used.

Why use a simple array instead of an array manager? Because in this case, simple is appropriate. If you look at the checkInteractions function, you will notice that it takes an incoming drug name and performs a sequential search against its array of drug names. The interactions array holds only 10 elements; the sequential search is as fast as any other type of search on such a small array. However, if you decided to increase the size of the array, you could always add a sort routine and a binary search to speed up interactions checking.

13.1.2 The Customer Class

The Customer class (Listing 13-3 and Listing 13-4) contains an array of the customer's prescriptions (called *scripts* by those in the medical field). Actually what's in the array aren't script objects, but information that will allow the program to locate a script object in the scripts data file. In this case, the data are the record numbers of the scripts. These data are not stored, but regenerated each time the program is launched. This keeps the list of scripts up to date, even if deletions have occurred between program runs.

```
#ifndef CUSTOMER
#define CUSTOMER

#include "stringclass.h"
#include "script.h"
#include "indexentry.h"
#include <fstream.h>

#define SCRIPT_ARRAY_SIZE 20

// for fixed field length I/O
#define FNAME_LENGTH 16
#define FNAME_OFFSET 0

#define LNAME_LENGTH 16
#define LNAME_OFFSET 16

#define STREET_LENGTH 31
#define STREET_OFFSET 32

#define CITY_LENGTH 21
#define CITY_OFFSET 63

#define STATE_LENGTH 3
#define STATE_OFFSET 84

#define ZIP_LENGTH 6
#define ZIP_OFFSET 87

#define PHONE_LENGTH 13
#define PHONE_OFFSET 93

#define DEL_FLAG_LENGTH 2
#define DEL_FLAG_OFFSET 106

#define NUMB_SCRIPTS_LENGTH 3
```

Listing 13-3   Declaration of the Customer class

```
#define NUMB_SCRIPTS_OFFSET 108

#define NUMB_LENGTH 6
#define SCRIPT_NUMB_START_OFFSET 111

#define CUST_REC_LENGTH 231

class Customer
{
    private:
        String fName, lName, street, city, state, zip, phone;
        int scripts[SCRIPT_ARRAY_SIZE], numbScripts;
        bool deleted;
    public:
        Customer(ifstream &, int);
        Customer(String, String, String, String, String, String,
            String, int, fstream &);
        void write (fstream &, int);
        String getZip ();
        String getLName ();
        String getFName ();
        String getStreet ();
        String getCity();
        String getState ();
        String getPhone ();
        bool getDeleted ();
        void addScript (int);
        void getKey (String &);
        void setDeleted ();
        void undelete ();
        int * getScriptArray ();
        int getNumbScripts ();
};

#endif
```

Listing 13-3 (Continued) Declaration of the Customer class

```
#include "customer.h"

Customer::Customer(ifstream & fin, int recNumb)
{
    long recStart = recNumb * CUST_REC_LENGTH;
    fin.seekg (recStart + FNAME_OFFSET);
    fin.getline (fName, FNAME_LENGTH, '\0');
    fin.seekg (recStart + LNAME_OFFSET);
    fin.getline (lName, LNAME_LENGTH, '\0');
    fin.seekg (recStart + STREET_OFFSET);
    fin.getline (street, STREET_LENGTH, '\0');
    fin.seekg (recStart + CITY_OFFSET);
    fin.getline (city, CITY_LENGTH, '\0');
    fin.seekg (recStart + STATE_OFFSET);
    fin.getline (state, STATE_LENGTH, '\0');
    fin.seekg (recStart + ZIP_OFFSET);
    fin.getline (zip, ZIP_LENGTH, '\0');
    fin.seekg (recStart + PHONE_OFFSET);
    fin.getline (phone, PHONE_LENGTH, '\0');
    fin.seekg (recStart + DEL_FLAG_OFFSET);
    fin >> deleted;
    fin.seekg (recStart + NUMB_SCRIPTS_OFFSET);
    fin >> numbScripts;

    for (int i = 0; i < numbScripts; i++)
    {
        fin.seekg (recStart + SCRIPT_NUMB_START_OFFSET +
            (i * NUMB_LENGTH));
        fin >> scripts[i];
    }
}

Customer::Customer(String ifname, String ilname, String istreet,
        String icity, String istate,
        String izip, String iphone, int recNumb, fstream & fout)
{
    fName = ifname;
    lName = ilname;
    street = istreet;
    city = icity;
```

Listing 13-4   Implementation of the Customer class

```
    state = istate;
    zip = izip;
    phone = iphone;
    deleted = false;
    numbScripts = 0;

    // store in data file
    write (fout, recNumb);
}

void Customer::write (fstream & fout, int recNumb)
{
    long recStart = recNumb * CUST_REC_LENGTH;
    fout.seekp (recStart + FNAME_OFFSET);
    fout << fName.getcString() << '\0';
    fout.seekp (recStart + LNAME_OFFSET);
    fout << lName.getcString() << '\0';
    fout.seekp (recStart + STREET_OFFSET);
    fout << street.getcString() << '\0';
    fout.seekp (recStart + CITY_OFFSET);
    fout << city.getcString() << '\0';
    fout.seekp (recStart + STATE_OFFSET);
    fout << state.getcString() << '\0';
    fout.seekp (recStart + ZIP_OFFSET);
    fout << zip.getcString()  << '\0';
    fout.seekp (recStart + PHONE_OFFSET);
    fout << phone.getcString() << '\0';
    fout.seekp (recStart + DEL_FLAG_OFFSET);
    fout << deleted << ' ';
    fout.seekp (recStart + NUMB_SCRIPTS_OFFSET);
    fout << numbScripts << ' ';

    for (int i = 0; i < numbScripts; i++)
    {
        fout.seekp (recStart + SCRIPT_NUMB_START_OFFSET +
            (i * NUMB_LENGTH));
        fout << scripts[i] << ' ';
    }
}
```

Listing 13-4 (Continued) Implementation of the Customer class

```
String Customer::getZip ()
    { return zip; }

String Customer::getLName ()
    { return lName; }

String Customer::getFName ()
    { return fName; }

String Customer::getStreet ()
    { return street; }

String Customer::getCity ()
    { return city; }

String Customer::getState ()
    { return state; }

String Customer::getPhone ()
    { return phone; }

bool Customer::getDeleted ()
    { return deleted; }

void Customer::getKey (String & theKey)
{
    theKey = lName;
    theKey += fName;
}

void Customer::setDeleted ()
    { deleted = true; }

void Customer::undelete ()
    { deleted = false; }

void Customer::addScript (int iscriptNumb)
    { scripts[numbScripts++] = iscriptNumb;}

int * Customer::getScriptArray ()
```

Listing 13-4 (Continued) Implementation of the Customer class

```
   { return scripts; }

int Customer::getNumbScripts ()
   { return numbScripts; }
```

Listing 13-4 (Continued) Implementation of the Customer class

13.1.3 The Script Class

The Script class can be found in Listing 13-5 and Listing 13-6. This class has no internal data structures. In fact, the most complicated action it performs is to handle a refill, which requires writing the date of the refill and the modified number of refills remaining back to the data file.

```
#ifndef SCRIPT
#define SCRIPT

#include "date.h"
#include "stringclass.h"
#include <fstream.h>

#define MAX_REFILLS 12

#define SCRIPT_DRUG_NUMB_LENGTH 6
#define SCRIPT_DRUG_NUMB_OFFSET 0

#define SCRIPT_NUMB_LENGTH 6
#define SCRIPT_NUMB_OFFSET 6

#define NUMB_REFILLS_LENGTH 3
#define NUMB_REFILLS_OFFSET 12

#define REFILLS_LEFT_LENGTH 3
#define REFILLS_LEFT_OFFSET 15

#define PRESCRIBER_LENGTH 50
#define PRESCRIBER_OFFSET 18
```

Listing 13-5 Declaration of the Script class

```
#define PRESCRIBER_PHONE_LENGTH 13
#define PRESCRIBER_PHONE_OFFSET 68

#define CUST_FNAME_LENGTH 16
#define CUST_FNAME_OFFSET 81

#define CUST_LNAME_LENGTH 16
#define CUST_LNAME_OFFSET 97

#define DOSE_LENGTH 30
#define DOSE_OFFSET 113

#define INSTRUCTIONS_LENGTH 255
#define INSTRUCTIONS_OFFSET 143

#define QUANTITY_LENGTH 4
#define QUANTITY_OFFSET 398

#define DATE_LENGTH 9
#define SCRIPT_DATE_OFFSET 402

#define REFILL_DATE_START_OFFSET 411

#define SCRIPT_DEL_FLAG_LENGTH 2
#define SCRIPT_DEL_FLAG_OFFSET 591

#define SCRIPT_REC_LENGTH 593

class Script
{
    private:
        int drugNumb;
        int scriptNumb, numbRefills, refillsLeft;
        String prescriber, prescriberPhone, custFName, custLName;
        String dose, instructions;
        int quantity;
        Date * scriptDate, * refillDates[MAX_REFILLS];
        bool deleted;
```

Listing 13-5 (Continued) Declaration of the Script class

```
public:
    Script (ifstream &, int);
    Script (int, int, int, String, String, String, String,
        String, String, int, String, fstream &, int);
    void write (fstream &, int);
    bool refill(String, fstream &, int);
    String getFName ();
    String getLName ();
    String getPrescriber();
    String getPrescriberPhone();
    int getScriptNumb ();
    int getDrugNumb ();
    String getDose ();
    String getInstructions ();
    int getQuantity ();
    Date * getScriptDate ();
    int getNumbRefills ();
    int getRefillsLeft ();
    Date ** getRefillDates ();
    void getKey (int &);
    bool getDeleted ();
    void setDeleted ();
    void undelete ();
};

#endif
```

Listing 13-5 (Continued) Declaration of the Script class

```
#include "script.h"
#include "customer.h"

Script::Script (ifstream & fin, int recNumb)
{
    String dateString;
    long recStart = recNumb * SCRIPT_REC_LENGTH;
    fin.seekg (recStart + SCRIPT_DRUG_NUMB_OFFSET);
    fin >> drugNumb;
    if (fin.eof())
        return;
```

Listing 13-6   Implementation of the Script class

```
    fin.seekg (recStart + SCRIPT_NUMB_OFFSET);
    fin >> scriptNumb;
    fin.seekg (recStart + NUMB_REFILLS_OFFSET);
    fin >> numbRefills;
    fin.seekg (recStart + REFILLS_LEFT_OFFSET);
    fin >> refillsLeft;
    fin.seekg (recStart + PRESCRIBER_OFFSET);
    fin.getline (prescriber, PRESCRIBER_LENGTH,'\0');
    fin.seekg (recStart + PRESCRIBER_PHONE_OFFSET);
    fin.getline (prescriberPhone, PRESCRIBER_PHONE_LENGTH,'\0');
    fin.seekg (recStart + CUST_FNAME_OFFSET);
    fin.getline (custFName, CUST_FNAME_LENGTH, '\0');
    fin.seekg (recStart + CUST_LNAME_OFFSET);
    fin.getline (custLName, CUST_LNAME_LENGTH, '\0');
    fin.seekg (recStart + DOSE_OFFSET);
    fin.getline (dose, DOSE_LENGTH, '\0');
    fin.seekg (recStart + INSTRUCTIONS_OFFSET);
    fin.getline (instructions, INSTRUCTIONS_LENGTH, '\0');
    fin.seekg (recStart + QUANTITY_OFFSET);
    fin >> quantity;
    fin.seekg (recStart + SCRIPT_DATE_OFFSET);
    fin.getline (dateString, DATE_LENGTH,'\0');
    if (dateString.len() > 0)
        scriptDate = new Date (dateString);

    for (int i = 0; i < (numbRefills - refillsLeft); i++)
    {
        fin.seekg (recStart + REFILL_DATE_START_OFFSET +
            (i * DATE_LENGTH));
        fin.getline (dateString, DATE_LENGTH,'\0');
        refillDates[i] = new Date (dateString);
    }

    fin.seekg (recStart + SCRIPT_DEL_FLAG_OFFSET);
    fin >> deleted;
}
```

Listing 13-6 (Continued) Implementation of the Script class

```
Script::Script (int idrugNumb, int iscriptNumb, int inumbRefills,
        String iprescriber, String iprescriberPhone,
        String iFName, String iLName, String idose,
        String iinstructions, int iquantity,
        String iprescriptionDate, fstream & fout, int recNumb)
{
    drugNumb = idrugNumb;
    scriptNumb = iscriptNumb;
    numbRefills = inumbRefills;
    refillsLeft = numbRefills;
    prescriber = iprescriber;
    prescriberPhone = iprescriberPhone;
    custFName = iFName;
    custLName = iLName;
    dose  = idose;
    instructions = iinstructions;
    quantity = iquantity;
    scriptDate = new Date (iprescriptionDate);
    deleted = false;

    write (fout, recNumb);
}

void Script::write (fstream & fout, int recNumb)
{
    String dateString;
    long recStart = recNumb * SCRIPT_REC_LENGTH;

    fout.seekp (recStart + SCRIPT_DRUG_NUMB_OFFSET);
    fout << drugNumb << ' ';
    fout.seekp (recStart + SCRIPT_NUMB_OFFSET);
    fout << scriptNumb << ' ';
    fout.seekp (recStart + NUMB_REFILLS_OFFSET);
    fout << numbRefills << ' ';
    fout.seekp (recStart + REFILLS_LEFT_OFFSET);
    fout << refillsLeft << ' ';
    fout.seekp (recStart + PRESCRIBER_OFFSET);
    fout << prescriber.getcString() << '\0';
    fout.seekp (recStart + PRESCRIBER_PHONE_OFFSET);
    fout << prescriberPhone.getcString() << '\0';
```

Listing 13-6 (Continued) Implementation of the Script class

```
    fout.seekp (recStart + CUST_FNAME_OFFSET);
    fout << custFName.getcString() << '\0';
    fout.seekp (recStart + CUST_LNAME_OFFSET);
    fout << custLName.getcString() << '\0';
    fout.seekp (recStart + DOSE_OFFSET);
    fout << dose.getcString() << '\0';
    fout.seekp (recStart + INSTRUCTIONS_OFFSET);
    fout << instructions.getcString() << '\0';
    fout.seekp (recStart + QUANTITY_OFFSET);
    fout << quantity << ' ';
    fout.seekp (recStart + SCRIPT_DATE_OFFSET);
    fout << scriptDate->showDate (dateString) << '\0';

    for (int i = 0; i < (numbRefills - refillsLeft); i++)
    {
        fout.seekp (recStart + REFILL_DATE_START_OFFSET +
            (i * DATE_LENGTH));
        fout << refillDates[i]->showDate (dateString) << '\0';
    }
    fout.seekp (recStart + SCRIPT_DEL_FLAG_OFFSET);
    fout << deleted << ' ';
}


bool Script::refill(String refillDate, fstream & fout,
        int recNumb)
{
    if (refillsLeft > 0)
    {
        int index = numbRefills - refillsLeft;
        refillDates [index] = new Date (refillDate);
        fout.seekp (recNumb * SCRIPT_REC_LENGTH +
            index * DATE_LENGTH + REFILL_DATE_START_OFFSET);
        int pos = fout.tellp();
        String dateString;
        fout << refillDates[index]->showDate (dateString) << '\0';
        refillsLeft--;
        fout.seekp (recNumb * SCRIPT_REC_LENGTH +
            REFILLS_LEFT_OFFSET);
        pos = fout.tellp ();
```

Listing 13-6 (Continued) Implementation of the Script class

```
        fout << refillsLeft << ' ';
        return true;
    }
    else
        return false;
}

// no mutators; can't modify script; must write a new one
String Script::getFName()
    { return custFName; }

String Script::getLName ()
    { return custLName; }

String Script::getPrescriber ()
    { return prescriber; }

String Script::getPrescriberPhone ()
    { return prescriberPhone; }

int Script::getScriptNumb()
    { return scriptNumb; }

int Script::getDrugNumb()
    { return drugNumb; }

String Script::getDose ()
    { return dose; }

String Script::getInstructions ()
    { return instructions; }

int Script::getQuantity ()
    { return quantity; }

Date * Script::getScriptDate ()
    { return scriptDate; }

int Script::getNumbRefills ()
    { return numbRefills; }
```

Listing 13-6 (Continued) Implementation of the Script class

```
int Script::getRefillsLeft ()
    { return refillsLeft; }

Date ** Script::getRefillDates ()
    { return refillDates; }

void Script::getKey (int & key)
    { key = scriptNumb; }
```

Listing 13-6 (Continued) Implementation of the Script class

13.1.4 Note on Deletions

Although the pharmacy will seldom delete data, the classes you have just seen are designed to support deletion. Each has a `deleted` flag that indicates whether an object has been deleted. The intent is that deletion merely flags the object as deleted but doesn't bother to remove it from the file. Until the files are rewritten without deleted objects, they can be undeleted by simply changing the value of the flag.

When deletion support is added to the program, the following two things must happen:

- The `buildIndexes` function must check the `deleted` flag for each object as it is read from the file and must ignore deleted objects.
- A `pack` function must be added. This function rewrites the data files, omitting deleted objects. It must then rebuild all the RAM-based indexes.

> **Note:** The pharmacy program also uses the `String` (Listing 12-22 on page 369 and Listing 12-23 on page 371) and `Date` (Listing 12-24 on page 374 and Listing 12-25 on page 374) utility classes from the video store program.

13.2 Choosing the Data Structures for File Access

The biggest choice that must be made for a program of this type is deciding how to provide access to the data in the files. To read the data, you have to know where an object is stored in a file. In this example, which uses a simple file organization, an object's record number provides enough information to locate it—well, that plus the object's own knowledge of how data are laid out in a record. The constants in each entity class header file provide that information as well as the total length of a record.

Therefore, an index to a data file needs a key on which you can search and a record number. Given that this is a pair of two values, you might at first consider using an `Association`. An association, however, may be too restrictive for use in a data structure other than a dictionary.

Therefore, the index entries are objects of the class `IndexEntry` (Listing 13-7). This class supports a mutable key. However, keep in mind that if you modify the key, you will in all likelihood end up with the object in the wrong location in its data structure. You will therefore need to remove the object, modify its key, and then reinsert it into the data structure so that it is in the correct place.

```
#ifndef INDEXENTRY
#define INDEXENTRY

#include "stringclass.h"

template <class V, class K>
class IndexEntry
{
    private:
        V theValue;
        K theKey;
    public:
        IndexEntry (V, K);
        V getValue ();
        K getKey ();
```

Listing 13-7   *The IndexEntry template class*

```
        void getKey (K &);
        void setValue (V);
        void setKey (K);
};

template <class V, class K>
IndexEntry<V, K>::IndexEntry (V ivalue, K ikey)
{
    theValue = ivalue;
    theKey = ikey;
}

template <class V, class K>
V IndexEntry<V, K>::getValue ()
    { return theValue; }

template <class V, class K>
K IndexEntry<V, K>::getKey ()
    { return theKey; }

template <class V, class K>
void IndexEntry<V, K>::getKey (K & rkey)
    { rkey = theKey; }

template <class V, class K>
void IndexEntry<V, K>::setValue (V ivalue)
    { theValue = ivalue; }

template <class V, class K>
void IndexEntry<V, K>::setKey (K ikey)
    { theKey = ikey; }

#endif
```

Listing 13-7 (Continued) The IndexEntry template class

The most commonly used data structures for file indexes are B-Trees. The pharmacy program maintains three B-Trees, one for each entity class. You can find the template version of the B-Tree node in Listing 13-8. The B-Tree template class itself appears in Listing 13-9. Other than being turned into templates these classes are unmodified from the original classes you first saw in Chapter 7.

```
#ifndef B_NODE
#define B_NODE

#include "stringclass.h"

#define MAX 4   // maximum keys per node
#define MIN 2   // minimum keys per new subtree

template <class E, class K>
class BNode
{
    private:
        int numbElements;
        BNode<E, K> * branches [MAX+1];
        // elements[0] is not used
        E * elements [MAX+1]; // use getKey() to retrieve keys
    public:
        BNode ();
        int getNumbElements ();
        K getKey (int); // gets key for a specified  object
        E * getElement (int);
        BNode<E, K> * getBranch (int);
        void setNumbElements (int);
        void setBranch (int, BNode<E, K> *);
        void setElement (int, E *);
};

template <class E, class K>
BNode<E, K>::BNode ()
{
    for (int i = 0; i <= MAX; i++)
        branches[i] = 0;
    for (int i = 0; i < MAX; i++)
        elements[i] = 0;
    numbElements = 0;
}
```

Listing 13-8   The BNode template class

```
template <class E, class K>
int BNode<E, K>::getNumbElements ()
    { return numbElements; }

template <class E, class K>
K BNode<E, K>::getKey (int index)
{
    K key;
    elements[index]->getKey(key);
    return key;
}

template <class E, class K>
E * BNode<E, K>::getElement (int index)
    { return elements[index]; }

template <class E, class K>
BNode<E, K> * BNode<E, K>::getBranch (int index)
    { return branches[index]; }

template <class E, class K>
void BNode<E, K>::setNumbElements (int value)
    { numbElements = value; }

template <class E, class K>
void BNode<E, K>::setBranch (int index, BNode * theNode)
    { branches[index] = theNode; }

template <class E, class K>
void BNode<E,K>::setElement (int index, E * theElement)
    { elements[index] = theElement; }

#endif
```

Listing 13-8 (Continued) *The BNode template class*

```
#ifndef B_TREE
#define B_TREE

#include "bnode.h"
#include "stringclass.h"
#include <iostream.h>

template <class E, class K>
class BTree
{
    private:
        BNode<E, K> * root;
        // used by find function
        bool search (K, BNode<E, K> *, BNode<E, K> * &, int &);
        bool searchNode (K, BNode<E, K> *, int &);
        // used by insert function
        bool pushDown (E *, BNode<E, K> *, E * &, BNode<E, K> * &);
        void pushIn (E *, BNode<E, K> *, BNode<E, K> *, int);
        void split (E *, BNode<E, K> *, BNode<E, K> *, int, E * &,
            BNode<E, K> * &);
        // used by deleteElement function
        bool recursiveDelete (K, BNode<E, K> *);
        void remove (BNode<E, K> *, int);
        void successor (BNode<E, K> *, int);
        void restore (BNode<E, K> *, int);
        void moveRight (BNode<E, K> *, int);
        void moveLeft (BNode<E, K> *, int);
        void combine (BNode<E, K> *, int);
    public:
        BTree ();
        void insert (E *); // initiate an insertion
        E * find (K); // initiate a search
        bool isEmpty ();
        bool deleteElement (K); // initiate a deletion
};

template <class E, class K>
BTree<E, K>::BTree ()
{
    root = 0;
}
```

Listing 13-9   The BTree template class

435

```
template <class E, class K>
void BTree<E, K>::insert (E * newElement)
{
    BNode<E, K> * rightSubtree;
    E * insertedElement;
    bool pushUp = pushDown (newElement, root, insertedElement,
        rightSubtree);
    if (pushUp)
    {
        BNode<E, K> * newNode = new BNode<E, K> ();
        newNode->setNumbElements (1);
        newNode->setElement (1, insertedElement);
        newNode->setBranch (0, root);
        newNode->setBranch (1, rightSubtree);
        root = newNode;
    }
}

template <class E, class K>
bool BTree<E, K>::pushDown (E * newElement,
        BNode<E, K> * currentNode, E * & insertedElement,
        BNode<E, K> * & rightSubtree)
{
    int position;
    bool found, pushUp;
    if (currentNode == 0)
    {
        pushUp = true;
        insertedElement = newElement;
        rightSubtree = 0;
    }
    else
    {
        K key;
        newElement->getKey (key);
        found = searchNode (key, currentNode, position);
        if (found)
            cout << "\nWarning: Inserting duplicate key.";
        pushUp = pushDown (newElement,
            currentNode->getBranch(position),insertedElement,
            rightSubtree);
```

Listing 13-9 (Continued) The BTree template class

```
        if (pushUp)
        {
            if (currentNode->getNumbElements() < MAX)
            {
                pushUp = false;
                pushIn (insertedElement, rightSubtree, currentNode,
                    position);
            }
            else
            {
                pushUp = true;
                split (newElement, rightSubtree, currentNode,
                    position, insertedElement, rightSubtree);
            }
        }
    }
    return pushUp;
}

template <class E, class K>
void BTree<E, K>::pushIn (E * newElement,
        BNode<E, K> * rightSubtree, BNode<E, K> * currentNode,
        int position)
{
    int elements = currentNode->getNumbElements();
    int i;
    for (i = elements; i >= position + 1; i--)
    {
        currentNode->setElement (i + 1,
            currentNode->getElement (i));
        currentNode->setBranch (i + 1, currentNode->getBranch (i));
    }
    currentNode->setElement (i + 1, newElement);
    currentNode->setBranch (position + 1, rightSubtree);
    currentNode->setNumbElements (elements + 1);
}

template <class E, class K>
void BTree<E, K>::split (E * newElement,
        BNode<E, K> * rightSubtree, BNode<E, K> * currentNode,
        int position,
```

Listing 13-9 (Continued) The BTree template class

```
      E * & medianElement, BNode<E, K> * & newRightSubtree)
{
    int median;

    if (position <= MIN)
        median = MIN;
    else
        median = MIN + 1;
    newRightSubtree = new BNode<E, K> ();
    for (int i = median + 1; i <= MAX; i++)
    {
        newRightSubtree->setElement (i - median,
            currentNode->getElement (i));
        newRightSubtree->setBranch (i - median,
            currentNode->getBranch (i));
    }
    newRightSubtree->setNumbElements (MAX - median);

    currentNode->setNumbElements (median);

    if (position <= MIN)
        pushIn (newElement, rightSubtree, currentNode, position);
    else
        pushIn (newElement, rightSubtree, newRightSubtree,
            position - median);
    int elements = currentNode->getNumbElements();
    medianElement = currentNode->getElement (elements);
    newRightSubtree->setBranch
        (0, currentNode->getBranch (elements));
    currentNode->setNumbElements (elements - 1);
}

template <class E, class K>
E * BTree<E, K>::find (K key)
{
    // start search
    BNode<E, K> * foundNode = 0;
    int position;
    bool found = search (key, root, foundNode, position);
    // handle result
    if (found)
```

Listing 13-9 (Continued) The BTree template class

```
            return foundNode->getElement (position);
    else
        return 0;
}


template <class E, class K>
bool BTree<E, K>::search (K key, BNode<E, K> * currentNode,
        BNode<E, K> * & foundNode, int & position)
{
    bool found;
    if (currentNode == 0)
        found = false;
    else
    {
        found = searchNode (key, currentNode, position);
        if (found)
            foundNode = currentNode;
        else
            found = search (key, currentNode->getBranch(position),
                foundNode, position) ;
    }
    return found;
}


// sequential search of a single node
template <class E, class K>
bool BTree<E, K>::searchNode (K key, BNode<E, K> * currentNode,
        int & position)
{
    bool found = false;
    if (key < currentNode->getKey(1))
        position = 0;
    else
    {
        position = currentNode->getNumbElements();
        while (key < currentNode->getKey(position) && position > 1)
            position--;
        found = (key == currentNode->getKey(position));
    }
    return found;
}
```

Listing 13-9 (Continued) The BTree template class

```
template <class E, class K>
bool BTree<E, K>::isEmpty ()
   { return (root == 0); }

template <class E, class K>
bool BTree<E, K>::deleteElement (K key)
{
   bool found;
   found = recursiveDelete (key, root);
   if (found && root->getNumbElements() == 0)
      root = root->getBranch(0);
   return found;
}

template <class E, class K>
bool BTree<E, K>::recursiveDelete (K key,
      BNode<E, K> * currentNode)
{
   int position;
   bool found;

   if (currentNode == 0)
      found = false;
   else
   {
      found = searchNode (key, currentNode, position);
      if (found)
      {
         if (currentNode->getBranch (position - 1) == 0)
            remove (currentNode, position);
         else
         {
            successor (currentNode, position);
            found = recursiveDelete
               (currentNode->getKey (position),
               currentNode->getBranch (position));
         }
      }
      else
      {
```

Listing 13-9 (Continued) The BTree template class

```
                found = recursiveDelete (key,
                    currentNode->getBranch (position));
            }
            BNode * branchNode = currentNode->getBranch (position);
            if (branchNode != 0 && branchNode->getNumbElements () < MIN)
                restore (currentNode, position);
        }
        return found;
}

template <class E, class K>
void BTree<E, K>::remove (BNode<E, K> * currentNode, int position)
{
    for (int i = position + 1; i <= currentNode->getNumbElements();
            i++)
    {
        currentNode->setElement (i-1, currentNode->getElement (i));
        currentNode->setBranch (i-1, currentNode->getBranch (i));
    }
    currentNode->setNumbElements
        (currentNode->getNumbElements() - 1);
}

template <class E, class K>
void BTree<E, K>::successor (BNode<E, K> * currentNode,
        int position)
{
    BNode<E, K> * branchNode = currentNode->getBranch (position);
    while (branchNode->getBranch (0) != 0)
        branchNode = branchNode->getBranch (0);
    currentNode->setElement (position, branchNode->getElement (1));
}

template <class E, class K>
void BTree<E, K>::restore (BNode<E, K> * currentNode,
        int position)
{
    if (position == 0) // leftmost element
    {
        BNode<E, K> * branchNode = currentNode->getBranch (1);
        if (branchNode->getNumbElements() > MIN)
```

Listing 13-9 (Continued) The BTree template class

```
            moveLeft (currentNode, 1);
        else
            combine (currentNode, 1);
    }
    // rightmost element
    else if (position == currentNode->getNumbElements())
    {
        BNode<E, K> * branchNode = currentNode->getBranch
        (position - 1);
        if (branchNode->getNumbElements() > MIN)
            moveRight (currentNode, position);
        else
            combine (currentNode, position);
    }
    else // middle elements
    {
        BNode<E, K> * branchNode = currentNode->getBranch
            (position - 1);
        if (branchNode->getNumbElements() > MIN)
            moveRight (currentNode, position);
        else
        {
            branchNode = currentNode->getBranch (position + 1);
            if (branchNode->getNumbElements () > MIN)
                moveLeft (currentNode, position + 1);
            else
                combine (currentNode, position);
        }
    }
}

template <class E, class K>
void BTree<E, K>::moveRight (BNode<E, K> * currentNode,
      int position)
{
    BNode<E, K> * branchNode = currentNode->getBranch (position);
    for (int i = branchNode->getNumbElements(); i >= 1; i++)
    {
        branchNode->setElement (i + 1, branchNode->getElement (i));
        branchNode->setBranch (i +  1, branchNode->getBranch (i));
    }
```

Listing 13-9 (Continued) The BTree template class

```
    branchNode->setBranch (1, branchNode->getBranch (0));
    branchNode->setNumbElements (branchNode->getNumbElements() +
1);
    branchNode->setElement (1, currentNode->getElement (position));

    BNode<E, K> * branchNode2 = currentNode->getBranch
        (position - 1);
    currentNode->setElement (position,
        branchNode2->getElement (branchNode2->getNumbElements()));

    branchNode->setBranch
        (0, branchNode2->getBranch
        (branchNode2->getNumbElements()));
    branchNode2->setNumbElements
        (branchNode2->getNumbElements() - 1);
}

template <class E, class K>
void BTree<E, K>::moveLeft (BNode<E, K> * currentNode,
        int position)
{
    BNode * branchNode = currentNode->getBranch (position - 1);
    branchNode->setNumbElements
        (branchNode->getNumbElements() + 1);
    branchNode->setElement
        (branchNode->getNumbElements(),
        currentNode->getElement (position));
    BNode * branchNode2 = currentNode->getBranch (position);
    branchNode->setBranch (branchNode->getNumbElements(),
        branchNode2->getBranch (0));

    currentNode->setElement (position,
        branchNode2->getElement (1));
    branchNode2->setBranch (0, branchNode2->getBranch (1));
    branchNode2->setNumbElements
        (branchNode2->getNumbElements() - 1);

    for (int i = 1; i <= branchNode2->getNumbElements(); i++)
    {
        branchNode2->setElement
            (i, branchNode2->getElement (i + 1));
```

Listing 13-9 (Continued) The BTree template class

443

```
            branchNode2->setBranch (i, branchNode2->getBranch (i + 1));
    }
}

template <class E, class K>
void BTree<E, K>::combine (BNode<E, K> * currentNode,
        int position)
{
    BNode<E, K> * branchNode = currentNode->getBranch (position);
    BNode<E, K> * branchNode2 =
        currentNode->getBranch (position - 1);

    branchNode2->setNumbElements
        (branchNode2->getNumbElements() + 1);
    branchNode2->setElement
        (branchNode2->getNumbElements(),
        currentNode->getElement (position));
    branchNode2->setBranch
        (branchNode2->getNumbElements (),
        branchNode->getBranch (0));
    for (int i = 1; i <= branchNode->getNumbElements (); i++)
    {
        branchNode2->setNumbElements
            (branchNode2->getNumbElements() + 1);
        branchNode2->setElement
            (branchNode2->getNumbElements(),
            branchNode->getElement (i));
        branchNode2->setBranch (branchNode2->getNumbElements(),
            branchNode->getBranch (i));
    }
    for (int i = position;
            i <= currentNode->getNumbElements () - 1; i++)
    {
        currentNode->setElement
            (i, currentNode->getElement (i + 1));
        currentNode->setBranch (i, currentNode->getBranch (i + 1));
    }
    currentNode->setNumbElements(currentNode->getNumbElements()-1);
}

#endif
```

Listing 13-9 (Continued) The BTree template class

The pharmacy program also uses one dictionary to store a combination of the generic and brand names of drugs. The association object that is used in the dictionary has a drug name as its key and a drug number that can be used to search the drugs B-Tree as its value. The Association (Listing 13-10) and Dictionary (Listing 13-11) classes have been turned into templates without requiring any code changes.

```
#ifndef ASSOCIATION
#define ASSOCIATION

#include "stringclass.h"

template <class K, class V>
class Association
{
   private:
      K key; // key cannot be modified
      V value;
   public:
      Association (K, V);
      void getKey (K &);
      V getValue ();
      void setValue (V);
};

template <class K, class V>
Association<K, V>::Association (K iKey, V iValue)
{
   key = iKey;
   value = iValue;
}

template <class K, class V>
void Association<K, V>::getKey (K & oKey)
   { oKey = key; }

template <class K, class V>
V Association<K, V>::getValue ()
   { return value; }
```

Listing 13-10   The Association template class

```
template <class K, class V>
void Association<K, V>::setValue (V iValue)
   { value = iValue; }

#endif
```

Listing 13-10 (Continued) The Association template class

```
#ifndef DICTIONARY
#define DICTIONARY

#include "association.h"
#include "tree.h" // template for binary search tree; includes
node.h
#include "stringclass.h"
#include "preorderitr.h"

template <class V, class K>
class Dictionary
{
   private:
      V defaultValue;
      Tree <Association<K, V>, K> * theTree;
   public:
      Dictionary ();
      // sets default value
      Dictionary (V);
      V operator [] (K);
      Association<K, V> * getAssociation (K);
      // Lets dictionary do the work rather than asking
application class
      // to make a call to the association object.
      // Similar to operator [] but doesn't create an assoication
if the
      // key isn't found.
      V getValue (K);
      void insert (Association<K, V> *);
      void deleteAllValues ();
      bool includesKey (K);
      bool isEmpty ();
```

Listing 13-11 The Dictionary template class

```
        bool removeKey (K);
        // set a default value for new associations
        void setDefault (V);
        Tree<Association<K, V>, int> * getTree ();
};

template <class V, class K>
Dictionary<V, K>::Dictionary ()
{
    theTree = new Tree<Association<K, V>, K> ();
}

template <class V, class K>
Dictionary<V, K>::Dictionary (V iDefault)
{
    theTree = new Tree<Association<K, V>, K> ();
    defaultValue = iDefault;
}

template <class V, class K>
void Dictionary<V, K>::insert (Association<K, V> * newAssociation)
    { theTree->insert (newAssociation); }

template <class V, class K>
V Dictionary<V, K>::operator[] (K key)
{
    Association<K, V> * theAssociation = getAssociation (key);
    // if not already in tree, create an association for this key
    if (!theAssociation)
    {
        theAssociation = new Association<K, V> (key, defaultValue);
        theTree->insert (theAssociation);
    }
    return theAssociation->getValue();
}

template <class V, class K>
void Dictionary<V, K>::deleteAllValues()
{
    PreOrderItr<Association<K, V>, int> theItr;
```

Listing 13-11 (Continued) The Dictionary template class

```
    // traverse the tree
    Association<K, V> * theAssociation;
    for (theItr.init (theTree); !theItr; ++theItr)
    {
        theAssociation = theItr();
        if (theAssociation)
            theAssociation->setValue ("/0");
    }
}

template <class V, class K>
bool Dictionary<V, K>::includesKey (K key)
    { return (getAssociation (key) != 0); }

template <class V, class K>
bool Dictionary<V, K>::isEmpty ()
    { return theTree->isEmpty(); }

template <class V, class K>
bool Dictionary<V, K>::removeKey (K key)
    { return (theTree->deleteNode (key)); }

template <class V, class K>
void Dictionary<V, K>::setDefault (V iValue)
    { defaultValue = iValue; }

template <class V, class K>
Association<K, V> * Dictionary<V, K>::getAssociation (K key)
    { return (theTree->find (key)); }

template <class V, class K>
Tree <Association<K, V>, int> * Dictionary<V, K>::getTree ()
    { return theTree; }

template <class V, class K>
V Dictionary<V, K>::getValue (K key)
{
    Association<K, V> * theAssociation = getAssociation (key);
    if (theAssociation)
        return theAssociation->getValue ();
```

Listing 13-11 (Continued) The Dictionary template class

```
    else
        return 0;
}

#endif
```

Listing 13-11 (Continued) The Dictionary template class

The B-Tree indexes and the dictionary are declared as objects of the application class (Listing 13-12). That in itself isn't a hard decision to make. But how do you maintain the indexes? Should they be stored on disk or should they be kept in RAM and therefore rebuilt each time the program is run?

```
#include "script.h"
#include "customer.h"
#include "drug.h"
#include "btree.h"
#include "dictionary.h"
#include "menu.h"
#include "indexentry.h"
#include "stringclass.h"
#include <iostream.h>
#include <fstream.h>

class AppClass
{
    private:
        // Indexes
        // element = valuekeypair; key = script #
        BTree<IndexEntry<int, int>, int> * scripts;
        // element = valuekeypair; key = drug #
        BTree<IndexEntry<int, int>, int> * drugs;
        // element = valuekeypair; key = lname + fname
        BTree<IndexEntry<int, String>, String> * customers;
        // Key is brand and generic drug names
        // Value is drug #
        Dictionary<int, String> * drugNames;

        // Menus
```

Listing 13-12 Declaration of the application class

```
        Menu * mainMenu;
        Menu * custMenu;
        Menu * drugMenu;
        Menu * scriptMenu;

        // next record numbers to be used
        // need not be stored in a file
        // regenerated when indexes are built at program startup
        int nextCustomerRecNumb;
        int nextDrugRecNumb;
        int nextScriptRecNumb;

        // auto-numbered items
        int nextScriptNumb;
        int nextDrugNumb;

        // internal functions
        bool buildIndexes ();

        void manageCustomers ();
        void addCustomer ();
        void findCustomer ();

        void manageDrugs ();
        void addDrug ();
        void findDrug ();

        void manageScripts ();
        void addScript ();
        void refillScript ();
        void findScript ();

    public:
        AppClass ();
        // writes ending auto-numbered values to text file
        ~AppClass ();
        void run ();
};
```

Listing 13-12 (Continued) Declaration of the application class

This is a situation in which there are significant trade-offs:

- You can keep all indexes in RAM and rebuild them each time the program is run. This takes a little extra time at program launch, but as the amount of data grows, speeds up both data entry and retrieval. (Keep in mind that indexes have to be updated as data are entered.) This is a good strategy when the data set is relatively small.

- You can keep all indexes in RAM while the program is running but store them in a disk file. This gives you the benefit of the speed of RAM-based indexes, but takes time to load the indexes at program startup and to write them either as they are modified or at the end of the program run.

- You can keep all indexes on disk, reading from the disk as needed for searching. (In fact, if your data set is very large, this may be your only viable option.) There is little or no overhead at program startup or termination. The drawback to this approach is that index searches require disk I/O. The same is true of any modifications to data: Not only do the entity object changes need to be written to disk, but index changes need to be written as well.

Because the purpose of the pharmacy program in this book is to demonstrate the use of data structures and the data set will remain small, the program uses the first option: All indexes are maintained in RAM and rebuilt each time the program starts.

13.3 The Application Class

A well-designed object-oriented program isolates its entity objects from the data structures that manage them. The pharmacy program attempts to act in this way by placing the responsibility of maintaining indexes to the data files on the application class.

The application class begins by loading some global data from a master file and then rebuilds its indexes. Conversely, on program termination it must rewrite the master file.

13.3.1 Program Startup and Termination

The pharmacy program's application class constructor can be found in Listing 13-13. In preparation for building the indexes, it does the following:

- Reads the next values to be assigned to auto-numbered keys (drug number and prescription number).
- Creates objects for the three B-Trees and one dictionary that will hold the data file indexes.
- Creates menu objects.

```
AppClass::AppClass ()
{
    ifstream fin ("master");
    if (!fin.is_open())
    {
        cout << "Master file not found. OK to continue? (y/n) ";
        char yes_no;
        cin >> yes_no;
        if (yes_no == 'n')
        {
            nextScriptNumb = 0;
            return;
        }
        else
        {
            nextScriptNumb = 1;
            nextDrugNumb = 1;
        }
    }
    else
    {
        fin >> nextScriptNumb;
        fin >> nextDrugNumb;
    }

    customers = new BTree<IndexEntry<int, String>, String> ();
    drugs = new BTree<IndexEntry<int, int>, int> ();
    scripts = new BTree<IndexEntry<int, int>, int> ();
```

Listing 13-13 The application class constructor

```
drugNames = new Dictionary<int, String> (0);

mainMenu = new Menu (maintitle, mainmenu, mainmenucount);
custMenu = new Menu (custtitle, custmenu, custmenucount);
drugMenu = new Menu (drugtitle, drugmenu, drugmenucount);
scriptMenu = new Menu (scripttitle, scriptmenu,
    scriptmenucount);
}
```

Listing 13-13 (Continued) The application class constructor

The destructor (Listing 13-14) reverses the process, saving the next script number and next drug number back in the master file.

```
AppClass::~AppClass ()
{
    // no master file at startup; user didn't want to continue.
    if (nextScriptNumb == 0)
        return;
    // save start for auto-numbered items in text file
    ofstream fout ("master");
    fout << nextScriptNumb << ' ';
    fout << nextDrugNumb << ' ';
    fout.close();
}
```

Listing 13-14 The application class destructor

13.3.2 The Run Function

As you would expect, overall control of the pharmacy program is handled by the run function (Listing 13-15). The most important thing to notice about this function is the initial call to buildIndexes. If a problem occurs while building indexes and the user decides not to continue, a false return from buildIndexes exits run and ultimately terminates the program run.

```
void AppClass::run ()
{
    bool result = buildIndexes ();
    if (!result)
        return;

    mainMenu->displaymenu();
    int choice = mainMenu->chooseoption ();
    while (choice != MAIN_QUIT)
    {
        switch (choice)
        {
            case CUSTOMERS:
                manageCustomers ();
                break;
            case DRUGS:
                manageDrugs ();
                break;
            case SCRIPTS:
                manageScripts ();
                break;
        }
        mainMenu->displaymenu();
        choice = mainMenu->chooseoption();
    }
}
```

Listing 13-15 The application class's run function

13.3.3 Building the Indexes

The buildIndexes function (Listing 13-16) must read through each data file sequentially, creating objects, extracting the necessary information, and then deleting the objects. Once the function has the necessary data, it can insert it into the appropriate indexes.

```cpp
bool AppClass::buildIndexes ()
{
    char yes_no;
    int recNumb;
    String key;

    // build customer index
    Customer * theCustomer;
    IndexEntry<int, String> * custEntry;
    ifstream fin ("customers");

    if (!fin.is_open ())
    {
        cout <<
            "Cannot open customers file. OK to continue? (y/n) ";
        cin >> yes_no;
        if (yes_no == 'n')
            return false;
        else
            recNumb = 0;
    }
    else
    {
        recNumb = 0;
        theCustomer = new Customer (fin, recNumb);
        while (!fin.eof())
        {
            theCustomer->getKey (key);
            custEntry = new IndexEntry<int, String> (recNumb, key);
            customers->insert (custEntry);
            delete theCustomer;
            recNumb++;
            theCustomer = new Customer (fin, recNumb);
        }
    }
    nextCustomerRecNumb = recNumb;
    fin.close ();

    // build drug index
    Drug * theDrug;
```

Listing 13-16   Building the main memory indexes

```
IndexEntry<int, int> * drugEntry;
ifstream drugsin ("drugs");

if (!drugsin.is_open())
{
    cout << "\nCannot open drugs file. OK to continue? (y/n) ";
    cin >> yes_no;
    if (yes_no == 'n')
        return false;
    else
        recNumb = 0;
}
else
{
    recNumb = 0;
    theDrug = new Drug (drugsin, recNumb);
    int intKey;
    while (!drugsin.eof())
    {
        theDrug->getKey (intKey);
        drugEntry = new IndexEntry<int, int> (recNumb, intKey);
        drugs->insert (drugEntry);
        Association<String, int> * theAssociation =
            new Association<String, int>
            (theDrug->getBrandName(), theDrug->getDrugNumb());
        drugNames->insert (theAssociation);
        theAssociation = new Association<String, int>
            (theDrug->getGenericName(), theDrug->getDrugNumb());
        drugNames->insert (theAssociation);
        delete theDrug;
        recNumb++;
        theDrug = new Drug (drugsin, recNumb);
    }
}
nextDrugRecNumb = recNumb;
drugsin.close ();

// build script index
Script * theScript;
IndexEntry<int, int> * scriptEntry;
```

Listing 13-16 (Continued) Building the main memory indexes

```
ifstream scriptsin ("prescriptions");

if (!scriptsin.is_open())
{
    cout << "Can't open scripts file. OK to continue? (y/n) ";
    cin >> yes_no;
    if (yes_no == 'n')
        return false;
    else
        recNumb = 0;
}
else
{
    recNumb = 0;
    theScript = new Script (scriptsin, recNumb);
    int intKey;
    while (!scriptsin.eof())
    {
        theScript->getKey (intKey);
        scriptEntry = new IndexEntry<int, int>
            (recNumb, intKey);
        scripts->insert (scriptEntry);
        delete theScript;
        recNumb++;
        theScript = new Script (scriptsin, recNumb);
    }
}
nextScriptRecNumb = recNumb;
scriptsin.close();

return true;
}
```

Listing 13-16 (Continued) Building the main memory indexes

As an example, let's look at what occurs when building the indexes for drugs, as this is the most complex case. This portion of the `buildIndex` function works in the following way:

1. Open the drug file for input.
2. If the drug file has been opened successfully, go to step 5.

3. Tell the user that the drug file can't be opened and ask if the user wants to continue.

4. If the user does not want to continue, return `false` and exit the function. Otherwise set the record number to 0 and go to step 19.

5. Set the current record number to 0.

6. Create a new drug object by reading it from the drug file.

7. Enter a loop that continues until the end of the drug file. When the end of file is reached, go to step 19.

8. Retrieve the drug object's key (its drug number).

9. Create an `IndexEntry` object that contains the current record number and the key.

10. Insert the `IndexEntry` object into the drug index (`drugs`).

11. Create an `Association` object that has the drug's brand name as its key and the drug number as its value.

12. Insert the `Association` object into the dictionary (`drugNames`).

13. Create a second `Association` object that has the drug's generic name as its key and the drug number as its value.

14. Insert the second `Association` object into the dictionary.

15. Delete the drug object.

16. Increment the record number.

17. Read another drug from the data file.

18. Go to step 7.

19. Initialize the next drug record number as the current record number, which will be one greater than the last valid record read from the file. (This step avoids having to store the value of the next drug record number in the master file.)

20. Close the drugs file.

13.3.4 Managing the Drugs

You can find the three functions that handle drug data in Listing 13-17. The actions for adding new data and finding data are similar to those of the other entity objects.

```
void AppClass::manageDrugs ()
{
    drugMenu->displaymenu();
    int choice = drugMenu->chooseoption ();
    while (choice != DRUG_QUIT)
    {
        switch (choice)
        {
            case NEW_DRUG:
                addDrug ();
                break;
            case FIND_DRUG:
                findDrug ();
                break;
        }
        drugMenu->displaymenu();
        choice = drugMenu->chooseoption ();
    }
}

void AppClass::addDrug ()
{
    int idrugNumb, inumbConflicts;
    String conflicts[MAX_INTERACTIONS];
    String ibrandName, igenericName;

    idrugNumb = nextDrugNumb++;
    cin.get();
    cout << "\nBrand name: ";
    cin.getline (ibrandName,BRAND_NAME_LENGTH);
    cout << "Generic name: ";
    cin.getline (igenericName, GENERIC_NAME_LENGTH);

    cout << "\nType the names of interacting drugs. ";
    cout << "Press Enter on empty line to end." << endl;
    inumbConflicts = 0;
    cout << "\nInteracting drug: ";
    cin.getline (conflicts[0], INTERACTION_LENGTH);
    if (conflicts[0].len() == 0)
        inumbConflicts = -1; // none
```

Listing 13-17 Managing drug data

459

```
    while (conflicts[inumbConflicts].len ()  > 0)
    {
        inumbConflicts++;
        cout << "Interacting drug: ";
        cin.getline (conflicts[inumbConflicts],
            INTERACTION_LENGTH);
    }

    fstream fout ("drugs", ios::in | ios::out);
    Drug * theDrug = new Drug (idrugNumb, inumbConflicts,
        ibrandName, igenericName, conflicts, fout,
        nextDrugRecNumb);
    int intKey;
    theDrug->getKey (intKey);
    IndexEntry<int, int> * drugEntry = new IndexEntry<int, int>
        (nextDrugRecNumb, intKey);
    drugs->insert (drugEntry);
    Association<String, int> * theAssociation =
        new Association<String, int> (theDrug->getBrandName(),
        theDrug->getDrugNumb());
    drugNames->insert (theAssociation);
    theAssociation = new Association<String, int>
        (theDrug->getGenericName(), theDrug->getDrugNumb());
    drugNames->insert (theAssociation);

    nextDrugRecNumb++;
    delete theDrug;
    fout.close();
}

void AppClass::findDrug ()
{
    String searchName;

    cin.get();
    cout << "\nDrug name: ";
    cin.getline (searchName, BRAND_NAME_LENGTH);
    int drugNumb = drugNames->getValue (searchName);
    IndexEntry<int, int> * drugEntry = drugs->find (drugNumb);
    ifstream fin ("drugs");
```

Listing 13-17 (Continued) Managing drug data

```
Drug * theDrug = new Drug (fin, drugEntry->getValue());
fin.close ();
if (!theDrug)
    cout << "\nThe drug you requested isn't in the database.";
else
{
    cout << "\nBrand name: " << theDrug->getBrandName ()
        << endl;
    cout << "\nGeneric name: " << theDrug->getGenericName ()
        << endl;
}
    delete theDrug;
}
```

Listing 13-17 (Continued) Managing drug data

To add a new drug, the `addDrug` function does the following:

1. Store the next drug number in a local variable and increments the global variable.

2. Get the brand and generic names from the user.

3. Get the names of interacting drugs from the user. These can be either generic or brand names.

4. Open the data file as an `fstream` object for input and output. This is essential to prevent truncation of the file. (An `ofstream` object is truncated by default; the only alternative is to append to the file, which will not place data in their correct locations.)

5. Create a new drug object, calling the drug's interactive constructor, which also calls the `write` function.

6. Get the new drug's key.

7. Create an `IndexEntry` object for the new drug.

8. Insert the index entry into the B-Tree index.

9. Create an `Association` object for the new drug's brand name.

10. Insert the association into the dictionary.

11. Create an `Association` object for the new drug's generic name.

12. Insert the association into the dictionary.

13. Increment the next drug record number.

14. Delete the new drug from memory. Only its index and dictionary entries remain in RAM.

15. Close the drugs file.

Finding a drug by name requires using both the dictionary and the B-Tree index:

1. Enter the drug name. This can be either a brand or generic name, since both are intermixed in the dictionary.

2. Use the `Dictionary` class's `getValue` function to search the dictionary for the drug name, returning the drug number.

3. Find the drug's index entry in the drugs B-Tree index.

4. Open the drugs file for input.

5. Create a new drug object, using the record number from the index entry to locate the object's data in the data file.

6. Close the input file.

7. If the pointer to the drug object is undefined (i.e., equal to 0), then the drug isn't in the database.

8. Otherwise, display drug data.

9. Delete the drug object.

13.3.5 Managing the Customers

The functions for handling customers appear in Listing 13-18. As you can see, they are virtually identical to those that handle the drugs. The major difference is that customer objects are referenced only by a single B-Tree index, which simplifies both storing and retrieving somewhat.

```
void AppClass::manageCustomers ()
{
    custMenu->displaymenu();
    int choice = custMenu->chooseoption ();
    while (choice != CUST_QUIT)
    {
        switch (choice)
        {
```

Listing 13-18   *Managing customer data*

```
        case NEW_CUST:
            addCustomer ();
            break;
        case FIND_CUST:
            findCustomer ();
            break;
    }
    custMenu->displaymenu();
    choice = custMenu->chooseoption ();
    }
}

void AppClass::addCustomer ()
{
    String ifname, ilname, istreet, icity, istate, izip, iphone;

    cin.get ();
    cout << "\nFirst name: ";
    cin.getline (ifname, FNAME_LENGTH);
    cout << "Last name: ";
    cin.getline (ilname, LNAME_LENGTH);
    cout << "Street: ";
    cin.getline (istreet, STREET_LENGTH);
    cout << "City: ";
    cin.getline (icity, CITY_LENGTH);
    cout << "State: ";
    cin.getline (istate, STATE_LENGTH);
    cout << "Zip: ";
    cin.getline (izip, ZIP_LENGTH);
    cout << "Phone: ";
    cin.getline (iphone, PHONE_LENGTH);

    fstream fout ("customers",ios::in | ios::out);
    if (!fout.is_open ())
    {
        cout <<
        "\nCould not open customer file. New customer not stored.";
        return;
    }
```

Listing 13-18 (Continued) Managing customer data

```
    Customer * newCust = new Customer (ifname, ilname, istreet,
        icity, istate, izip,iphone, nextCustomerRecNumb, fout);
    String key;
    newCust->getKey (key);
    IndexEntry<int, String> * custEntry =
        new IndexEntry<int, String> (nextCustomerRecNumb, key);
    customers->insert (custEntry);

    nextCustomerRecNumb++;
    fout.close();
    delete newCust;
}

void AppClass::findCustomer ()
{
    String fname, lname, key;

    cin.get();
    cout << "\nFirst name: ";
    cin.getline (fname, FNAME_LENGTH);
    cout << "Last name: ";
    cin.getline (lname, LNAME_LENGTH);

    key = lname;
    key += fname;

    IndexEntry<int,String> * indexInfo = customers->find (key);
    ifstream fin ("customers");
    Customer * theCustomer = new Customer
        (fin, indexInfo->getValue ());
    fin.close();
    if (!theCustomer)
        cout << "\nThe customer you entered isn't in the database.";
    else
    {
        cout << endl << fname << " " << lname << endl;
        cout << theCustomer->getStreet ()  << endl;
        cout << theCustomer->getCity () << ", " <<
            theCustomer->getState() << " " <<
            theCustomer->getZip () << endl;
```

Listing 13-18 (Continued) Managing customer data

```
    }
    delete theCustomer;
}
```

Listing 13-18 (Continued) Managing customer data

13.3.6 Managing the Prescriptions

With the exception of finding a prescription by its prescription number, handling prescriptions (Listing 13-19) is more complex than managing drugs or customers. Adding a new prescription requires several data integrity checks; handling refills involves writing specific pieces of modified data back to the prescription data file.

```
void AppClass::manageScripts ()
{
    scriptMenu->displaymenu();
    int choice = scriptMenu->chooseoption ();
    while (choice != SCRIPT_QUIT)
    {
        switch (choice)
        {
            case NEW_SCRIPT:
                addScript ();
                break;
            case REFILL:
                refillScript ();
                break;
            case FIND_SCRIPT:
                findScript ();
                break;
        }
        scriptMenu->displaymenu();
        choice = scriptMenu->chooseoption ();
    }
}

void AppClass::addScript ()
{
```

Listing 13-19 Managing prescription data

```
int irefills, idrugNumb, iscriptNumb, iquantity;
String iprescriber, iprescriberPhone, icustFName, icustLName,
    idose, stringDate;
String drugName, iinstructions, idate;

// Locate the drug
cin.get();
cout << "\nDrug name: ";
cin.getline (drugName, BRAND_NAME_LENGTH);
idrugNumb = drugNames->getValue (drugName);
if (!idrugNumb)
{
    cout << "\nWe don't stock this drug.";
    return;
}
IndexEntry<int, int> * drugEntry = drugs->find (idrugNumb);
ifstream fin ("drugs");
Drug * theDrug = new Drug (fin, drugEntry->getValue());
fin.close();

// Locate the customer
cout << "\nCustomer's first name: ";
cin.getline (icustFName, CUST_FNAME_LENGTH);
cout << "Customer's last name: ";
cin.getline (icustLName, CUST_LNAME_LENGTH);
String key = icustLName;
key += icustFName;
IndexEntry<int, String> * custEntry = customers->find (key);
if (!custEntry)
{
    cout << "\nThat customer isn't in the database." << endl;
    cout << "Please create a customer entry first.";
    return;
}
ifstream custin ("customers");
Customer * theCustomer = new Customer
    (custin, custEntry->getValue());
custin.close();

// Check for drug interactions
```

Listing 13-19 (Continued) Managing prescription data

```
Script * theScript;
int recNumb, drugNumb;
Drug * scriptDrug;
bool result;
IndexEntry<int, int> * entry;

if (nextScriptNumb > 1)
{
    ifstream scriptsin ("prescriptions");
    if (!scriptsin.is_open() )
    {
        cout <<
"\nCan't open scripts file to check for drug interactions.";
        return;
    }
    ifstream drugsin ("drugs");
    if (!drugsin.is_open())
    {
        cout <<
    "\nCan't open drugs file to check for drug interactions.";
        return;
    }

    int * scriptArray = theCustomer->getScriptArray();
    for (int i = 0; i < theCustomer->getNumbScripts(); i++)
    {
        entry = scripts->find (scriptArray[i]);
        recNumb = entry->getValue();
        theScript = new Script (scriptsin, recNumb);
        drugNumb = theScript->getDrugNumb();
        entry = drugs->find (drugNumb);
        recNumb = entry->getValue();
        scriptDrug = new Drug (drugsin, recNumb);
        result = theDrug->checkInteraction
            (scriptDrug->getBrandName());
        if (!result)
            break;
        result = theDrug->checkInteraction
            (scriptDrug->getGenericName());
        if (!result)
```

Listing 13-19 (Continued) Managing prescription data

```
            break;
        delete theScript;
        delete scriptDrug;
    }
    drugsin.close();
    scriptsin.close();
    if (!result)
    {
        cout <<
            "\nAn interaction between this drug and a drug ";
        cout << "already prescribed --" << endl;
        cout << scriptDrug->getBrandName() << "/" <<
            scriptDrug->getGenericName() <<
            " -- has been found." << endl;
        cout <<
    "Please check with the person who prescribed this drug.";
        delete theScript;
        delete scriptDrug;
        return;
    }
}
delete theDrug;

// Get rest of script info and create object
iscriptNumb = nextScriptNumb++;
cout << "\nPrescriber: ";
cin.getline (iprescriber, PRESCRIBER_LENGTH);
cout << "Prescriber phone: ";
cin.getline (iprescriberPhone, PRESCRIBER_PHONE_LENGTH);
cout << "Quantity to despense: ";
cin >> iquantity;
cin.get();
cout << "Dose: ";
cin.getline (idose, DOSE_LENGTH);
cout << "Instructions: ";
cin.getline (iinstructions, INSTRUCTIONS_LENGTH);
cout << "Number of refills: ";
cin >> irefills;
cin.get();
cout << "Prescription date: ";
```

Listing 13-19 (Continued) Managing prescription data

```
    cin.getline (idate, DATE_LENGTH);

    fstream scriptout ("prescriptions",ios::in | ios::out);
    if (!scriptout.is_open())
    {
        cout << "\nCan't open scripts file.";
        return;
    }

    Script * newScript = new Script (drugNumb, iscriptNumb,
        irefills, iprescriber, iprescriberPhone,
        icustFName, icustLName, idose, iinstructions, iquantity,
        idate, scriptout, nextScriptRecNumb);
    scriptout.close();

    // Insert into all necessary data structures
    entry = new IndexEntry<int, int>
        (nextScriptRecNumb, iscriptNumb);
    scripts->insert (entry);
    theCustomer->addScript (iscriptNumb);

    delete newScript;
    delete theCustomer;
    nextScriptRecNumb++;
}

void AppClass::refillScript ()
{
    int scriptNumb;
    bool OK;

    cin.get();
    cout << "\Prescription #: ";
    cin >> scriptNumb;

    IndexEntry<int, int> * scriptEntry =
        scripts->find (scriptNumb);
    if (!scriptEntry)
    {
        cout << "\nThere is no prescription with that number.";
```

Listing 13-19 (Continued) Managing prescription data

```
        return;
    }

    int recNumb = scriptEntry->getValue();
    ifstream fin ("prescriptions");
    if (!fin.is_open())
    {
        cout << "\nCan't open scripts file.";
        return;
    }
    Script * theScript = new Script (fin, recNumb);
    fin.close ();

    cin.get();
    String refillDate;
    cout << "\nRefill date: ";
    cin.getline (refillDate, DATE_LENGTH);
    fstream file ("prescriptions", ios::in | ios::out);
    OK = theScript->refill (refillDate, file, recNumb);
    if (!OK)
        cout << "\nThere are no refills left.";
    file.close();
    delete theScript;
}

void AppClass::findScript ()
{
    int scriptNumb;

    cin.get();
    cout << "\Prescription #: ";
    cin >> scriptNumb;

    IndexEntry<int, int> * scriptEntry =
        scripts->find (scriptNumb);
    if (!scriptEntry)
    {
        cout << "\nThere is no prescription with that number.";
        return;
    }
```

Listing 13-19 (Continued) Managing prescription data

```
    int recNumb = scriptEntry->getValue ();
    ifstream fin ("prescriptions");
    if (!fin.is_open())
    {
        cout << "\nCan't open scripts file.";
        return;
    }
    Script * theScript = new Script (fin, recNumb);

    Date * theDate = theScript->getScriptDate ();
    String dateString;
    cout << "\nCustomer: " << theScript->getFName() << " "
        << theScript->getLName() << endl;
    cout << "Prescription date: "
        << theDate->showDate (dateString) << endl;
    cout << "Number of refills left: " <<
        theScript->getRefillsLeft() << endl;

    fin.close();
    delete theScript;
}
```

Listing 13-19 (Continued) Managing prescription data

To enter a new prescription, the application class does the following:

1. Get the drug name from the user. Either a generic or brand name will do.

2. Find the drug number by searching the dictionary.

3. If the search fails, exit the function.

Note: There are many better ways to handle the user interface here, especially when it comes to drugs and customers that aren't in the files. However, they have been omitted from this demonstration program to keep the code as short as possible.

4. Find the drug's index entry in its B-Tree index.

5. Create a drug object using the record number from the index entry to locate the data in the data file.

6. Get the customer's first and last names from the user.

7. Find the customer's entry in the B-Tree index using the concatenation of the last and first names as the key.

8. If the search fails, exit the function.

9. Create a customer object, using the record number from the index entry to locate the data in the data file.

10. Open the prescription and drug files for input.

11. Retrieve a pointer to the customer's scripts array. (This array stores prescription numbers.)

12. Enter a loop that continues until all of the customer's existing prescriptions have been checked for interactions with the new drug. When all existing scripts have been checked, go to step 25.

13. Find the prescription's index entry in its B-Tree index.

14. Create a new script object using the script's record number from the index entry to locate the data in the data file.

15. Retrieve the drug number from the script object.

16. Find the drug's index entry in its B-Tree index.

17. Create a new drug object using the drug's record number from the index entry.

18. Check the brand name of the drug being prescribed against the list of drug interactions with the drug object created in step 17.

19. If interactions are found, exit the loop and continue with step 25.

20. Check the generic name of the drug being prescribed against the list of drug interactions with the drug object created in step 17.

21. If interactions are found, exit the loop at continue with step 25.

22. Delete the script object.

23. Delete the drug object created in step 17.

24. Return to Step 12.

25. If interactions were found, display an appropriate message to the user, delete objects, and exit the function.

26. Otherwise, delete the object for the drug being prescribed.

27. Store the script number in a local variable and increment the global variable.

28. Get the remainder of the script data from the user.

29. Open the scripts file.

30. Create a new script object, which includes writing it to the data file.

31. Close the scripts file.

32. Create an index entry object for the new script.

33. Insert the index entry into the customer's B-Tree index.

34. Add the script to the customer's array of prescriptions.

35. Delete the script and customer objects.

36. Increment the next script record number.

Fortunately, refilling a prescription is much easier on the user (and the computer):

1. Get the script number from the user.

2. Retrieve the script's index entry from its B-Tree index.

3. Open the scripts file.

4. Create a new script object, reading its data from the file.

5. Close the scripts file.

6. Get the refill date from the user.

7. Open the scripts file for input and output.

8. Call the script object's `refill` function to process the refill. This involves adding the date to the array of refill dates, decrementing the number of refills remaining, and writing both pieces of modified data back to the data file.

9. If there are no refills remaining, the `Script` class's `refill` function returns `false`, in which case no modifications have been made to the data file. Display an appropriate error message to the user.

10. Close the scripts data file.

11. Delete the script object.

13.4 Summary

When working with data that reside in data files except when they are being actively processed by a program, the program must maintain indexes to those data files. The indexes—most typically B-Trees—can be kept in RAM or on disk. RAM-based indexes can be either rebuilt each time a program is launched or read into RAM from a disk file at program launch.

Disk-based indexes are slower than RAM-based indexes, but may be the only feasible solution when data sets are very large.

Part V: Appendix—Code Listings

APPENDIX A *Templates*

This appendix contains template code for those data structure classes whose templates are not used in the body of the book. To find the source code of a template, first consult the template index in Section A.1 below. It contains the location of each template, both those in the body of the book and those in this appendix.

A.1 *Template Index*

A.2 Array Manager Iterator

```
#ifndef ARRAY_ITR
#define ARRAY_ITR

#include "ArrayMgr.h"

template <class A, class B>
class ArrayItr
{
    private:
        ArrayMgr<A, B> * theArray;
        int numb_elements;
        int current_index;

    public:
        // pass in the array manager and total elements
        // pass in the array manager and total elements
        ArrayItr (ArrayMgr<A, B> *, int);
        bool getNext (A * &);
};

template <class A, class B>
ArrayItr<A, B>::ArrayItr (ArrayMgr<A, B> * inArray, int iElements)
{
    theArray = inArray;
    numb_elements = iElements;
    current_index = O;
}

template <class A, class B>
bool ArrayItr<A, B>::getNext (A * & nextObject)
{
    bool result = false;
    if (current_index <numb_elements)
    {
        theArray->getElement (current_index, nextObject);
```

Listing A-1   Array iterator template class

```
        result = true;
        current_index++;
    }
    return result;
}

#endif
```

Listing A-1 (Continued) Array iterator template class

A.3 AVL Tree

```
#ifndef AVLTREE
#define AVLTREE

#include "tree.h"
#include "avlnode.h"

template <class E, class K>
class AVLTree : public Tree<E, K>
{
    public:
        AVLTree ();
        void insert (E *);
        bool deleteNode (K);
};

template <class E, class K>
AVLTree<E, K>::AVLTree ()
    : Tree ()
    {  }

template <class E, class K>
void AVLTree<E, K>::insert (E * theElement)
{
```

Listing A-2   AVL tree template class

```
    AVLNode<E, K> * theRoot = (AVLNode<E, K> *) root;
    if (theRoot)
        root = theRoot->insert (theElement);
    else
        root = new AVLNode<E, K> (theElement);
}

template <class E, class K>
bool AVLTree<E, K>::deleteNode (K key)
{
    AVLNode<E, K> * deletedNode = 0;
    AVLNode<E, K> * theRoot = (AVLNode<E, K> *) root;

    if (theRoot)
        root = theRoot->deleteNode (key, deletedNode);
    if (deletedNode)
    {
        delete deletedNode;
        return true;
    }
    else
        return false;
}

#endif
```

Listing A-2 (Continued) AVL tree template class

A.4 AVL Tree Node

```
#ifndef AVLNODE
#define AVLNODE

#include "node.h"

template <class E, class K>
class AVLNode : public Node<E, K>
{
    private:
        int balanceFactor;
        AVLNode<E, K> * singleRotateLeft ();
        AVLNode<E, K> * singleRotateRight ();
        AVLNode<E, K> * restoreLeftBalance (int);
        AVLNode<E, K> * restoreRightBalance (int);
        AVLNode<E, K> * balance ();
        AVLNode<E, K> * removeLeftChild (AVLNode<E, K> * &);
    public:
        AVLNode (E *);
        void setLeft (AVLNode<E, K> *);
        void setRight (AVLNode<E, K> *);
        AVLNode<E, K> * getLeft ();
        AVLNode<E, K> * getRight ();
        int getBalanceFactor ();
        void setBalanceFactor (int);
        AVLNode<E, K> * insert (E *);
        AVLNode<E, K> * deleteNode (K, AVLNode<E, K> * &);
};

template <class E, class K>
AVLNode<E, K>::AVLNode (E * theElement)
    : Node (theElement)
{
    balanceFactor = 0;
}
```

Listing A-3   AVL tree node template class

```
template <class E, class K>
AVLNode<E, K> * AVLNode<E, K>::singleRotateLeft ()
{
    AVLNode<E, K> * current = this;
    AVLNode<E, K> * child = (AVLNode<E, K> *) right_child;

    // perform the rotation
    current->setRight (child->getLeft());
    child->setLeft (current);

    // recompute balance factors
    int currentBF = current->balanceFactor;
    int childBF = child->getBalanceFactor();
    if (childBF <= 0)
    {
        if (currentBF >= 1)
            child->setBalanceFactor (childBF - 1);
        else
            child->setBalanceFactor (currentBF + childBF - 2);
        current->balanceFactor = currentBF - 1;
    }
    else
    {
        if (currentBF <= childBF)
            child->setBalanceFactor (currentBF - 2);
        else
            child->setBalanceFactor (childBF - 1);
        current->balanceFactor = (currentBF - childBF) - 1;
    }
    return child;
}

// single right_child rotation of current node
template <class E, class K>
AVLNode<E, K> * AVLNode<E, K>::singleRotateRight ()
{
    AVLNode<E, K> * current = this;
    AVLNode<E, K> * child = (AVLNode<E, K> *) left_child;

    //perform the rotation
```

Listing A-3 (Continued) AVL tree node template class

```
    current->setLeft (child->getRight());
    child->setRight (current);

    //recompute balance factors
    int currentBF = current->balanceFactor;
    int childBF = child->getBalanceFactor();
    if (childBF <= 0)
    {
        if (childBF > currentBF)
            child->setBalanceFactor (childBF + 1);
        else
            child->setBalanceFactor (currentBF + 2);
        current->balanceFactor = 1 + currentBF - childBF;
    }
    else
    {
        if (currentBF <= -1)
            child->setBalanceFactor (childBF + 1);
        else
            child->setBalanceFactor (currentBF + childBF + 2);
        current->balanceFactor = 1 + currentBF;
    }
    return child;
}

template <class E, class K>
AVLNode<E, K> * AVLNode<E, K>::restoreLeftBalance (int oldBF)
{
    AVLNode<E, K> * left = (AVLNode<E, K> *) left_child;

    if (!left)
        balanceFactor++;
    else
        if ((left->getBalanceFactor() != oldBF) && (left-
>getBalanceFactor() == 0))
            balanceFactor++;

    if (balanceFactor > 1)
        return balance();
    return this;
```

Listing A-3 (Continued) AVL tree node template class

```
}

template <class E, class K>
AVLNode<E, K> * AVLNode<E, K>::restoreRightBalance (int oldBF)
{
    AVLNode<E, K> * right = (AVLNode<E, K> *) right_child;

    if (!right)
        balanceFactor--;
    else
        if ((right->getBalanceFactor() != oldBF) && (right-
>getBalanceFactor() == 0))
            balanceFactor--;

    if (balanceFactor < -1)
        return balance();
    return this;
}

template <class E, class K>
AVLNode<E, K> * AVLNode<E, K>::balance ()
{
    AVLNode<E, K> * left = (AVLNode<E, K> *) left_child;
    AVLNode<E, K> * right = (AVLNode<E, K> *) right_child;
    if (balanceFactor < 0)
    {
        if (left->getBalanceFactor() <= 0)
            return singleRotateRight ();
        else
        {
            setLeft (left->singleRotateLeft());
            return singleRotateRight();
        }
    }
    else
    {
        if (right->getBalanceFactor() >= 0)
            return singleRotateLeft();
        else
        {
```

Listing A-3 (Continued) AVL tree node template class

```
            setRight (right->singleRotateRight());
            return singleRotateLeft();
        }
    }
}

template <class E, class K>
AVLNode<E, K> * AVLNode<E, K>::removeLeftChild
        (AVLNode<E, K> * & childNode)
{
    AVLNode<E, K> * left = (AVLNode<E, K> *) left_child;

    if (!left)
    {
        childNode = this;
        return (AVLNode<E, K> *) right_child;
    }

    int oldBF = left->getBalanceFactor();
    setLeft (left->removeLeftChild (childNode));
    return restoreLeftBalance (oldBF);
}

template <class E, class K>
void AVLNode<E, K>::setLeft (AVLNode<E, K> * node)
    { left_child = (Node<E, K> *) node; }

template <class E, class K>
void AVLNode<E, K>::setRight (AVLNode<E, K> * node)
    { right_child = (Node<E, K> *) node; }

template <class E, class K>
AVLNode<E, K> * AVLNode<E, K>::getLeft ()
    { return (AVLNode<E, K> *) left_child; }

template <class E, class K>
AVLNode<E, K> * AVLNode<E, K>::getRight ()
    { return (AVLNode<E, K> *) right_child; }

template <class E, class K>
```

Listing A-3 (Continued) AVL tree node template class

```
int AVLNode<E, K>::getBalanceFactor ()
   { return balanceFactor; }

template <class E, class K>
void AVLNode<E, K>::setBalanceFactor (int factor)
   { balanceFactor = factor; }

template <class E, class K>
AVLNode<E, K> * AVLNode<E, K>::insert (E * theElement)
{
   K newKey, currentKey;
   theElement->getKey (newKey);
   getKey (currentKey);

   AVLNode<E, K> * left = (AVLNode<E, K> *) left_child;
   AVLNode<E, K> * right = (AVLNode<E, K> *) right_child;

   if (newKey < currentKey) // insert into left subtree
   {
      if (left) // if there is a left child
      {
         int oldBF = left->getBalanceFactor ();
         setLeft (left->insert (theElement));
         // determine whether tree is larger
         if ((left->getBalanceFactor () != oldBF) &&
            left->getBalanceFactor())
            balanceFactor--;
      }
      else
      {
         setLeft (new AVLNode<E, K> (theElement));
         balanceFactor--;
      }
   }
   else // insert into right subtree
   {
      if (right) // if there is a right child
      {
         int oldBF = right->getBalanceFactor ();
         setRight (right->insert (theElement));
```

Listing A-3 (Continued) AVL tree node template class

```
            // determine whether tree is larger
            if ((right->getBalanceFactor () != oldBF) &&
                right->getBalanceFactor())
                balanceFactor++;
        }
        else
        {
            setRight (new AVLNode<E, K> (theElement));
            balanceFactor++;
        }
    }

    //determine whether tree is balanced
    if (balanceFactor < -1 || balanceFactor > 1)
        return balance ();
    return this;
}

template <class E, class K>
AVLNode<E, K> * AVLNode<E, K>::deleteNode
        (K key, AVLNode<E, K> * & deletedNode)
{
    AVLNode<E, K> * right = (AVLNode<E, K> *) right_child;
    AVLNode<E, K> * left = (AVLNode<E, K> *) left_child;

    if (key == intKey)  // this is where the deletion occurs
    {
        deletedNode = this;
        if (!right)
            return left;

        int oldBF = right->getBalanceFactor();
        AVLNode<E, K> * newRoot;
        setRight (right->removeLeftChild (newRoot));
        newRoot->setLeft ((AVLNode<E, K> *) left_child);
        newRoot->setRight ((AVLNode<E, K> *) right_child);
        newRoot->setBalanceFactor (balanceFactor);
        return newRoot->restoreRightBalance (oldBF);
    }
    else if (key < intKey)
```

Listing A-3 (Continued) AVL tree node template class

```
    {
        if (!left)
            return this;

        int oldBF = left->getBalanceFactor();
        setLeft (left->deleteNode (key, deletedNode));
        return restoreLeftBalance (oldBF);
    }
    else
    {
        if (!right)
            return this;

        int oldBF = right->getBalanceFactor();
        setRight (right->deleteNode (key, deletedNode));
        return restoreRightBalance (oldBF);
    }
}

#endif
```

Listing A-3 (Continued) AVL tree node template class

A.5 Binary Search

There are at least two ways to include a binary search in a program. The first is simply to include a search or find function in whatever class you are writing, copying in the code on page 293 and modifying it for the specific data type being used. An alternative is to use the stand-alone binary search class template in Listing A-4.

```
#ifndef BINARY_SEARCH
#define BINARY_SEARCH

template <class A, class K>
class BinarySearch
{
```

Listing A-4 Binary search class template

```
    private:
        A ** theArray;
        int size;
    public:
        BinarySearch (A **, int);
        A * search (K);
};

template <class A, class K>
BinarySearch<A, K>::BinarySearch (A ** inArray, int iSize)
{
    theArray = iArray;
    size = iSize;
}

template <class A, class K>
A * BinarySearch<A, K>::search (K searchKey)
{
    int top, bottom, middle;
    top = 0;
    bottom = size - 1;

    bool found = false;
    A * result = 0;

    while (top <= bottom && !found)
    {
        middle = (top + bottom) / 2; // find a new middle element
        K middleKey;
        theArray[middle]->getKey(middleKey);
        if (middleKey == searchKey)
        {
            result = theArray[middle]; // found it!
            found = true;
        }
        else if (middleKey < key)
            top = middle + 1; // in bottom half; move top down
        else
            bottom = middle - 1; // must be in top half; move bottom
up
```

Listing A-4 (Continued) Binary search class template

```
    }
    return result; // desired element wasn't found
}

#endif
```

Listing A-4 (Continued) Binary search class template

To use the template, create an object from the class, specifying the data type of the array that will be sorted and the data type of the key. Pass a pointer to an array of pointers and the number of elements in the array to the constructor. Then, call the search function with a key value to perform a search.

A.6 Bubble Sort

For comments on how to use the bubble sort in a program, see the instructions for the binary search (Section A.5 on page 490).

```
#ifndef BUBBLE_SORT
#define BUBBLE_SORT

template <class A, class K>
class BubbleSort
{
    private:
        A ** theArray;
        int size;
    public:
        BubbleSort (A **, int);
        void sort ();
};

template <class A, class K>
BubbleSort<A, K>::BubbleSort (A ** iArray, int iSize)
```

Listing A-5 Bubble sort template class

```
{
    theArray = iArray;
    size = iSize;
}

template <class A, class K>
void BubbleSort<A, K>::sort ()
{
    bool swap_made = true;
    A * tempElement;
    K key1, key2;
    while (swap_made)
    {
        swap_made = false;
        count++;
        for (int i = 0; i < size - 1; i++) // one pass
        {
            theArray[i]->getKey(key1);
            theArray[i+1]->getKey(key2);
            if (key1 > key2) //swap
            {
                swap_made = true;
                tempElement = theArray[i];
                theArray[i] = thetArray[i+1];
                theArray[i+1] = tempElement;
            }
        }
    }
}
```

Listing A-5 (Continued) Bubble sort template class

A.7 Double Linked List Descending Order Iterator

```
#ifndef LISTITR_DESC
#define LISTITR_DESC

#include "doublelistmgr.h"

template <class E>
class ListItrDesc
{
   private:
       DoubleNode<E> * current;
       DoubleListMgr<E> * theList;
   public:
       ListItrDesc (DoubleListMgr<E> *);
       E * getNext ();
};

template <class E>
ListItrDesc<E>::ListItrDesc (DoubleListMgr<E> * whichList)
{
   current = 0;
   theList = whichList;
}

template <class E>
E * ListItrDesc<E>::getNext ()
{
   if (current == 0)
      current = theList->getLast ();
   else
      current = current->getPrior ();
   if (current != 0)
      return current->getElement();
   else
      return 0;
}

#endif
```

Listing A-6   Double linked list descending order iterator template class

A.8 Hash Table (Adjacent Elements for Collisions)

This hash table template differs from the demonstration version in the body of the book in one way: it uses a dynamically allocated array for the table. The user must therefore give the constructor the size of the array when creating a hash table object.

```
#ifndef HASHTABLE
#define HASHTABLE

// requires a string key (any char * or string class that can be
// used in place of char * will do).
template <class E, class K>
class Hashtable
{
    private:
        E ** table;
        int tableSize;
        int computeIndex (K key);
    public:
        Hashtable(int);
        ~Hashtable ();
        bool insert (E *);
        E * find (K);
        E * getElement (int);
};

template <class E, class K>
Hashtable<E, K>::Hashtable (int size)
{
    tableSize = size;
    // Note: Class E must have a default constructor
    table = new E * [tableSize];
    for (int i = 0; i < tableSize; i++)
        table[i] = 0;
}
```

Listing A-7 *Template class for a hash table that uses adjacent elements for collisions*

```
template<class E, class K>
Hashtable<E, K>::~Hashtable ()
    { delete table; }

template <class E, class K>
bool Hashtable<E, K>::insert (E * newElement)
{
    K key;
    newElement->getKey (key);
    int index = computeIndex (key);
    int computedindex = index;
    bool result = true;

    if (table[index] == 0) // first entry at that hash value
        table[index] = newElement;
    else
    {
        while (table[++index] != 0 && index < tableSize)
            ; // find next open spot
        if (index == tableSize)
        {
            int index = -1;
            // start at top
            while (table[++index] != 0 && index < computedindex -1)
                ;
            if (index == computedindex)
                result = false; //  table is full
            else
                table[index] = newElement;
        }
        else
            table[index] = newElement;
    }
    return result;
}

template <class E, class K>
int Hashtable<E, K>::computeIndex (K key)
{
    long sum = 0;
```

Listing A-7 (Continued) Template class for a hash table that uses adjacent elements for collisions

```
    for (int i = 0; i < key.len(); i++)
        sum += key[i];
    return sum % tableSize;
}


template <class E, class K>
E * Hashtable<E, K>::find (K key)
{
    int index = computeIndex (key);
    int computedIndex = index;
    E * theElement = 0;
    K theKey;
    table[index]->getKey (theKey);

    if (theKey != key)
    {
        while (theKey != key && table[index] !=0 &&
            index < tableSize)
            table[++index]->getKey (theKey);

        if (theKey == key)
            theElement = table[index];
        else if (index == tableSize)
        {
            // start at beginning again
            index = -1;
            while (theKey != key && table[++index] != 0 &&
                index < computedIndex)
                table[index]->getKey (theKey);
            if (theKey == key)
                theElement = table[index];
        }
    }
    else
        theElement = table[index];
    return theElement;
}

template <class E, class K>
```

Listing A-7 (Continued) Template class for a hash table that uses adjacent elements for collisions

```
E * Hashtable::getElement (int index)
    { return table[index]; }
```

```
#endif
```

Listing A-7 (Continued) Template class for a hash table that uses adjacent elements for collisions

A.9 Hash Table (Linked Lists for Collisions)

This hash table template differs from the version that appears in the body of the book in two ways: it uses a dynamically allocated array and it uses the linked link template class that appears in this appendix. The user must therefore pass the constructor the initial size of the array.

```
#ifndef HASHTABLE
#define HASHTABLE

#include "listmgr.h"

// requires a string key (any char * or class that
// can be used in place of a char * will do)
template <class E, class K>
class Hashtable
{
    private:
        // uses list manager template class
        ListMgr<E, K> ** table;
        int tableSize;
        int computeIndex (String key);
    public:
        Hashtable(int);
        ~Hashtable ();
        void insert (E *);
        bool remove (K);
        E * find (K);
        ListMgr<E, K> * getList (int);
};
```

Listing A-8   Template class for a hash table that uses linked lists for collisions

```
template <class E, class K>
Hashtable<E, K>::Hashtable (int size)
{
    tableSize = size;
    // Class E must have a default constructor
    table = new E * [size];
    for (int i = 0; i < tableSize; i++)
        table[i] = 0;
}

template <class E, class K>
Hashtable<E, K>::~Hashtable ()
    { delete table; }

template <class E, class K>
void Hashtable<E, K>::insert (E * newElement)
{
    K key;
    newElement->getKey (key);
    int index = computeIndex (key);

    if (table[index] == 0) // first entry at that hash value
        table[index] = new ListMgr ();
    table[index]->insert (newElement);
}

template <class E, class K>
int Hashtable<E, K>::computeIndex (K key)
{
    long sum = 0;
    for (int i = 0; i < key.len(); i++)
        sum += key[i];
    return sum % tableSize;
}

template <class E, class K>
bool Hashtable<E, K>::remove (K key)
{
    E * theElement;
```

Listing A-8 (Continued) Template class for a hash table that uses linked lists for collisions

```
    bool result = false;
    K elementKey;

    int index = computeIndex (key);
    if (table[index] != 0)
        theElement = table[index]->find (key);
    if (theElement != 0)
    {
        theElement->getKey (elementKey);
        result = table[index]->remove (elementKey);
    }
    return result;
}

template <class E, class K>
E * Hashtable<E, K>::find (K key)
{
    int index = computeIndex (key);
    E * theElement = 0;
    if (table[index] != 0)
        theElement = table[index]->find (key);
    return theElement;
}

template <class E, class K>
ListMgr<E, K> * Hashtable<E, K>::getList (int index)
    { return table[index]; }

#endif
```

Listing A-8 (Continued) Template class for a hash table that uses linked lists for collisions

A.10 Hash Table Iterator (Adjacent Elements)

```cpp
#ifndef HASHTABLEITR
#define HASHTABLEITR

#include "hashtable.h"

template <class E, class K>
class HashtableItr
{
    private:
        Hashtable<E, K> * theTable;
        int index, tableSize;
    public:
        HashtableItr (Hashtable<E, K> *, int);
        bool getNext (E * &);
};

template <class E, class K>
HashtableItr<E, K>::HashtableItr (Hashtable<E, K> * whichTable,
        int size)
{
    theTable = whichTable;
    tableSize = size;
    index = -1;
}

template <class E, class K>
bool HashtableItr<E, K>::getNext (E * & theElement)
{
    bool done = false;

    // find next used position in table
    while (theTable->getElement(++index) == 0 && index < tableSize)
        ;

        if (index == tableSize)
```

Listing A-9   Template class for a hash table iterator that uses adjacent elements for collisions

```
            done = true;
        else
            theElement = theTable->getThing(index);
    return done;
}

#endif
```

Listing A-9 (Continued) Template class for a hash table iterator that uses adjacent elements for

A.11 Hash Table Iterator (Linked Lists)

```
#ifndef HASHTABLEITR
#define HASHTABLEITR

#include "hashtable.h"
#include "listitr.h"

template <class E, class K>
class HashtableItr
{
    private:
        Hashtable<E, K> * theTable;
        int index, tableSize;
        bool newList;
        ListItr<E, K> * theItr;
    public:
        HashtableItr (Hashtable<E, K> *, int);
        bool getNext (E * &);
};

template <class E, class K>
HashtableItr<E, K>::HashtableItr (Hashtable * whichTable,
        int size)
{
```

Listing A-10 Template class for a hash table iterator that uses linked lists for collisions

```
    theTable = whichTable;
    tableSize = size;
    index = -1;
    newList = true;
}

template <class E, class K>
bool HashtableItr<E, K>::getNext (E * & theElement)
{
    bool done = false;

    if (newList)
    {
        while (theTable->getList(++index) == 0 && index < tableSize)
            // find next used position in table ;

        if (index == tableSize)
            done = true;
        else
        {
            theItr = new ListItr<E, K> (theTable->getList(index));
            newList = false;
        }
    }

    if (!done)
    {
        theElement = theItr->getNext();
        if (theItr->getNextNode() == 0) // if last in list
            newList = true; // need new list next time
    }
    return done;
}


#endif
```

Listing A-10 (Continued) Template class for a hash table iterator that uses linked lists for collisions

A.12 Heap Sort

For comments on how to use the bubble sort in a program, see the instructions for the binary search (Section A.5 on page 490).

```
#ifndef HEAP_SORT
#define HEAP_SORT

template <class E, class K>
class HeapSort
{
    private:
        VectorMgr<E, K> * theVector;
        void buildHeap (int, int, VectorMgr<E, K> *);
    public:
        HeapSort (VectorMgr<E, K> *);
        void sort ();
};

template <class E, class K>
HeapSort<E, K>::HeapSort (VectorMgr<E, K> * iVector)
    { theVector = iVector; }

template <class E, class K>
void HeapSort<E, K>::sort ()
{
    int numbElements = theVector->getNumbElements();

    for (int i = numbElements - 1; i > 0; i--)
    {
        E * tempElement, iElement, firstElement;
        theVector->getElement (i, iElement);
        theVector->getElement (0, firstElement);
        tempElement = firstElement;
        theVector->setElement (iElement, 0);
        theVector->setElement (tempElement, i);

        buildHeap (0, i, theVector);
    }
```

Listing A-11   Heap sort template class

```
}

template <class E, class K>
void HeapSort<E, K>::buildHeap (int position, int size,
      VectorMgr<E, K> * buildVector)
{
    int key, key0, key1;

    E * theElement, theElement1, theElement0;
    buildVector->getElement (position, theElement);
    theElement->getKey (key);

    int childPosition;
    while (position < size)
    {
        childPosition = position * 2 + 1;
        if (childPosition < size)
        {
            buildVector->getElement (childPosition, theElement0);
            theElement0->getKey (key0);
            buildVector->getElement (childPosition + 1,
                theElement1);
            theElement1->getKey (key1);
            if ((childPosition + 1 < size) && key1 > key0)
                childPosition += 1;

            if (key > key0)
            {
                buildVector->setElement (theElement, position);
                return;
            }
            else
            {
                E * childElement;
                buildVector->getElement (childPosition,
                    childElement);
                buildVector->setElement (childElement, position);
                position = childPosition;
            }
        }
    }
```

Listing A-11 (Continued) Heap sort template class

```
        else
        {
                buildVector->setElement (theElement, position);
                return;
        }
    }
}

#endif
```

Listing A-11 (Continued) Heap sort template class

A.13 Insertion Sort (New Array)

For comments on how to use the insertion sort in a program, see the instructions for the binary search (Section A.5 on page 490)

```
#ifndef INSERTION_SORT1
#define INSERTION_SORT1

template <class A, class K>
class InsertionSort
{
    private:
        A ** sourceArray;
        int size;
    public:
        InsertionSort (A **, int);
        void sort (A **);
};

template <class A, class K>
InsertionSort<A, K>::InsertionSort (A ** iArray, int iSize)
{
    sourceArray = iArray;
    size = iSize;
}
```

Listing A-12   Template class for an insertion sort into a new array

```
template <class A, class K>
void InsertionSort<A, K>::sort (A ** targetArray)
{
    K sourceKey, targetKey;

    targettArray[0] = sourceArray[0];
    int sortCount = 0; // last element used in sort array
    for (int i = 1; i < size; i++) //loop through original array
    {
        int insert_spot = -1;
        for (int j = sortCount; j >= 0; j--)
        {
            sourceArray[i]->getKey(sourceKey);
            targetArray[j]->getKey(targetKey);
            if (sourceKey > targetKey) // find insert spot
                insert_spot = j + 1;
            if (insert_spot > -1)
                break;
        }
        if (insert_spot == -1)
            insert_spot = 0;

        for (int k = sortCount; k >= insert_spot; k--)
            targetArray[k+1] = targetArray[k]; //move down
        targetArray[insert_spot] = sourceArray[i]; // insert
        sortCount++;
    }
}

#endif
```

Listing A-12 (Continued) Template class for an insertion sort into a new array

A.14 Insertion Sort (Source Array)

For comments on how to use the insertion sort in a program, see the instructions for the binary search (Section A.5 on page 490).

```
#ifndef INSERTION_SORT2
#define INSERTION_SORT2

template <class A, class K>
class InsertionSort
{
    private:
        A ** theArray;
        int size;
    public:
        InsertionSort (A **, int);
        void sort ();
};

template <class A, class K>
InsertionSort<A, K>::InsertionSort (A ** iArray, int iSize)
{
    theArray = iArray;
    size = iSize;
}

template <class A, class K:
void InsertionSort<A, K>::sort ()
{
    K key1, key2;
    A * tempElement;

    for (int i = 1; i < size; i++)
    {
        theArray[i]->getKey(key1);
        theArray[i-1]->getKey(key2);
        if (key1 < key2) // if out of order
        {
            tempElement = theArray[i]; // save element to be moved
```

Listing A-13   Template class for an insertion sort using a single array

```
        // index into sorted portion of array
        int sortedIndex = i;
        bool found = false;
        while (!found) // look for place to insert element
        {
            // move an element up
            theArray [sortedIndex] = theArray[sortedIndex - 1];
            sortedIndex--;
            if (sortedIndex == 0)
                found = true;
            else
            {
                theArray[sortedIndex - 1]->getKey(key1);
                tempElement->getKey(key2);
                found = key1 <= key2;
            }
        }
        theArray[sortedIndex] = tempElement;
    }

    }
}

#endif
```

Listing A-13 (Continued) Template class for an insertion sort using a single array

A.15 Merge Sort

For comments on how to use the insertion sort in a program, see the instructions for the binary search (Section A.5 on page 490).

```
#ifndef MERGE_SORT
#define MERGE_SORT

template <class A, class K>
class MergeSort
```

Listing A-14 Merge sort template class

```
{
    private:
        A ** sortArray ();
        int size;
        void mergesort (A **, const int &, const int &);
        void domerge (A **, const int &, const int &, const int &);
    public:
        MergeSort (A **, int);
        void merge ();
};

template<class A, class K>
MergeSort<A, K>::MergeSort (A ** sourceArray, int iSize)
{
    sortArray = sourceArray;
    size = iSize;
}

template<class A, class K>
void MergeSort<A, K>::merge ()
    { mergesort (sortArray, 0, size - 1); }   // initiate the sort

template<class A, class K>
void MergeSort<A, K>::mergesort (A ** theArray, const int & low,
        const int & high)
{
    if (low < high)
    {
        int mid = (low + high) / 2; // find the middle element

        mergesort (theArray, low, mid); // sort top half
        mergesort (theArray, mid + 1, high); // sort bottom half
        // merge the halves back together
        domerge (theArray, low, mid, high);
    }
}

template<class A, class K>
void MergeSort<A, K>::domerge (A ** theArray, const int  & low,
        const int & mid, const int & high)
```

Listing A-14 (Continued) Merge sort template class

```
{
    int topPtr = low; // pointer to top half of array
    int midPtr = mid + 1; // pointer to middle; start of bottom half
    int resultPtr = 0;   // pointer to merged array
    A ** tempArray = new A * [size];
    K topKey, midKey;

    // copy into temporary array from two sorted
    // halves in correct order
    while (topPtr <= mid && midPtr <= high)
    {
        theArray[topPtr]->getKey(topKey);
        theArray[midPtr]->getKey(midKey);
        if (topKey < midKey)
        {
            tempArray[resultPtr] = theArray[topPtr];
            topPtr++;
        }
        else
        {
            tempArray[resultPtr] = theArray[midPtr];
            midPtr++;
        }
        resultPtr++;
    }

    // copy remaining elements; at most one of these
    // two loops will execute
    while (topPtr <= mid)
    {
        tempArray[resultPtr] = theArray[topPtr];
        topPtr++;
        resultPtr++;
    }
    while (midPtr <= high)
    {
        tempArray[resultPtr] = theArray[midPtr];
        midPtr++;
        resultPtr++;
    }
```

Listing A-14 (Continued) Merge sort template class

```
    // now copy back to original array
    topPtr = low;
    resultPtr = 0;
    while (topPtr <= high)
    {
        theArray[topPtr] = tempArray[resultPtr];
        topPtr++;
        resultPtr++;
    }
    delete tempArray;
}

#endif
```

Listing A-14 (Continued) Merge sort template class

A.16 Priority Queue

```
#ifndef PRIORITY_QUEUE
#define PRIORITY_QUEUE

#include "vectormgr.h"

#define INITIAL_SIZE 25
#define SIZE_INCREMENT 10

template <class E, class K>
class PQueue
{
    private:
        VectorMgr<E, K> * theVector; // implement as a vector
        void buildHeap (int, int, VectorMgr<E, K> *);
    public:
        PQueue ();
```

Listing A-15   Priority queue template class

```
          PQueue (int); // pass in initial size
          ~PQueue ();
          void insert (E *);
          bool remove (E *);
          VectorMgr<E, K> * getVector (); // used by iterator
    };

    template <class E, class K>
    PQueue<E, K>::PQueue ()
       { theVector = new VectorMgr<E, K> (INITIAL_SIZE); }

    template <class E, class K>
    PQueue<E, K>::PQueue (int initial_size)
       { theVector = new VectorMgr<E, K> (initial_size); }

    template <class E, class K>
    PQueue<E, K>::~PQueue ()
       { delete theVector; }

    template <class E, class K>
    void PQueue::insert (E * newElement)
    {
       K newKey;
       newElement->getKey (newKey);
       E * theElement;

       int numbElements = theVector->getNumbElements();

       // Add elements if vector is full
       if (numbElements + 1 >= theVector->getSize ())
          theVector->resize (theVector->getSize() + SIZE_INCREMENT);

       int position = numbElements++;
       K storedKey;
       theVector->getElement ((position-1)/2, theElement);
       theElement->getKey (storedKey);
       while (position > 0 && newKey >= storedKey)
       {
          theVector->setElement (theElement, position);
          position = (position - 1)/2;
```

Listing A-15 (Continued) Priority queue template class

```
        theVector->getElement ((position-1)/2, theThing);
        theElement->getKey (storedKey);
    }

    theVector->addElement (newElement, position);
}

template <class E, class K>
bool PQueue<E, K>::remove (E * removedElement)
{
    bool result = theVector->isEmpty();
    if (result)
        return false;

    theVector->getElement (0, removedElement);
    int lastIndex = theVector->getNumbElements() - 1;
    E lastElement;
    theVector->getElement (lastIndex, lastElement);
    theVector->setElement (lastElement, 0);
    theVector->decrementNumbElements ();

    buildHeap (0, theVector->getNumbElements(), theVector);
    return true;
}

template <class E, class K>
void PQueue<E, K>::buildHeap (int position, int size,
        VectorMgr<E, K> * buildVector)
{
    int key = 0, key0 = 0, key1 = 1;

    E * theElement, theElement1, theElement0;
    buildVector->getElement (position, theThing);
    theElement->getKey (key);

    int childPosition;
    while (position < size)
    {
        childPosition = position * 2 + 1;
        if (childPosition < size)
```

Listing A-15 (Continued) Priority queue template class

514

```
    {
        buildVector->getElement (childPosition, theElement0);
        theElement0->getKey (key0);
        buildVector->getElement (childPosition + 1,
            theElement1);
        if (theElement)
            theElement1.getKey (key1);
        if ((childPosition + 1 < size) && key1 > key0)
            childPosition += 1;

        if (key > key0 && key < key1)
        {
            buildVector->setElement (theElement, position);
            return;
        }
        else
        {
            E * childElement;
            buildVector->getElement (childPosition,
                childElement);
            buildVector->setElement (childElement, position);
            position = childPosition;
        }
    }
    else
    {
            buildVector->setElement (theElement, position);
            return;
    }
  }
}

template <class E, class K>
VectorMgr<E, K> * PQueue<E, K>::getVector ()
    { return theVector; }

#endif
```

Listing A-15 (Continued) Priority queue template class

A.17 Priority Queue Iterator

```
#ifndef PQ_ITR
#define PQ_ITR

#include "vectoritr.h"
#include "priorityqueue.H"

template <class E, class K>
class PQueueItr
{
    private:
        VectorMgr<E, K> * theVector;
        VectorItr<E, K> * theItr;
    public:
        PQueueItr (PQueue<E, K> *);
        ~PQueueItr ();
        bool getNext (E *);
};

template <class E, class K>
PQueueItr<E, K>::PQueueItr (PQueue<E, K> * thePQ)
{
    theVector = thePQ->getVector ();
    theItr<E, K> = new VectorItr<E, K> (theVector,
        theVector->getNumbElements());
}

template <class E, class K>
PQueueIt<E, K>r::~PQueueItr ()
    { delete theItr; }

template <class E, class K>
bool PQueueItr<E, K>::getNext (E * theElement)
{
    bool result = theItr->getNext (theElement);
    return result;
```

Listing A-16   *Priority queue iterator template class*

```
}

#endif
```

Listing A-16 (Continued) Priority queue iterator template class

A.18 Queue (Array)

```
#ifndef QUEUEMGR1
#define QUEUEMGR1

#include "queuenode1.h"

#define MAX_ELEMENTS 10

template class <E>
class QueueMgr
{
   private:
      int queue_end;
      QueueNode<E> * theQueue [MAX_ELEMENTS];

   public:
      QueueMgr ();
      bool enqueue (E *); // pass in a single element
      // pass in ordinal position of element
      bool getElement (int, E * &);
      bool dequeue (E * &);
      bool is_empty (); // true if queue is empty
      int getSize (); // return total elements in the array
};

template class <E>
QueueMgr<E>::QueueMgr ()
{
```

Listing A-17 Template class for a queue implemented as an array

```
    queue_end = 0;
}

template class <E>
bool QueueMgr<E>::enqueue (E * newElement)
{
    bool result;
    QueueNode<E> * theNode = new QueueNode<E> (newElement);
    if (queue_end < MAX_ELEMENTS)
    {
        theQueue[queue_end] = theNode;
        queue_end++;
        result = true;
    }
    else
        result = false;
    return result;
}

template class <E>
bool QueueMgr<E>::getElement (int position, E *  & element)
{
    int result = true;
    if (position > queue_end || queue_end == 0)
        result = false;
    else
    {
        QueueNode<E> * theNode = theQueue [position];
        element = theNode->getElement();
    }
    return result;
}

template class <E>
bool QueueMgr::dequeue (E * & element)
{
    bool result = true;
    if (queue_end == 0)
        result = false;
    else
```

Listing A-17 (Continued) Template class for a queue implemented as an array

```
    {
        QueueNode<E> * theNode = theQueue [0];
        element = theNode->getElement ();
        delete theNode;
        for (int i = 0; i < queue_end - 1; i++)
            theQueue[i] = theQueue[i+1];
        queue_end--;
    }
    return result;
}

template class <E>
bool QueueMgr<E>::is_empty ()
{
    return (queue_end == 0);
}

template class <E>
int QueueMgr<E>::getSize ()
    { return queue_end; }

#endif
```

Listing A-17 (Continued) Template class for a queue implemented as an array

A.19 Queue (Linked List)

```
#ifndef QUEUEMGR2
#define QUEUEMGR2

#include "queuenode2.h"

template <class E>
class QueueMfr
{
```

Listing A-18   Template class for a queue implemented as a linked list

```
    private:
        QueueNode<E> * head, * tail;
    public:
        Queue ();
        int is_empty ();
        bool enqueue (E *);
        E * dequeue ();
        QueueNode<E> * getHead ();
};

template <class E>
QueueMgr<E>::Queue ()
    { head = 0; }

template <class E>
int QueueMgr<E>::is_empty()
    { return (head == 0); }

template <class E>
bool QueueMgr<E>::enqueue (E * theElement)
{
    QueueNode<E> * theNode = new QueueNode<E> (theElement);
    if (!theNode)
    {
        cout << "\nCannot create node.";
        return;
    }
    if (is_empty())
    {
        head = theNode;
        tail = theNode;
    }
    else
    {
        tail->setNext (theNode);
        tail = theNode;
    }
    return true;
}
```

Listing A-18 (Continued) Template class for a queue implemented as a linked list

```
template <class E>
E * QueueMgr<E>::dequeue ()
{
    QueueNode<E> * theNode = head;
    head = theNode->getNext();
    E * theElement = theNode->getElement ();
    delete theNode;
    return theElement;
}

template <class E>
QueueNodeMgr<E> * QueueMgrMgr<E>::getHead ()
{
    QueueNode<E> * theNode = head;
    return theNode;
}

#endif
```

Listing A-18 (Continued) Template class for a queue implemented as a linked list

A.20 Queue Node (Array)

```
#ifndef QUEUE_NODE1
#define QUEUE_NODE1

template <class E>
class QueueNode
{
    private:
        E * theElement;
    public:
        QueueNode (E *);
        E * getElement();
};
```

Listing A-19   A queue node template class for a queue implemented as an array

```
template <class E>
QueueNode<E>::QueueNode (E * iElement)
{
    theElement = iElement;
}

E * QueueNode<E>::getElement()
    { return theElement; }

#endif
```

Listing A-19 (Continued) A queue node template class for a queue implemented as an array

A.21 Queue Node (Linked List)

```
#ifndef QUEUE_NODE2
#define QUEUE_NODEw

template <class E>
class QueueNode
{
    private:
        E * theElement;
        QueueNode<E> * next;
    public:
        QueueNode (E *);
        E * getThing();
        QueueNode<E> * getNext ();
        void setNext (QueueNode<E> *);
};

template <class E>
QueueNode<E>::QueueNode (E * iElement)
{
```

Listing A-20 A queue node template class for a queue implemented as a linked list

```
    theElement = iElement;
    next = 0;
}

template <class E>
E * QueueNode<E>::getElement()
    { return theElement; }

template <class E>
QueueNode<E> * QueueNode<E>::getNext ()
    { return next; }

template <class E>
void QueueNode<E>::setNext (QueueNode<E> * iNode)
    { next = iNode; }

#endif
```

Listing A-20 (Continued) A queue node template class for a queue implemented as a linked list

A.22 Queue Iterator (Array)

```
#ifndef QUEUEITR1
#define QUEUEITR1

#include "QueueMgr1.h"

template <class E>
class QueueItr
{
    private:
        QueueMgr<E> * theQueue;
        int queue_end;
        int current_index;
```

Listing A-21   Template class for a queue iterator that traverses a queue implemented as an array

```
    public:
        QueueItr (QueueMgr<E> *, int); // pass in the queue manager
and total elements
        bool getNext (E * &);
};

template <class E>
QueueItr<E>::QueueItr (QueueMgr<E> * inQueue, int iElements)
{
    theQueue = inQueue;
    queue_end = iElements;
    current_index = 0;
}

template <class E>
bool QueueItr<E>::getNext (E * & nextElement)
{
    bool result = false;
    if (current_index < queue_end)
    {
        theQueue->getElement (current_index, nextElement);
        result = true;
        current_index++;
    }
    return result;
}

#endif
```

Listing A-21 (Continued) Template class for a queue iterator that traverses a queue implemented as

A.23 Queue Iterator (Linked List)

```
#ifndef QUEUE__ITR2
#define QUEUEITR2

#include "queuenode2.h"
#include "queue2.h"

template <class E>
class QueueItr
{
    private:
        QueueNode<E> * current;
        Queue<E> * theQueue;
    public:
        QueueItr (Queue<E> *);
        QueueNode<E> * getNext ();
};

template <class E>
QueueItr<E>::QueueItr (Queue<E> * iQueue)
{
    theQueue = iQueue;
    current = theQueue->getHead();
}

template <class E>
QueueNode<E> * QueueIt<E>r::getNext ()
{

    QueueNode<E> * theNode = current;
    current = current->getNext();
    return theNode;
}

#endif
```

Listing A-22   Iterator template class for a queue implemented as a linked list

A.24 Quicksort (Recursive)

For comments on how to use the recurisve quicksort in a program, see the instructions for the binary search (Section A.5 on page 490).

```
#ifndef QUICKSORT1
#define QUICKSORT1

template<class A, class K>
class QuickSort
{
    private:
        A ** sortArray;
        int size;
        void quicksort (A **, int, int)
        void parition (A **, int, int, int &);
    public:
        QuickSort (A **, int);
        void sort ();
};

template<class A, class K>
QuickSort<A, K>::QuickSort (A ** iArray, int iSize)
{
    sortArray = iArray;
    size = iSize;
}

void QuickSort<A, K>::sort ()
    // initiate the sort
    { quicksort (sortArray, 0, size - 1); }
}

void QuickSort<A, K>::quicksort (A ** theArray, int low, int high)
{
    int pivotPoint;
    if (low < high)
    {
        // partition the array
        partition (theArray, low, high, pivotPoint);
```

Listing A-23   Template class for a recursive quicksort

```
      // sort the top half
      quicksort (theArray, low, pivotPoint - 1);
      // sort the bottom half
      quicksort (theArray, pivotPoint + 1, high);
   }
}

void QuickSort<A, K>::partition (A ** theArray, int low, int high,
      int & pivotPoint)
{
   A * tempElement;
   pivotPoint = low;
   k lowKey, highKey;
   int pivotKey = key;

   while (low <= high)
   {
      theArray[low]->getKey(lowKey);
      theArray[high]->getKey(highKey);
      if (lowKey <= pivotKey)
         low++;
      else if (highKey >= pivotKey)
         high--;
      else
      {
         tempElement = theArray[high]; //swap
         theArray[high] = theArray[low];
         theArray[low] = tempElement;
         low++;
         high--;
      }
   }
   ElementThing = theArray[high];
   theArray[high] = theArray[pivotPoint];
   theArray[pivotPoint] = tempElement;
   // this is the spot between the two partitions
   pivotPoint = high;
}

#endif
```

Listing A-23 (Continued) Template class for a recursive quicksort

A.25 Quicksort (Nonrecursive)

For comments on how to use the nonrecurisve quicksort in a program, see the instructions for the binary search (Section A.5 on page 490).

```
#ifndef QUICKSORT2
#define QUICKSORT2

#define STACK_SIZE 25

template <class A, class K>
class QuickSort
{
    private:
        A ** sortArray;
        int size;
        void partition (A **, int, int, int &);
    public:
        QuickSort (A **, int);
        void sort ();
};

template<class A, class K>
Quicksort<A, K>::QuickSort (A ** iArray, int iSize)
{
    sortArray = iArray;
    size = iSize;
}

template <class A, class K>
void QuickSort<A, K>::sort ()
{
    int low = 0;
    int high = size - 1;
    int pivotPoint;
    int stackPtr = -1;
    int lowStack [STACK_SIZE], highStack [STACK_SIZE]; // up to 1
million elements
```

Listing A-24   Template class for a nonrecursive quicksort

```
    do
    {
       if (stackPtr > -1)
       {
          low = lowStack [stackPtr];
          high = highStack [stackPtr];
          stackPtr--;
       }

       while (low < high)
       {
          partition (sortArray, low, high, pivotPoint);
          if (pivotPoint - low < high - pivotPoint)
          {
             if (stackPtr >= STACK_SIZE)
             {
                cout << "\nStack overflow. Cannot complete sort.";
                return;
             }
             stackPtr++;
             lowStack[stackPtr] = pivotPoint + 1;
             highStack[stackPtr] = high;
             high = pivotPoint - 1;
          }
          else
          {
             if (stackPtr >= STACK_SIZE)
             {
                cout << "\nStack overflow. Cannot complete sort.";
                return;
             }
             stackPtr++;
             lowStack[stackPtr] = low;
             highStack[stackPtr] = pivotPoint - 1;
             low = pivotPoint + 1;
          }
       }
    } while (stackPtr > -1);
}
```

Listing A-24 (Continued) Template class for a nonrecursive quicksort

```
template <class A, class K>
void QuickSort<A, K>::partition (A ** theArray, int low, int high,
int & pivotPoint)
{
    A * tempElement;
    pivotPoint = low;
    int pivotKey = theArray[low]->getKey();
    K lowKey, highKey;

    while (low <= high)
    {
        theArray[low]->getKey(lowKey);
        theArray[high]->getKey(highKey);
        if (lowKey <= pivotKey)
            low++;
        else if (highKey >= pivotKey)
            high--;
        else
        {
            tempElement = theArray[high]; //swap
            theArray[high] = theArray[low];
            theArray[low] = tempElement;
            low++;
            high--;
        }
    }
    tempElement = theArray[high];
    theArray[high] = theArray[pivotPoint];
    theArray[pivotPoint] = tempElement;
    pivotPoint = high; // this is the spot between the two
partitions
}

#endif
```

Listing A-24 (Continued) Template class for a nonrecursive quicksort

A.26 Radix Sort

This radix sort requires an integer key (either int or long). For comments on how to use the radix sort in a program, see the instructions for the binary search (Section A.5 on page 490).

```
#ifndef RADIX_SORT
#define RADIX_SORT

// Requires an integer key

#include <math.h>

template <class A, class K>
class RadixSort
{
    private:
        A ** sourceArray;
        int size;
        void radixsort (int, A **, A**);
    public:
        RadixSort (A **, int);
        void sort ();
};

template <class A, class K>
RadixSort<A,K>::RadixSort (A ** iArray, int iSize)
{
    sourceArray = iArray;
    size = iSize;
}

template <class A, class K>
void RadixSort<A,K>::sort ()
{
    A ** destArray [size];

    // first find largest key
    K maxKey, sourceKey;
```

Listing A-25 Radix sort template class

```
    sourceArray[0]->getKey(maxKey);
    for (int i = 1; i < total_elements; i++)
    {
        sourceArray[i]->getKey(sourceKey);
        if (sourceKey > maxKey)
        {
            maxKey = sourceKey;
            break;
        }
    }

    int numb_digits = log10 (maxKey) + 1;
    for (int i = 0; i <= numb_digits; i+=2)
    {
        radixsort (i, destArray, sourceArray);
        radixsort (i+1, sourceArray, destArray);
    }
}

template <class A, class K>
void RadixSort<A,K>::radixsort (int theDigit, A ** destArray,
        A ** sourceArray)
{
    int frequency [10];
    for (int i = 0; i < 10; i++)   // initialize frequency counting
array
        frequency[i] = 0;

    int digit;
    float value;
    K key;
    // count occurrences of each value
    for (int i = 0; i < size; i++)
    {
        sourceArray[i]->getKey(key);
        value = ((float) key / (pow (10, theDigit)));
        digit = (int) ((float) key / (pow (10, theDigit)));
        digit = (int) ((value - (float) digit) * 10);
        frequency [digit]++;
    }
```

Listing A-25 (Continued) Radix sort template class

```
    int index [size];
    index[0] = 0;
    for (int i = 1; i < size; i++)
        index[i] = index[i-1]+frequency[i-1];

    for (int i = 0; i < size; i++)
    {
        sourceArray[i]->getKey(key);
        value = ((float) key / (pow (10, theDigit)));
        digit = (int) ((float) key / (pow (10, theDigit)));
        digit = (int) ((value - (float) digit) * 10);
        destArray[index[digit]++] = sortArray[i];
    }
}

#endif
```

Listing A-25 (Continued) Radix sort template class

A.27 Selection Sort

For comments on how to use the selection sort in a program, see the instructions for the binary search (Section A.5 on page 490).

```
#ifndef SELECTION_SORT
#define SELECTION_SORT

template <class A, class K>
class SelectionSort
{
    private:
        A ** sortArray;
        int size;
    public:
        SelectionSort (A **, int);
        void sort ();
```

Listing A-26 Selection sort template class

```
};

template <class A, class K>
SelectionSort<A, K>::SelectionSort (A ** iArray, int iSize)
{
    sortArray = iArray;
    size = iSize;
}

template <class A, class K>
void SelectionSort<A, K>::sort ()
{
    A * tempElement;
    int maxIndex;
    K maxKey, sortKey; // index of maximum element

    // if all items are in place except the last one, then last one
must be too.
    // therefore can stop loop at 1 rather than 0.
    for (int i = size - 1; i >= 1; i--)
    {
        // find element with max key value
        // that isn't in the right place yet
        sortArray[0]->getKey(maxKey);
        maxIndex = 0;
        for (int j = 1; j <= i; j++)
        {
            sortArray[j]->getKey(sortKey);
            if (sortKey > maxKey)
            {
                maxKey = sortKey;
                maxIndex = j;
                break;
            }
        }

        // move it to the bottom; i represents bottom of array
        tempElement = sortArray[maxIndex];
        sortArray[maxIndex] = sortArray[i];
        sortArray[i] = tempElement;
```

Listing A-26 (Continued) Selection sort template class

```
    }
}

#endif
```

Listing A-26 (Continued) Selection sort template class

A.28 Shell Sort

For comments on how to use the Shell sort in a program, see the instructions for the binary search (Section A.5 on page 490).

```
#ifndef SHELL_SORT
#define SHELL_SORT

template <class A, class K>
class ShellSort
{
    private:
        A ** sortArray;
        int size;
    public:
        ShellSort (A **, int);
        void sort ();
};

template <class A, class K>
ShellSort<A, K>::ShellSort (A ** iArray, int iSize)
{
    sortArray = iArray;
    size = iSize;
}

template <class A, class K>
void ShellSort<A, K>::sort ()
{
    A * tempElement;
```

Listing A-27 Shell sort template class

```
K tempKey, sortKey;
int increment = size /2;
int sortIndex;

while (increment >= 1)
{
    for (int i = increment; i < size; i++)
    {
        tempElement = sortArray[i];
        tempElement->getKey(tempKey);
        sortArray[i - increment]->getKey(sortKey);
        for (sortIndex = i - increment; sortIndex >= 0 && tempKey
< sortKey; sortIndex -= increment)
        {
            sortArray[sortIndex + increment] =
sortArray[sortIndex];
            sortArray[sortIndex]->getKey(sortKey);
        }
        sortArray[sortIndex + increment] = tempElement;
    }
    // compute new increment
    if (increment == 2)  // last increment must be 1
        increment = 1;
    else
        increment = increment / 2.2;
}
}

#endif
```

Listing A-27 (Continued) Shell sort template class

A.29 Single Linked List

```
#ifndef LISTMGR
#define LISTMGR

#include "listnode.h"

template <class E, class K>
class ListMgr
{
    private:
        ListNode<E, K> * first;
    public:
        ListMgr ();
        void insert (E *);
        E * find (K); // traverse list to locate by key
        int remove (K); // use key to locate for removal
        ListNode<E, K> * getFirst();
};

template <class E, class K>
ListMgr<E, K>::ListMgr()
{
    first = 0;
}

template <class E, class K>
void ListMgr<E, K>::insert (E * theElement)
{
    ListNode<E, K> * newNode, * current, * previous;
    E * currentElement;

    // create a node object
    newNode = new ListNode<E, K> (theElement);
    if (!newNode)
    {
        cout << "\nCannot create node." << endl
```

Listing A-28   Single linked list template class

```
        return;
    }

    K newKey, currentKey;
    theElement->getKey(newKey);

    if (first == 0) // list is empty
        first = newNode;
    else
    {
        int firstNode = true;
        current = first; // start at head of list
        while (current != 0)
        {
            currentElement = current->getElement();
            currentElement->getKey(currentKey);
            if (newKey < currentKey)
        // spot found (between current and current's previous node
                break;
            // save preceding because there aren't backward pointers
            previous = current;
            current = current->getNext ();
            firstNode = false; // not the first node
        }

        // set previous node to point to new node except
        //when first in list
        if (!firstNode)
            previous->setNext (newNode);
        else
            first = newNode; // have new first in list

        // set new node to point to following node
        newNode->setNext (current);
    }
}

template <class E, class K>
E * ListMgr<E, K>::find (K searchKey)
{
```

Listing A-28 (Continued) Single linked list template class

```
    E * currentElement;
    ListNode * current;
    K currentKey;
    current = first; // start at head of list

    while (current != 0)
    {
        currentElement = current->getElement();
        currentThing->getKey(currentKey);
        if (searchKey == currentKey)
            return currentElement;
        current = current->getNext ();
    }
    return 0; // not found
}

template <class E, class K>
int ListMgr<E, K>::remove (K searchKey)
{
    E * currentElement;
    ListNode * current, * previous, * next;
    K currentKey;

    if (first == 0)
        return false; // list is empty

    int firstNode = true;
    current = first;

    while (current != 0)
    {
        currentElement = current->getElement();
        currentThing->getKey(currentKey);
        if (searchKey == currentKey)
            break; // jump out of loop
        // save preceding because there aren't backward pointers
        previous = current;
        current = current->getNext ();
        firstNode = false; // not the first node
    }
```

Listing A-28 (Continued) Single linked list template class

```
    if (current == 0)
        return false; // node not found

    if (!firstNode)
    {
        // gets node after node being removed
        next = current->getNext ();
        previous->setNext (next);
    }
    else
        // sets first to node after node being removed
        first = current->getNext ();

    delete current; // remove node object from memory
    return true; // remove was successful
}

template <class E, class K>
ListNode * ListMgr<E, K>::getFirst()
    { return first; }

#endif
```

Listing A-28 (Continued) Single linked list template class

A.30 Single Linked List Iterator

```
#ifndef LISTITR
#define LISTITR

#include "listmgr.h"

template <class E, class K>
class ListItr
```

Listing A-29 Single linked list iterator template class

```
{
    private:
        Node<E, K> * current;
        ListMgr<E, K> * theList;
    public:
        ListItr (ListMgr<E, K> *);
        E * getNext ();
};

template <class E, class K>
ListItr<E, K>::ListItr (ListMgr<E, K> * whichList)
{
    current = 0;
    theList = whichList;
}

template <class E, class K>
E * ListItr<E, K>::getNext ()
{
    if (current == 0)
        current = theList->getFirst ();
    else
        current = current->getNext ();

    if (current != 0)
        return current->getElement();
    else
        return 0;
}

#endif
```

Listing A-29 (Continued) Single linked list iterator template class

A.31 Single Linked List Node

```
#ifndef LIST_NODE
#define LIST_NODE

template <class E, class K>
class ListNode
{
    private:
        K key;
        ListNode * next;
        E * theElement;
    public:
        ListNode (E *);
        void getKey (K &);
        E * getElement ();
        ListNode * getNext();
        void setNext (ListNode *);
};

template <class E, class K>
ListNode<E, K>::ListNode (E * iElement)
{
    theElement = iElement;
    theElement->getKey(key);
    next = 0;
}

template <class E, class K>
void ListNode<E, K>::getKey(K & oKey)
    { oKey = key; }

template <class E, class K>
E * ListNode<E, K>::getElement ()
    { return theElement; }

template <class E, class K>
```

Listing A-30   Single linked list node template class

```
ListNode<E, K> * ListNode<E, K>::getNext ()
   { return next; }

template <class E, class K>
void ListNode<E, K>::setNext (ListNode * iNode)
   { right_child = iNode; }

#endif
```

Listing A-30 (Continued) Single linked list node template class

A.32 Stack (Linked List)

```
#ifndef STACK2
#define STACK2

#include "listnode.h"

template <class E, class K>
class Stack
{
   private:
      int stackPtr;
      Node<E, K> * first;
   public:
      Stack ();
      int is_empty ();
      bool push (E *);
      E * pop ();
      Node<E, K> * getTop ();
};

template <class E, class K>
Stack<E, K>::Stack ()
   { first = 0; }
```

Listing A-31 Template class for a stack implemented as a linked list

```
template <class E, class K>
int Stack<E, K>::is_empty()
   { return (first == 0); }

template <class E, class K>
bool Stack<E, K>::push (E * theElement)
{
    Node<E, K> * theNode = new Node<E, K> (theElement);
    if (!newNode)
    {
        cout << "\nCannot create node." << endl
        return;
    }

    theNode->setNext (first);
    first = theNode;
    return true;
}

template <class E, class K>
E * Stack<E, K>::pop ()
{
    Node<E, K> * theNode = first;
    E * theElement = theNode->getElement();
    first = theNode->getNext();
    delete theNode;
    return theElement;
}

template <class E, class K>
Node<E, K> * Stack<E, K>::getTop ()
   { return first; }

#endif
```

Listing A-31 (Continued) Template class for a stack implemented as a linked list

A.33 Stack Iterator (Array)

```
#ifndef STACKITR1
#define STACKITR1

#include "stack1.h"

template <class E, class K>
class StackItr
{
    private:
        int current;
        Stack<E, K> * theStack;
    public:
        StackItr (Stack<E, K> *);
        Node<E, K> * getNext ();
};

template <class E, class K>
StackItr<E, K>::StackItr (Stack<E, K> * iStack)
{
    theStack = iStack;
    current = theStack->getStackPtr();
}

template <class E, class K>
Node<E, K> * StackItr<E, K>::getNext ()
{
    Node<E, K> * theNode = theStack->getElement (current);
    current--;
    return theNode;
}

#endif
```

Listing A-32 Stack iterator template class for a stack implemented as an array

A.34 Stack Iterator (Linked List)

```
#ifndef STACKITR2
#define STACKITR2

#include "stack2.h"

template <class E, class K>
class StackItr
{
    private:
        Node<E, K> * current;
        Stack<E, K> * theStack;
    public:
        StackItr (Stack<E, K> *);
        Node<E, K> * getNext ();
};

template <class E, class K>
StackItr<E, K>::StackItr (Stack<E, K> * iStack)
{
    theStack = iStack;
    current = theStack->getTop();
}

template <class E, class K>
Node<E, K> * StackItr<E, K>::getNext ()
{
    Node<E, K> * theNode = current;
    current = current->getNext();
    return theNode;
}

#endif
```

Listing A-33 Stack iterator template class for a stack implemented as a linked list

Index